TRUDEAU'S SHADOW

TRUDEAU'S SHADOW

THE LIFE AND LEGACY OF PIERRE ELLIOTT TRUDEAU

Jean-Marc Carisse

EDITED BY

ANDREW COHEN AND

J. L. GRANATSTEIN

Vintage Canada

A Division of Random House of Canada Ltd.

FIRST VINTAGE CANADA EDITION, 1999

Copyright © 1998 by Andrew Cohen and J. L Granatstein.

Duncan Macpherson cartoons reprinted with
permission — The Toronto Star Syndicate

Canadian Cataloguing in Publication Data

Main entry under title:

Trudeau's shadow: the life and legacy of Pierre Elliott Trudeau

ISBN 0-679-31006-1

1. Trudeau, Pierre Elliott, 1919-   . 2. Canada - Politics and government -
1963-1984.* 3. Prime ministers - Canada - Biography.
I. Cohen, Andrew, 1955-   . II. Granatstein, J. L., 1939-   .

FC626.T7T794 1999   971.064'4'092   C99-931179-4
FI034.3.T7T78 1999

Printed and bound in the United States of America

10 9 8 7 6 5 4 3 2 1

*We are grateful to our agent, Linda McKnight, to our editor,
Rosemary Shipton, and to our long-suffering spouses,
Elaine Granatstein and Mary Gooderham.*

CONTENTS

Introduction

∎

SPRING 1968: The huge crowd waiting in the city centre was festive, the red banners and posters waving. Party workers passed through the throng handing out buttons and pamphlets, especially to children and young women in miniskirts, of whom there were far more than usual at political rallies. When members of the official party finally made their way to the stage to begin reciting their prepared texts, the people became impatient. Shouts of "We want the prime minister!" began to be heard, and soon the whole crowd was clapping in unison, drowning out the local nabobs.

At last, the time had come: "Ladies and gentlemen, the prime minister of Canada." As the slight, natty figure appeared from the rear of the stage, young and old alike went wild, everyone pressing closer to the stage, reaching out to touch him, throwing flowers, shouting his name. The leader's attempts to calm them did not really succeed, and not until he began his speech was quiet restored. Canadians had never had a politician like this before, and the election campaign of 1968 was not a contest but the coronation of Canada's new king, Pierre Elliott Trudeau.

Incredibly, that was thirty years ago, a full generation. The adolescents in the crowds who turned out to greet the new Liberal leader are today's adults. Trudeau was then forty-eight years old, and now he is almost eighty. Much has changed in Canada, but what has not, despite all the vicissitudes of partisan politics, is that Trudeau in 1998, just as in 1968, remains a force in Canada. In 1968 he inspired Canadians—academics, politicians, and teeny-boppers alike—with his charismatic appeal for participatory democracy and a new style of politics. In 1998, with Canada and Quebec still on a collision course, politicians continue to fear that Trudeau might again make a speech or issue a statement that suddenly swings public opinion in Canada, exactly as he did during the Meech and Charlottetown debates. No other Canadian public figure has ever retained such power to move his country almost fifteen years after leaving office.

No one else in office either has ever had his power to galvanize opinion. While he was prime minister, Trudeau was the most loved and most hated of leaders, sometimes simultaneously. He burst onto the scene in 1965, a virtual political novice. He had come to Ottawa after a lifetime as a political gadfly, student, and lawyer, but he was still so little known that people could argue over the spelling of his middle name—was it Eliot, Elliot, or Elliott? He had written a book, published in English as *Federalism and the French Canadians*, but though many had heard of it, almost no one had read it. What was important was that he was a federalist. When he was chosen party leader and prime minister in 1968, the issue of the day was Quebec and its place in Canada. The man and the subject came together perfectly and, after the respected but dull Lester Pearson, he was youthful, intellectual, irreverent, and sexy.

Trudeau was born in 1919 in Montreal, and he grew up in a family that went in a few years from being comfortable to being rich. He was fluently bilingual; he was educated by the Jesuits at the Collège Jean-de-Brébeuf, and then at Harvard, the London School of Economics, and École des sciences politiques in Paris; and he travelled widely. During the Second World War he had taken part in anti-conscription demonstrations and did not serve in the forces, but in the long era of Maurice Duplessis he resisted the know-nothing nationalism that kept French Canada in blinkers. He became a founder of *Cité libre* in 1950, a small magazine that tried to light up the darkness. He lined up with the workers during the great Asbestos strike of 1949, a climactic event in the struggle against Duplessis, and he soon began to write powerful essays that attacked the attitudes and predilections of the *nationalistes* and their friends in and out of power. This exposure gave him contacts throughout opposition circles in Quebec, and eventually, once Duplessis was gone, led to the life of a law professor at Université de Montréal.

Trudeau had no party politics as yet. He leaned towards the New Democratic Party and its predecessor, the Co-operative Commonwealth Federation, but never joined. He denounced the Liberals under Pearson for their nuclear policy, and showed no interest at all in the Conservatives of John Diefenbaker. But in 1965, when Pearson was trying to find attractive new candidates in Quebec, Trudeau's name came up and, with Jean Marchand and Gérard Pelletier, he went to Ottawa. Very quickly, he was parliamentary secretary to the prime minister, and then a reforming justice minister. In eighteen months he modernized the Criminal Code and the nation's antiquated divorce and sex laws. In April 1968 he won the party leadership against the titans of Liberalism on the fourth ballot.

Trudeau set out to remake Canada. The federal position on Quebec—cooperative federalism it had been called under Pearson—hardened under Trudeau. At the same time, the prime minister set off on a long quest for a patriated Constitution and a Charter of Rights and Freedoms. Canadian foreign policy was examined root and branch, Canada recognized China, and Trudeau unilaterally altered defence policy. In October 1970 he reacted with cold remorselessness and the War Measures Act to put down the terrorism unleashed by militant Quebec separatists. His government completed the social welfare state—and the Treasury spent public funds as if there were no tomorrow.

Through it all, the voters' love affair with Trudeau waxed and waned. The leader's sharp tongue—"Fuddle-Duddle," he told opposition MPs—annoyed many, and his arrogance was jarring. The great majority of 1968 was, by 1972, reduced to a minority government dependent for its life on NDP support. In 1974 Trudeau regained his majority but, growing ever more unpopular, narrowly lost power to Joe Clark's Conservatives in 1979. Clark missed his chance to consolidate his hold on power, however, and lost a vote of confidence in the House in December 1979. Trudeau, who had given up the leadership, was persuaded to return. On February 18, 1980, he won another majority.

"Welcome to the 1980s!" Trudeau said to the enthusiastic Liberal crowd that evening. For much of the next four years, his preoccupation was Quebec and the Constitution. It began with his commitment to renew federalism during the referendum campaign of 1980, in which Trudeau's forceful, timely intervention rallied flagging federalists and routed René Lévesque's separatists. For the next eighteen months, the Constitution was his *idée fixe*. Finally, after bitter debate in parliament, after a reference to the Supreme Court, and after protracted negotiations with the premiers, the federal government and nine provinces agreed to patriate the British North America Act of 1867 and to entrench the Charter of Rights and Freedoms. It was Trudeau's greatest moment, dimmed only by the refusal of Lévesque's government to sign, thus leaving the issue of Quebec's place in Canada unresolved.

In his last years in office, with the Constitution home and the economy in recession, Trudeau became bored with everything except foreign policy. On February 29, 1984, after a solitary walk in a snowstorm the evening before, Trudeau announced his retirement from politics. It was, he said, the first day of the rest of his life.

Inevitably, his influence endured. While Trudeau returned to Montreal and private life, doting on his three sons, he kept a watchful eye on the national discourse. Twice he returned to public life, both times to defend his vision of Canada: first to denounce the Meech Lake accord in 1987, and then to attack the Charlottetown accord in 1992. Both times, his eloquent, effective opposition was critical to the defeat of the measures.

In power and out, Trudeau was a primeval force, the only Canadian leader who could dominate the agenda simply by his presence. His mind was sharp, and his instincts and timing shrewd. Canada had never seen his like before or since. For good or ill, his shadow dominates—or darkens—the Canadian landscape.

This book examines the legacy of Pierre Trudeau, thirty years after he came to power. We approached former politicians and associates of Trudeau, as well as historians, political scientists, novelists, journalists, and philosophers, and asked them to reflect on Trudeau a generation later in the context of the 1990s. Some sought to put Trudeau in the broadest context, examining him as part of the Canadian political tradition or compared with other leaders. Here, in Part One, is Trudeau in history. Others put him into a personal context: in Part Two we see Trudeau as lover, outdoorsman, communicator, cultural icon. Still others looked at the Trudeau record, studying his political record in an effort to understand what he got right—and wrong. In Part Three we find Trudeau as reformer, diplomat, liberal, and constitutionalist. Finally, the last essay reflects on Trudeau today, certainly older, perhaps sadder, perhaps wiser.

Winter 1998: The occasion is the Toronto launch of the English edition of *Cité libre*. At a reception at the Metro Centre, the editors and their supporters gather to celebrate the renewal of the journal that launched so many crusades. Hundreds have come, admirers all, and they mob the now wizened, almost frail man. Students seek autographs, former colleagues shake his hand, reporters press forward with questions. "I am no longer in politics," he responds with his famous shrug to their entreaties, "you can't be half in and half out." Then again, for Canadians, perhaps Pierre Elliott Trudeau never left.

1

TRUDEAU'S PLACE

Guarding a Most Famous Stream: Trudeau and the Canadian Political Tradition

■

MICHAEL BLISS

Michael Bliss is one of Canada's best-known business, *medical, and political historians. A professor at the University of Toronto, he has won both the Sir John A. Macdonald and the F.-X. Garneau medals of the Canadian Historical Association and the J.B. Tyrrell medal of the Royal Society of Canada. Among his many books is* Right Honourable Men: The Descent of Canadian Politics from Macdonald to Mulroney. *He was an early and active opponent of the Meech Lake and Charlottetown accords.*

I T SEEMS EASY TO LOCATE Pierre Elliott Trudeau against the mainstream of Canadian political leadership. He was surely an outsider, a stranger, a maverick, a self-proclaimed contrarian. *Against the Current*, the title of his most recent book, says it all.

From the beginning, his style was unconventional. Trudeau was either a playboy dabbling in politics or a breath of fresh air, or perhaps a little of both, as he thumbed his nose at parliamentary protocol. Then, less than three years after entering politics, he was prime minister. No one else had ever come in from the cold so fast. No one ever received a warmer welcome than Trudeau, in the outpouring of Trudeaumania in the 1968 election campaign. His style seemed unique and charismatic. "Had there ever been in Canada a national party leader quite like this?" historian Roger Graham later wrote. "Sir Wilfrid Laurier, let us say, sliding down a banister? Sir Robert Borden in goggles and flippers? Arthur Meighen in a Mercedes? Mackenzie King at judo? R.B. Bennett on skis?"

Had there ever been a prime minister who seemed so aloof and arrogant in office? A prime minister who told his political opponents to "fuck off" and "eat shit"? A prime minister who raised his middle finger to protesting constituents? A prime minister who taunted opposition MPs as "nobodies"? A prime minister who told Canadians to stop expecting that government should be Santa Claus? A prime minister who said, "I'm not really governing to be re-elected. If the Canadian people don't like it, they can lump it."

Was there ever a prime minister as tough as Trudeau during the October Crisis of 1970? A prime minister as determined to bring about a constitutional revolution as Trudeau in 1981? One of the provincial premiers told Stephen Clarkson and Christina McCall that Trudeau was "so diamond-hard he glittered" during the negotiations on constitutional renewal. These were not so much negotiations as ultimata, laid down by a prime minister determined to force Britain to amend Canada's constitution against the wishes of eight provincial premiers, determined to declare unilateral independence if Britain baulked, determined to fulfil his promise to Quebeckers whether the province of Quebec liked it or not. Just watch him.

And then watch him come out of retirement to attack the entire political élite of the country when they agree to water down his constitution in the Meech Lake accord. Watch him come out of retirement again to condemn the second unanimous deal, the Charlottetown accord. By the 1990s he was fighting for his principles virtually without followers, as most of his party abandoned him to lust after renewed power.

In his heyday the Liberal Party's image makers liked to play up Trudeau the gunslinger, jacket open, thumbs hooked in his belt, heading down Main Street for the showdown. His own favourite metaphor, splendidly displayed in his television memoirs, was solo canoeing, coming in from the wilderness, returning to it by himself. Cincinnatus, the saviour of Rome, had his plough; Pierre Trudeau, of Canada, his paddle.

Most politicians believe that the key to their art is compromise. When there are differences of opinion, conflicting interests, clashing personalities, the wise and successful leader is the one who finds a common denominator, brokers a deal, brings people together. Most students of Canadian politics would agree that brokerage has been central to the mainstream tradition. Macdonald, Laurier, and King were all great compromisers. They had to be, given the tremendous diversity of regional, religious, ethnic, and class interests that compose the stew of Canadian politics. If Macdonald made the Conservative Party a haven for any interest group with forty votes, Laurier read from his recipes, applied them to the Liberals, and haunted Mackenzie King with reminders of the need to conciliate Quebec, the West, and everyone else with a grievance.

Purists hated the apparent surrender of principle that seemed to accompany political success in Canada. How could Macdonald consort with the ultramontane papists in Quebec on Monday and the Loyal Orange Lodge on Tuesday? If "Waffly Willy" Laurier went to heaven, Henri Bourassa complained, he would immediately propose a compromise between God and Satan. To Frank Scott of the Co-operative Commonwealth Federation, Mackenzie King would do nothing by halves that he could do by quarters. When Lester Pearson decided in 1963 to abandon the Liberal Party's principled opposition to nuclear weapons for Canadian forces, one of his most outraged critics was Trudeau. "Power offered itself to Mr. Pearson," Trudeau wrote in *Cité libre*. "He had nothing to lose except his honor. He lost it."

The alternative approach to leadership, frequently advocated by New Democratic Party politicians and their predecessors, and to whom the young Trudeau seemed most sympathetic, was to cling to your principles, confront those who disagreed with you, and argue, persuade, claw, and fight your way to victory. If you lost at the power game, at least you went out with honour intact.

The trouble was that most Canadian politicians who took strong stands on issues of principle did lose. Not only J.S. Woodsworth and practically everyone else on the left but also their true-blue counterparts, ostensibly principled Tories like Arthur Meighen and R.B. Bennett. Trudeau did appear to stand in a kind of prime ministerial tradition as he shrugged instead of compromised, hammered the Front de Libération du Québec with the War Measures Act, rammed through patriation and the Charter of Rights and Freedoms, hissed and mocked the media—and anyone else who got in his way. It was indeed the tradition of Meighen and Bennett, two of the least popular prime ministers in Canadian history. It was also the tradition of one remarkably successful contemporary Conservative politician, Britain's Margaret Thatcher.

■

There is a way of challenging this conventional wisdom, a contrarian point of view.

Until his pathetic last days in office, when he, too, trumpeted the virtues of being unpopular, Brian Mulroney prided himself on having ousted Trudeau as the heir to Canada's mainstream political tradition. An experienced mediator in industrial disputes, Mulroney saw himself as a skilled practitioner in the politics of creative compromise, particularly with the Meech Lake accord. The rhetoric of Meech was an endless litany of the necessity of compromise, of finding common ground, of remembering the tradeoffs of 1867, of scorning those whose principles would divide and rupture the nation. The first ministers who made Meech saw themselves as direct successors to the Fathers of Confederation. They were the statesmen of Re-confederation. Trudeau was the outsider, the spoiler, the fanatic.

But where exactly was the mainstream Canadian tradition as it poured into the muck of Meech Lake? Would Macdonald ever have conceded control of the Senate and the Supreme Court to the provinces? Would Laurier or King or St. Laurent ever have given special status to Quebec? Would the leader of the federal government at any previous time in Canadian history have made as many concessions for the sake of a deal as Mulroney did at Meech Lake? When the premiers of Manitoba and Ontario found themselves urging the prime minister to speak up for the national interest in the final Meech bargaining, it was clear that a mainstream tradition of resisting the power-hungry provinces had collapsed. In his desperation to make a deal at any cost, Mulroney had abandoned prime ministerial stewardship of the national interest.

The sense of a mainstream brokerage tradition in Canadian politics must not imply that prime ministers have never been firm or tough. Macdonald was at least as contemptuous of the provincial governments as Trudeau ever was, and usually acted accordingly. When respect for the rule of law was at stake, in the North-West Rebellion and the trial of Louis Riel, Macdonald could be rock solid. His perhaps apocryphal comment "Riel shall hang, though every dog in Quebec bark in his favour," certainly bears compari-

son with Trudeau's "Let them bleed" interview during the October Crisis. Laurier and St. Laurent, who governed Canada under
very favourable circumstances, were perhaps never fully tested.
Robert Borden, whose "unholy alliance" with Henri Bourassa and
the Quebec nationalists in 1911 anticipated the partnership between Mulroney and Lucien Bouchard, rose to his duty in giving
Canada Thatcher-like leadership during the conscription crisis of
1917–18. Even King, possibly the flabbiest of all prime ministers
before Pearson, drew the line when Maurice Duplessis challenged
Canada's participation in the war against Hitler. Liberal legions intervened in a Quebec election to destroy their opponent, not deal
with him. Even Pearson, whose desire to be liked sometimes had
a frighteningly irresponsible dimension, could have a backbone on
occasion, specifically after Charles de Gaulle's "Vive le Québec
libre" speech. The prime minister sent the president home.

Much of Trudeau's toughness and unwillingness to compromise, at least at key moments in his career, was firmly in the mainstream of behaviour for Canadian prime ministers. As prime
minister, you make a lot of compromises, but you are careful not to
give away the shop. You always have a bottom line. You don't surrender control of the federation to the provinces. You don't let one
province, Quebec, become a state within a state. You don't allow
the rule of law to be undermined. In familiar words, you stand on
guard for Canada.

In this regard, the odd man out at Meech Lake and afterwards
was not Trudeau. He stood firmly in the grand Canadian political
tradition. Those who abandoned that tradition were the Conservatives Joe Clark and Mulroney. In hopes of forging alliances with
provincial governments on the one hand and Quebec nationalists
on the other, the Tories abandoned the notion of the supremacy of
the government of Canada in the federal system and the constitutional equality of all Canadians.

From a reverse angle, it should not be forgotten that when he
chose to, Trudeau could broker, buy off interests, and bribe voters
with their own money as readily as most of his predecessors. No
one has suggested, for example, that Trudeau's personal spartanism

had the slightest impact on the Ottawa circus he presided over. He made one or two good Senate appointments (out of several score), he had fewer sleazy personal friends than prime ministers before and since, and he seems intellectually to have begun to think about the limits of the Santa Claus state. Otherwise, in the Trudeau years, there was no fundamental change from Laurier or King's day in the outpouring of Liberal patronage, campaign promises, or spending on public works. Or perhaps there was: arguably, the cynical use of taxpayers' money to buy up regional, cultural, ethnic, and even gender interest groups may have reached a kind of apotheosis during the Trudeau years. The fact that bastard Keynesianism was everywhere in the ascendent and that no one seriously controlled government spending only lubricated the process.

Although they could never quite wean themselves from these practices, the Mulroney Tories at least recognized that the writing was on the wall. For all his sins, Mulroney did not leave office under the shadow of a last-minute orgy of cynical patronage appointments. Trudeau, like Sir Charles Tupper in 1896, did. He also left behind him the swimming pool at 24 Sussex Drive, donated by friends of the Liberal Party. If Mackenzie King had been a swimmer, he too might have appreciated such a favour. Robert Borden, I think, would have turned the pool down.

■

Canadian historian A.R.M. Lower once wrote a book entitled *This Most Famous Stream*, a meditation on the expansion of liberal democracy. A generation or two ago, before postmodern theory and the questioning of most traditional notions of "progress," there was a commonly held view that the mainstream of the Canadian political tradition was one of expanding freedom. It was usually a Liberal view. Its heroes included the rebels of 1837 and those who fought for responsible government against the British and the Family Compact. After Confederation, Liberals were far more concerned with expanding the franchise and moving Canada towards democracy and independance than were anti-American, imperialist Tories like Macdonald.

King situated himself firmly in the great Liberal tradition, begun for Canada by his rebel grandfather, William Lyon Mackenzie. With the achievement of universal suffrage and de facto Canadian independence by the early 1920s, advanced Liberalism concentrated on building a welfare state, of which King became the chief Canadian architect. Members of Pearson's government saw themselves as further broadening that mainstream Canadian tradition with their introduction of the Canada Pension Plan, the Canada Assistance Plan, and national health insurance. In fact, all Canadian politicians had become social welfare democrats by the 1950s, with John Diefenbaker serving as the Progressive Conservative who brought his party into the century of the common man and woman.

The first Trudeau government planned to continue to broaden the social welfare tradition. It vastly liberalized access to unemployment insurance, tinkered with experiments in a guaranteed annual income, and saw regional development and equalization programs as the key to its thrust towards a "just society." But by 1971 it was becoming clear that the state might have trouble financing existing welfare entitlements, let alone launching major new programs. The limits of welfare Liberalism were being reached.

Another major tradition in liberalism's challenge to authority in the Western world had been an emphasis on expanding individual rights, especially vis-à-vis the state. Although Canadian Liberals, led by the social conservative St. Laurent, were not particularly eager champions of human rights during and after the war years, other politicians began to ride wavelets of interest. With his Canadian Bill of Rights, legislated federally in 1960, Diefenbaker caught what turned out to be a rising tide of human rights concerns all across Canada.

The rights of the individual were central to Trudeau's early politics because he stood firmly in the old *rouge* tradition of having to fight for them in Quebec against the collectivist thrust of church-state hegemony. Trudeau's early politics, like Laurier's, revolved around the struggle to establish human rights and real democracy in Quebec. When, as prime minister of Canada, he began to be pushed on constitutional issues—somewhat against his will—he took up the idea of entrenching a bill or charter of rights to advance liberty across the whole country. In 1981–82 he won that struggle—his own determination clearly making the difference between success and failure—and became the father of Canada's Charter of Rights and Freedoms.

By the 1990s the Charter, while still controversial, had become a revered Canadian institution. It was impossible to return to pre-Charter days, except, possibly, in a secessionist Quebec. The Canadian Charter was being studied around the world as a milestone in human rights legislation. Canada's Constitution of 1982 had completed the long march to total independence, and its Charter, completing the transfer of power from the Crown to the people, was the first significant improvement Canadians had made on the political institutions they had inherited from Britain. It will probably be copied in the old motherland in the early years of the twenty-first century. Here, indeed, was the mainstream of modern human rights liberalism running broad and true.

■

Pierre Trudeau was undeniably more abrasive, arrogant, tough, aloof, solitary, and self-contained than traditional politicians in Canada or most other countries. Temperamentally, he began as an outsider and ended as one, most particularly in Quebec. But if he was not a back-slapper like Macdonald, a charmer like Laurier, a thoughtful fusser like King, or a diplomat like Pearson, neither was he an exotic European philosopher king, an inscrutable northern magus, or Cincinnatus in buckskin. He brought to the prime ministership intellectual skills, life experiences, and values different from those brought by most of his predecessors. Once in the office, however, he was not as unlike them as even his own ornery reflections imply. He brokered competing interests, bought political support, and doled out patronage in the grand Canadian manner. He stood firmly on guard for Canada when it was menaced. He greatly expanded the freedoms of Canadians. In these regards he was a true inheritor of the mantles of William Lyon Mackenzie, Sir John A. Macdonald, Wilfrid Laurier, Robert Borden, William Lyon Mackenzie King, Lester Pearson, even John Diefenbaker. Some maverick.

Trudeau: The Idea of Canadianism

■

RICHARD GWYN

Richard Gwyn is a regular columnist on national and international affairs for the Toronto Star. *As the syndicated Ottawa columnist for the* Star *from 1973 to 1985, he covered most of Trudeau's years in power, and he distilled these impressions and observations into his biography of Trudeau,* The Northern Magus. *His most recent book,* Nationalism without Walls, *was published in 1995.*

I N THE APRIL 21, 1997, edition of *Maclean's*, two dozen historians delivered their collective judgment on Pierre Elliott Trudeau. They concluded that his accomplishments ranked him as High Average, one rung below the single Near Great, Louis St. Laurent, and two below the predictable trio of the Great: William Lyon Mackenzie King, John A. Macdonald, and Wilfrid Laurier.

Even this comparatively modest assessment exaggerated the historians' appreciation of him. The writers noted that Trudeau's achievement in surviving in office for so long—his fifteen years has been exceeded since 1945 by only four other world democratic leaders—had earned him bonus marks in addition to the comparatively scanty number he had accumulated by his actual policies and programs. The historians were harsh, almost contemptuous, about his record. "The disappointment of the century . . . who left Canada dramatically more divided and drastically poorer than he found it," declared Desmond Morton of the McGill Institute for the Study of Canada. "A resounding failure, both on the grounds of public finance and national unity," concluded René Durocher of Université de Montréal.

This censoriousness by our historians about Canada's recent political leaders—Lester Pearson was likewise ranked in the B-minus category—provided useful fodder for argument among the chattering classes. Perhaps the historians were overcritical of contemporary figures who had to operate in the blinding glare of the media, cope with a much more sophisticated and demanding electorate, and deal with vocal and well-organized interest groups.

Conversely, they may have been more indulgent towards antiquities whose errors, when re-examined years later, tend to get overwhelmed by the gentilities of official papers and the self-serving circumlocutions of memoirs.

The real criticism to be made of the historians' judgment is that they were not behaving like historians. They were looking at the trees rather than the forest. Trudeau can only be judged by fitting him into the context of contemporary Canada and, as any analysis of things Canadian must do, by accepting the inevitability of paradox and ambiguity.

A severe critic of Trudeau, York University political scientist Kenneth McRoberts, has perhaps put the case best for the former prime minister, even while condemning him for "bringing Canada to the point of collapse." In *Misconceiving Canada*, McRoberts describes Trudeau's hostility to nationalism, specifically to the bicultural, *deux nations* concept. In McRoberts' view, this approach was, and is, the only one that might keep Quebec within Canada. Still, he admits that the devil has some good tunes. It is a "profound irony," he writes, that "Trudeau, the self-declared anti-nationalist, is embraced by much of English-Canada as the 'saviour' of the Canadian nation and ultimately emerges as the champion of Canadian nationalism." Trudeau's strategy, although aimed at Quebec, had the largely unforeseen effect of "transforming English Canada." Bilingualism, multiculturalism, and the Charter of Rights and Freedoms, as well as the notion of the equality of all citizens and provinces, have met the needs and aspirations of most Canadians outside Quebec. Yet, in McRoberts' view, because this vision leaves no space for Québécois to be fully themselves, it has brought the country to the brink of collapse.

But McRoberts misses the central point. Whether Canada is collapsing or not these days, it is most certainly inchoate as a nation-state, and deeply divided. Yet Canadianism has never been healthier. The idea of being Canadian now commands wide and deep appeal. For some new citizens it's a mere convenience; for the great majority it's a real achievement. The same can be said for the native-born. Canadianism means membership in a collective enterprise that, however diverse, pluralist, regionalized, or postmodern, inspires genuine pride, commands a real sense of belonging, and participates in a remarkable and virtually unparalled human enterprise.

Put simply, today's Canada is Trudeau's Canada. More accurately, today's concept of Canadianism is Trudeau's concept, plus other enduring aspects like Pearson's legacy of internationalism or the traditions of civility in public discourse which can be traced back to the peace, order, and good government of the Loyalists.

Before assessing Trudeau's legacy, it may be useful to address the lesser points cited by the historians to justify their judging Trudeau less consequential to Canadian affairs than the competent corporate lawyer St. Laurent.

■

Certainly, Trudeau left Canada "drastically poorer" than he found it in terms of public finances. But in the 1970s and 1980s, every country piled up its national debt, not least the United States under its free-marketeer president Ronald Reagan. The remedy—essentially of saying no—was not applied until the advent of Margaret Thatcher. The real closure on Thatcher's success did not occur until 1997, when a Labour government returned to power committed to maintaining her fiscal and economic policies while modulating her social and cultural ones. It is improbable that Trudeau, or anyone, could have sold fiscal restraint and a lowering of expectations about government in the way that Finance Minister Paul Martin was able to do in the mid-1990s. Not until the early years of that decade did public opinion switch from blaming government meanness to criticizing government fiscal indulgence for social and economic problems. During his nine years in office after Trudeau, Mulroney failed to make any dent on the deficit. South of the border, George Bush was equally helpless. Trudeau may well have been an economic dilettante, but most democratic leaders of his generation were the same.

The really serious judgment, and for Trudeau the wounding one personally, is that he left the country far more deeply divided than he found it and that he failed resoundingly on the issue of national unity. This cause was the focus of Trudeau's entire political existence. Assessing his contributions as destructive is the equivalent of saying that Macdonald bungled his opportunity to create a real country in 1867 and that King perpetuated the Depression. If true, Trudeau ought not be rated High Average but positioned below John Diefenbaker or bracketed with Kim Campbell.

The question is one of timing. In the spring of 1998 we are clearly more deeply divided than ever before. Had fewer than 30,000 Quebeckers, half the winning margin, changed their minds from No to Yes while in the ballot boxes on October 31, 1995, Canada today would not merely be divided but separated into two nation-states—assuming that Jacques Parizeau meant what he wrote in his memoirs. Before that came the failures of the Meech Lake and Charlottetown accords, the return to power in Quebec of the Parti Québécois, the emergence and near-triumph of the Bloc Québécois in Ottawa, and the rise of support for sovereignty in the polls to as much as 60 percent (it still hovers at the half-way mark). The charismatic Lucien Bouchard has replaced Parizeau, and he will almost certainly win re-election. Ahead looms another referendum, most probably in 1999. At that time, Canada's champion is again due to be Jean Chrétien.

A western regional party, at best uncomprehending about Quebec, at worst hostile to its aspirations, is now the official opposition. Its election campaign featured a TV commercial depicting Quebec politicians, whether federalist or separatist, as Guilty Men, along with a denunciation by its leader of "Quebec-based politicians." This saying out loud of the long unsayable has radically changed the tone of the national debate. The truth, unpalatable but undeniable, is that Reform and Preston Manning are echoing faithfully the sentiments of a large number of Canadians. These sentiments encompass an indifference to Quebeckers' aspirations and an irritated weariness with the entire topic. Seldom has there been so little in the centre holding the country together.

Some observers nevertheless claim to see shafts of light in the endless unity tunnel. A crashing federal miscalulation in the weeks before the last referendum was not to inform Quebec that separation meant separation. Already, Justice Minister Ann McClellan is co-opting into the official wisdom Manning's long-standing call for a Plan B. Never again will Quebeckers make up their minds on the basis of wishful thinking and blind ignorance, as happened in 1995, when 25 per cent and more of those intending to vote sovereigntist told pollsters they assumed that, after separation, they would still send MPs to Ottawa and experience no unsettling economic or financial consequences. Such realism may alter the outcome. So may the growing realization of the economic consequences, already so painfully visible in Montreal, of protracted political uncertainty. In this optimistic scenario, Quebeckers are approaching a mood when they will be ready to proclaim a victory and call the sovereigntist troops home, provided they are designated a symbolic, distinct society.

A contradictory, pessimistic scenario is equally plausible. Bouchard's emotional appeal is too powerful to be overcome. To be young in Quebec is to be a sovereigntist, and only the aged are federalists. Western and Reform opposition groups make a distinct society offer unfeasible, and, in humiliation, Quebeckers vote for sovereignty whether they want it or not.

The point here is not that one scenario will turn out to be more accurate than the other but that one of them will happen at some point in the near future. By that time Trudeau will have spent a decade and a half in retirement and be nearing eighty. He may not even be around to kick at all.

Only some extreme version of the victim theory, of politics and of life, can hold Trudeau responsible forever for everything that may happen long after he left command. It would certainly be glib to blame everything that has happened since upon Mulroney. His motives were generally honourable, if mixed, because they included envy of Trudeau. Nevertheless, at Meech Lake and at Charlottetown he reached too far, opening up a second front at a time when, by his war for free trade, he was alienating many of the English-Canadian nationalists whose support he needed to win his constitutional conflict. Similarly, Chrétien's hands-off approach to the 1995 referendum has been widely castigated. As always in politics,

accident played an important part. Premier Robert Bourassa turned
off other Canadians by his unilingual sign legislation, which seemed
like a turning away from the bilingualism into which many people
had poured their effort and idealism. The stubbornness and self-
conviction of Newfoundland Premier Clyde Wells was an x-factor
that few could have anticipated (although the massive public support for Wells, which powerfully reinforced his intellectual convictions, ought to have been detected and factored in). Later, almost
no one anticipated Bouchard's hypnotic appeal.

At the moment Trudeau actually left the bridge in 1984,
Canada's ship of state was headed towards safety. The recent referendum of 1980, for which he had been the federalist champion,
had ended in triumph. The overall result was convincing and even
seemed to be permanent. A majority of Québécois had voted No,
and the sovereignists were headed towards defeat and displacement
by the nominally federalist Robert Bourassa. Reform and the Bloc
Québécois did not exist, and Bouchard was still practising law in
Chicoutimi.

The link between that time and the present is that Trudeau's
patriation of the Constitution and enactment of the Charter of
Rights and Freedoms in 1982 constituted a political and emotional
land-mine that was bound to explode one day. This connection
is accurate enough in hindsight, but was far from certain then. Although the Quebec legislature roundly condemned the act as a deception and an intrusion, ordinary Quebeckers showed few signs
of shock. There were no public protests or demonstrations, and the
polls measured no increase in support for sovereignty. Quebeckers
quickly lost most of their interest in politics, whether nationalist or
federalist, turning instead to the phenomenon of Quebec Inc. and
the first ever crop of successful francophone entrepreneurs.

Because of all our succeeding troubles, the victim analysis—
Trudeau made us do everything that we've done—retains considerable appeal. The best expression of this view is contained in
two recent books, McRoberts' *Misconceiving Canada* (1997) and Guy
Laforest's *Trudeau and the End of a Canadian Dream* (1995). Both argue
that, by his "bitter struggle against duality" (Laforest's phrase) and

by wrongly "see[ing] the secession of Quebec in apocalyptic" terms (McRoberts' phrase, based on Trudeau's remark that the breakup of Canada would be "a crime against humanity"), Trudeau has straight-jacketed the country into a "One Canada" vision that precludes a solution based either on a Canada-Quebec condominium (Laforest) or a "con-federalism" (McRoberts). In short, Trudeau dashed sovereignty-association as an alternative to separation.

The obvious counter commentary is that though there may be a distinction between the two, there is no real difference. If the rest of the country does have to cease being "a nation that dares not speak its name," it may well do so more effectively when it does not have to look over its shoulder constantly to check how its partner is getting along. Rump Canada's national self-interests would call for a settlement—restoration of at least the native-occupied Nouveau Québec so that the new country would still stretch from sea to sea—that no Quebec negotiator could agree to. And other Canadians would never agree to any deal that did not encompass an immediate cutoff of all subsidies, at present worth several billion a year, and an immediate return of all federal agencies. The new con-federal Canadian family would quickly be as unhappy as the present one.

It is also far from certain that the mood of most Quebeckers in the next referendum will be as antagonistic and as reckless as it was in 1995.

■

The single most memorable comment on Trudeau was crafted by his biographers Stephen Clarkson and Christina McCall a decade after he retired: "He haunts us still." Another relevant comment was uttered two decades ago by a close friend: "He sucks all the oxygen from a room." While doing absolutely nothing, strolling down a street, shopping, standing patiently in a film queue, releasing familiar political thoughts about the Constitution to the press, Trudeau continues to hypnotize, intimidate, and inspire.

It is hard to think of any other contemporary figure who so dominates the national public consciousness. Or to name anyone, on the vital and uniquely Canadian issue of national unity, who still commands so much respect or so much hatred.

Asked to name a hero, Trudeau is the only one that young Canadians can think of, especially now that Wayne Gretzky is aging. Fading campaign posters, particularly the one of him in the gun-fighter's pose, can still be spotted in restaurants, shops, offices, homes, and, most especially, among ethnic admirers. His quite awful book of memoirs sold 150,000 copies, and a cottage industry keeps cranking out selections of his writings and speeches. His TV series drew millions to their screens. In the spring of 1997 two plays about him were performed in Toronto, a revival of Linda Griffiths' 1980 tour-de-force, *Maggie and Pierre*, and the latest in Michael Hollingsworth's historical chronicle, *Pierre Trudeau and the Quebec Question*. Both were sellouts. In the winter of 1997, when he attended the inaugural lecture of the series established to honour Senator Keith Davey, Trudeau upstaged the speaker, John Kenneth Galbraith, at the reception that followed, even while he determinedly stood aside. One political veteran remarked, "He's the one ex–prime minister everyone wants to be seen standing beside." Any time Trudeau flicks an eye, he becomes an item in *Frank* magazine.

Some of this attention is just nostalgia—a means to revive warm memories of Expo 67, of mini-skirts, of youth in the ascendency, and peace and love. It is a way to recall more innocent times, before the global economy, down-sizing, and fiscal constraint, when it was still credible to assume that governments could, and should, solve most of the country's problems. It is an entry to those years, before all our protective barriers came down, when there was substance to the cause of economic and cultural nationalism.

A large part of this attention is contemporary politics. Canadians are still voting for Trudeau. They did it in 1990 by their massive support for his surrogate, Clyde Wells. They did it during the 1992 Charlottetown referendum, when his Maison de Egg Roll manifesto told them that to oppose the accord was not to oppose Quebec. In the 1995 referendum, Chrétien's adamant opposition to distinct society, until the last frenetic week, had its source in

Trudeau. Now Manning's call for equality of the provinces anchors its single claim to political respectability in Trudeau's identical call, though for radically different motives.

Trudeau haunts us still because of his style, his elegance, his intellect, his fearlessness, and his ruthlessness. He teases, taunts, inspires, and bugs the hell out of Canadians because they know he is utterly un-Canadian, but exactly what they want other people to think Canadians are like. He haunts because he has given us an idea of what being Canadian means—the only idea that gives us any national cohesion now that the alternatives we face are an association of two sovereignties or further decentralization within a nation-state that is already the most-decentralized in the world.

Without doubt, Trudeau's patriation of the Constitution and enactment of the Charter of Rights and Freedoms was a provocation to and a humiliation of Quebec's highly influential political class. Not so to Quebeckers in general, who, represented by federal MPs in all parties, were strongly supportive of these acts. Of the four signatures on the new Constitution, all but one—Queen Elizabeth II's—are those of Quebec francophones. Here, many critics rest their case. Unexamined is what would have happened if the Constitution had remained at Westminster and if the Charter had remained a cabinet document.

At the cusp of the millennium, the Charter has become a surrogate citizenship, a summary description of Canadianism, for a clear majority of Canadians. If, as a nation-state, Canada is "not a real country," the Canadianism this society nurtures has become a passionately held conviction. Much of this Canadianism we owe to Trudeau: bilingualism; multiculturalism; cultural and racial diversity; regional variety; tolerance; civility; internationalism; the equality of all provinces, a presumption that does not require them to be treated as identical, but ensures that they will feel full partners in the whole; and the equality of all citizens, bracketed, in finely calibrated Canadian ambiguity, with a recognition of the need to nurture group rights and identities.

For a regionalized, decentralized, multinational, pluralist, and heterogenous nation-state without a distinctive language or a dominant ethnic group, condemned to be influenced deeply by its super-power neighbour, that list adds up to an inspirational *projet national*. If the United Nations is any credible judge, Canada is on track towards fulfilling that project. According to international agencies, it is also doing quite well in terms of global economic competitiveness, despite Trudeau's legacy of red ink.

This Canada, largely Trudeau's making, is so successful a nation-state—or, more accurately, a society—that for any group to leave it, Québécois or others, would be an act of collective idiocy. This accomplishment is the real reason for believing that there is light at the end of the unity tunnel.

In his person and by his ideas, Trudeau made a signal contribution to the evolution of the idea of Canadianism. Few other national leaders have left such a legacy—perhaps, Charles de Gaulle in rebuilding postwar France, Franklin D. Roosevelt by educating Americans to trust themselves rather than fear the Depression, and Lee Kwan Yew by inventing Singapore out of a barren island. The incomplete legacy that Trudeau leaves behind is the unity of Canada itself. Since we are responsible individuals rather than victims, the task of keeping the nation united is now up to us all.

2

TRUDEAU'S IMPACT

The Lover:
Dancing with Trudeau

■

LINDA GRIFFITHS

Writer/actor **Linda Griffiths** *might be described as a Canadian original. She not only writes plays like* Maggie & Pierre *and* The Duchess *★a.k.a. Wallis Simpson but often performs them too, in sold-out runs. In 1991 she was nominated for a Governor General's Award for* The Darling Family, *which was made into a feature film. She has won numerous awards, including four Dora Mavor Moore awards for both acting and writing, a Chalmers Award, a Gemini Award, and the Los Angeles A.G.A. Award for her title role in John Sayles' film* Lianna.

THEY PHONED and asked me to write about "Trudeau the Lover" for this book. I thought, "Trudeau the Lover?" I never knew Pierre Trudeau the lover, and even if I did, how crass to kiss and tell. But deep inside I knew exactly what they were talking about. I had a flash image of a slight figure in a perfect tux with a little bit of dandruff on the collar. There was music playing and a light touch on my shoulder. I remembered what it was to dance with Trudeau.

So many people have a story of meeting Trudeau. Even today they stop me in the street and tell of their encounters in excited whispers: "I met him when he was campaigning, and he smiled at me . . . I met him when I was twelve and had my picture taken with him." Well, I finagled, wrangled, and flirted my way into the Governor General's Ball and danced with him. Then I wrote a play, in which I acted Pierre, his wife, Margaret, and an Ottawa journalist called Henry. I travelled the country performing the play for two and half years, becoming a kind of unofficial jester in the court of the northern magus. But this is not a story about the play. It's a personal story I tell in the hope that, by pursuing the microcosm of my encounter, a piece of the macrocosm will emerge. This is the story of how I found one part of Pierre Trudeau, the part that could be called "The Lover."

It was 1979, and I was beginning to research the play. I knew I was going to play both Pierre and Margaret, but, somehow, I wasn't overwhelmed. The fact that I was young and female didn't faze me at all. Then I began to realize that I didn't know anything about them at all. I could imagine playing Maggie quite easily, but Pierre was going to be difficult. I read every conceivable book about Trudeau, but soon I knew that books were not enough. If I was going to write about and act the prime minister, I would have to meet him. I would have to "breathe him in." I had been trained in a new Canadian school of improvisation: We found characters, stole their personalities and stories, and put them on the stage. The reason for all this stealing was that there were no Canadian characters on either stages or screens. We had no models, so we studied people. A kind of alchemy was involved in this process—it was more than imitation. We watched bodies and listened for heartbeats; we followed the breath of our subjects; and, eventually, we "breathed them in." Then we started talking as if from their mouths, and that's how we made plays.

At the beginning I knew so little that when I wrote to Margaret Trudeau asking to meet her, I addressed the letter to "22 Sussex Drive." I never got a reply. I decided to go to Ottawa, armed with a list of the authors and journalists who were mentioned in the books I had read. People talked about Ottawa being boring, but to me it was a place of wonders. Inside the walls of those Gothic stone buildings was my goal; and all around, in the restaurants and bars, on the clean streets, were people who might know Trudeau or had heard personal things about him. Ottawa was the place where it all happened, or so it seemed to me that summer.

I called the Press Club number and started interviewing the journalists. Most were so eager to talk to me that our meetings lasted for hours. Out poured all those experiences they'd been having that no one had ever asked them about. I was surprised at the rawness of their emotions, at the intensity of the relationship between these professional watchers and their subject. And, like the two sisters in the fairy tale, one who spits out flowers and jewels and the other, toads and snails, I heard conflicting reports. I heard love, respect, admiration, and bile, hatred, and rumour. I heard that Trudeau was gay and regularly had it off in the bathroom with the conductor on the train to Montreal. One journalist refused to talk to me, saying what I was doing was immoral and disgusting.

Trudeau deserved better than that. I began to see that the emotions were those of a love affair.

I became more and more frightened that if I didn't meet Trudeau, I would end up with a cheap vaudeville impression—and that wasn't enough. I had to breathe him in. But how? Then one day I read that the fall parliamentary session began with something called the Governor General's Ball. And I knew I was going to get to that ball to dance with Pierre Trudeau. He would be as I imagined him to be, as millions imagined him to be, even though they were sick to death of him and felt betrayed and tormented by him. Every time the Lover would reveal himself in all his warmth and charm, the cold professorial élitist would appear, seeming to look down on them and say, "Suckers!" But the Trudeau I intended to meet would be the Trudeau of legend. The high cheek-bones would gleam; the blue eyes would shine; his tux would fit perfectly, with some small outrageous touch all his own; there would be patent leather pumps on his small, perfect feet; and he would dance divinely.

I found out the date of the ball and started to scheme. Of course I had nothing to wear, but my boyfriend had been left with a trunk of clothes when his ex-girlfriend moved out and in that trunk there was a dress—a vintage black lace gown. It was very old, probably from the twenties, and the lace was torn in places, held together with a rhinestone pin, but it had a kind of beauty. Shoes were a problem—but then, for the poor, shoes are always a problem.

I travelled to Ottawa by bus with the dress in a plastic bag. The ball was in two days and I had no concrete plans except my desire to get there. I phoned my "deep throat" at the Press Club. He was a friend of an actor I knew and he'd helped me a lot. It turned out the ball wasn't a cool event at all. None of the high-level journalists went, but he would see what he could do. He phoned back to say he could get me in with the reporters who were going, but they were allowed to stay only for the first dance. I would have to dance the first dance with Trudeau.

The afternoon of the ball, I went to the Parliament Buildings. I walked through the grey stone arches and peered at the carvings of grapes and leaves. I went to the visitors' gallery and looked down on the Commons chamber, at the bright green of the desk blotters on the dark wood. I looked at the mostly paunchy men slouched in their seats. I counted the women. Was that one? Or maybe two? I could almost have touched them. In the Canada that was then, there was no glass wall between the visitors and their MPs. There was open space; I could have thrown a spit ball or a bomb.

I sat in the visitors' gallery and watched Trudeau. He'd just lost what many called the "disco election," when Maggie ran off with the Rolling Stones and danced in New York at Studio 54 the night the votes came. I was hardly a Liberal. I was rebellious and critical of him, and I had abhorred the War Measures Act. But it was as if these things were not important. I watched him hovering in his chair as if he barely sat, as if he were a visitor himself. I saw, or imagined I saw, the man who could wink at me like Sean Connery in some cheesy movie and and say, "I know it's all bullshit, I'm just playing the game." I was so close. I decided to write him a note. I pulled a piece of scrap paper from my purse and scribbled: "Dear Pierre Trudeau. You don't know me, but I will be at the Governor General's Ball with the reporters, but I'm not a reporter. I have a very strange request. Would you dance the first dance with me? I have long dark hair and I will be wearing a black dress. I will explain all this later." I wandered through the corridors of the Parliament Buildings until it seemed I was in an Escher-like maze of stairways and archways. Finally I found a security guard in the hall and handed the note to him. "Would you give this to Pierre Trudeau?" He nodded calmly, as if he did this kind of thing all the time. I had done all I could. Now I had to change.

I was staying with my friend Nicky Guadagni, an actor with a great deal of common sense. As I changed, I noticed more holes in my dress, hidden at a distance by the lining, but close up? Nicky said it didn't matter as she curled my hair, trying to give it a natural twist. When we got to the makeup she said, "No, you're young, that's what you've got going for you. He'll be surrounded by old people. His wife's just left him, and he lost the election. Just do lipstick and a bit of powder."

When I got to the governor's residence, a group of reporters were huddled together, waiting to be let in. I knew none of them, and none of them was dressed up. I learned that there was first a dinner, then the dancing. We were led in as a group and we passed by the empty ballroom, cordoned off by a purple velvet cord. It was a classic Victorian room, with large gilt-framed pictures of former governors general and their wives, and it was lit by lights shaped like candles. With the inevitable chandelier dangling overhead, the ballroom looked both British and colonial, a combination that fit the antiquated nature of the occasion. Governor General, indeed.

Instead of being seated with the rest of the guests, we were put into another room and made to eat separately. I was beside myself. This was it? I would eat with a bunch of reporters, watch the first dance, and go home? I didn't have much hope that Trudeau had received my note. Hastily I scribbled another one, saying the same thing, but this time sounding more desperate. If he didn't dance the first dance with me I would be kicked out. Could he help? We were scheduled to eat first, isolating us still further. It was possible we would never even get near the guests, much less Trudeau. When the reporters, once more carefully escorted as a group, went to line up for the buffet, I held back. I went into the bathroom and waited until they had finished filling their plates. Then, with my note crumpled in my purse, I joined the line with the real guests of the night. I looked around, trying to see some cabinet minister I might recognize, but my knowledge was limited, and no one looked familiar. The man ahead of me in line looked nice and French, and I had nothing to lose. I asked him if he knew Pierre Trudeau. He laughed and said he did. Would he give Trudeau a note? He said he would. And so a second note may or may not have been passed on to the leader of the loyal opposition.

Back in the restricted room, I couldn't eat. Finally, the meal was over and we were herded to the ballroom. We bunched behind the velvet cord while the guests drifted in. All I could think of was that it looked like a high school prom, except everyone was older. Then Trudeau entered. I stared, trying to will him to notice me, but not a glance did I get. Almost immediately the first dance began. He danced with the governor general's daughter. I stood watching the scene, knowing that in a few minutes I would be gone. The dance ended and I prepared to go. Then Trudeau started walking towards us. He looked at me, smiled, and extended his hand over the velvet cord. I entered the ballroom.

There is a photograph of this moment which the society reporters took, unbeknownst to me. I am talking to Trudeau the Lover. It is the picture of a young girl, breathless, overwrought, excited and unbelieving, with a rather odd Indonesian purse dangling from her arm. The shoes actually don't look so bad. Am I going too far to think of myself as a metaphor for the country, wooed, desperate to be wooed, by the small, balding man in the perfectly cut tuxedo? Of course I am. But that night was about going too far. It was about trying to seek out this person and find his essence. About crossing the velvet cord in a country that was still protecting its leaders with something as ephemeral as a string of purple cloth.

I babbled, of course. I remember saying, "Thank you, oh, thank you, they were about to kick me out." I hope I didn't say "You saved me," but maybe I did. Yet somewhere I was thinking, "He's so little. He's just a fraction taller than me." He said, "I'm sorry I couldn't dance the first dance with you." "Oh, that's fine," I burbled, "I understand, I'm just so happy that you got my note." "Now, what's all this about? Why are they going to 'kick you out'?" The quizzical smile was on his lips, and suddenly I saw that part of him that loved to engage, that genuine curiosity about the world. I revelled in the intense focus of his interest. I'd met him through a combination of youth and chutzpah, and now I believed that, in spite of his marriage breakdown and election loss, or perhaps because of these things, he was interested in me. It was as if every word I said was a jewel, as if, by merely listening to me, he was massaging me from inside. I had the feeling I could tell him anything. But I couldn't tell him the truth. I wondered if Mata Hari had ever felt guilty.

Trudeau took my hand and led me deeper into the room. We started to dance as I was still trying to explain. "I'm writing a play

about Ottawa and . . ." "About Ottawa? That's a pretty strange subject." A bit of gentle irony. "Yes it is, and I wanted to come here
and get an idea . . . you know, research . . ." I could feel his body
underneath the suit. He held me lightly. I noticed there was dandruff on his shoulders. "Is there anyone here you would like to
meet?" I giggled; I couldn't help it. "No, that's fine, it's just so
wonderful that I'm here." We didn't have just one dance, we had
four or five. I wasn't used to this kind of pseudo-ballroom dancing.
It reminded me of being taught to dance by my father in our rec
room, with my mother at the record player. I laughed again. "What
are you laughing at?" "I'm just not used to dancing this way." I
wanted to squeeze him and feel his muscles. "You intimidate me
when you laugh." How did he say that? With absolute sincerity, in
the style of some old movie. Douglas Fairbanks? It didn't matter. I
intimidated Pierre Trudeau! "You have soft hair," he said quietly,
into my ear, his cheek at my hair, so recently curled by another
actor now waiting across town to hear the story. And then a classic:
"That's a lovely dress you're wearing." "It's full of holes." "But in
all the right places." In all the right places? Who could get away
with that?

I wanted to tell him about the play, about my dreams for it,
about my thoughts on the personal and the political and how they
connected. But I had read enough: This was Pierre the private
man, and I was going to tell the story of his marriage. I was going
to make fun of him, to play him and his wife, to strut their lives
across the stage. The more kind and courtly, the more lightly flirta-
tious and open he was with me, the more I felt like a shit. How
many times during those dances did I try to find a way to tell him?
I was dancing with Pierre the Lover, but he could turn on a dime.
What would I do if that grim, horrible Pierre showed himself? The
persona that emerged sometimes on the evening news, cold and
lethal, pockmarks pitted like the surface of the moon, his brilliance
sharpened as the proverbial blade, ready to skewer people like me?
A nasty kind of intelligence.

We seemed to dance for a very long time. I kept expecting him
to leave, for I knew he would have to mingle. Then I remembered

that he'd come alone, that he was here within a familiar group of
people who had few surprises to offer, and that I, at least, was a surprise. It occurred to me, with a tiny spear-point of pain in the pit of
my stomach, that he might be lonely. I did the only thing I could
do. I started to breathe again. As we danced, I began to take him in,
to try to remember everything, but more than that, to see the world
from inside his eyes. I tried to find his heartbeat and my own. I
breathed him in. And I knew that, because of this, I was bound, as if
to some unspoken pact with him, even though he knew nothing,
to rise above any easy instincts I might have about portraying him.
Not that I was in the business of getting cheap laughs, but a yuk or
two is worth a lot in my business. No, I wouldn't go for the easy
laughs. I would get the hard laughs, won from the inside. I was suddenly afraid. I felt responsible to him, the way no ordinary citizens
feel responsible to democratic leaders. They are supposed to be responsible to us. This sense of a pact grew, and I knew I was experiencing another side of Pierre the Lover, the side that bound people
to him: that strange vulnerability. And if I showed this vulnerability,
I must also embody his pain. If he ever saw the play, that's what he
would hate me for the most.

He asked me again if there was anyone else I would like to meet.
I said no, I was fine. He said he had to go. I said I understood. He
gave the number of his secretary and said I could call him there. I
thanked him, knowing I would not. He called over an aide de
camp, Captain St. Laurent, in a white uniform with gold epaulettes,
who he said would take care of me. So I danced with Captain St.
Laurent for a while. When I finally got back to Nicky's, she was
waiting for me. "Did you meet him? Did you dance?" Later, she
told me she didn't even need to ask. It was all on my face.

The play was successful in an overwhelming way—to me, at
least. The trick of it seemed to be this girl, playing both characters.
But the real trick was Trudeau. And, in spite of a few slightly cheap
laughs, it is Trudeau the Lover who is in that play. The man who
was rarely too tired to engage. And because of his ability to engage,
I learned to engage those audiences. I tried to be interested in them
and, more than that, curious.

For a long time I had a recurring dream. I dreamed I was dancing with Trudeau and trying to find a way to tell him about the play. In the dream I would feel guilty, cruelly aware of how abhorrent the whole idea would be to him. Recently, I had the dream again. I was dancing with Trudeau, I told him about the play, he understood, and it was wonderful. I felt relieved and free. But just as he walked away, I remembered I hadn't told him about the second act. There, the Trudeau character gets down on his knees and prays. As tears fall down his cheeks, he prays for strength, for the country, and for love. Even in a dream, I knew he wouldn't like hearing about that.

Perhaps it is this capacity to engage that is the essence of real charm. People who are known as charming have this quality, this outward gaze. The lover looks at every person as if that person is utterly unique and worthy—worthy of their total interest. And what is a lover but someone who is ultimately interested, down to the smallest detail, in everything about you? Perhaps that's the truth of Trudeau's ability to engage both men and women: that he loved contact, that he was genuinely interested. More than that, curious. Curiosity led him to love a young woman who seemed his antithesis. He wanted to know about the kind of person who operated entirely on her instincts and passions, whose charm was an openness as different from his own as could be. Trudeau the Lover was at his best when taking a chance on Margaret, for Trudeau the Lover was capable of real risk.

But even while I was experiencing this lover-like charm, even while I had the feeling that every word I said was a jewel he would treasure forever, I was aware he was never able to use this charm on the western farmers, who somehow seemed to feel that those patent leather pumps were dancing on their heads—even after he sold all that wheat to China. Journalists, too, feeling betrayed by the perverse enigma that was Pierre their lover, began to be exempt from the spell—but still he engaged with them. If they goaded him, he responded like a person, not a politician. He asked them questions, he questioned their questions, he got pissed off. He engaged, at times as if he was able to anticipate the inner needs and desires of whatever person he was speaking to; at other times he disengaged, as if that person was beneath his contempt. We can't forget this side of the Lover, the side that can hurt us as only our deepest relationships can hurt. As I listen to the barely simmering emotions people still have towards Trudeau—of anger, admiration, and betrayal—it is like a love affair that's never really ended. Real love never goes away, but remains in the mind and the heart forever, full of subconscious yearnings and perversions, forever confused and faithful.

Humble Arrogance:
A Cautionary Tale of
Trudeau and the Media

■

LARRY ZOLF

Larry Zolf is the host-writer for "Inside Zolf," a weekly CBC Newsworld Online program. He writes on present day politics, on Canadian history and culture, and all aspects of the Canadian scene. He has been a writer, a reporter, a host, a producer, a consultant to CBC News and Current Affairs and Newsworld since 1962. He is the author of Dance of the Dialectic, Survival of the Fattest: An Irreverent View of the Senate, *and* Just Watch Me: Remember Pierre Trudeau. Scorpions For Sale, *his first fiction, was nominated for the Stephen Leacock Award for Humour in 1989.*

THERE WERE NO SCREAMING, mini-skirted, mini-minded women shouting the praises of the Great Man's godly powers or charismatic talents when I first met Pierre Elliott Trudeau in the fall of 1964. The encounter took place in a Montreal hotel room booked by Trudeau's friend Patrick Watson, the executive producer of the CBC's investigative television news program *This Hour Has Seven Days*.

Trudeau sprawled over one of the twin beds in the room, but I could see he was short, almost elfin-like in appearance, and dressed entirely in the British mode. His pock-marked face gave him a tough street-kid look, accentuated by his cold blue eyes. Oddly enough, given his later heart-throb image, he exuded little sexuality. If anything, he seemed asexual. In his shyness and aloofness, he resembled the Jesuits who had trained him at the classical Collège Jean-de-Brébeuf. Above all, there was a wonderful humble arrogance about him. A special kind of languid air about Trudeau suggested that he had better things to do than sit in a hotel room that afternoon and a Radio-Canada studio that night.

Watson was then thirty-seven years old and the boy wonder of Canadian television. In a matter of weeks, *This Hour Has Seven Days* had completely captured the media agenda and shoved newspapers and radio aside. Cabinet ministers and political leaders who accepted invitations to occupy its "hot seat" had a long shotgun microphone thrust before their mouths and soon found themselves exposed as bogeymen feeding voraciously at the public trough. The Salem witch hunt had come to Canada, to the delight of the lynch-mob viewers. René Lévesque, who was a minister in the Quebec

Liberal government, was the bogeyman who had gathered Trudeau,
Watson, and me together in that hotel room in Montreal.

Lévesque even then had a reputation as a separatist. *This Hour*
would put the boot to him and his crooked ways. Once again it
would save the country—at least for seven days. Watson's strategy
was simple enough. Lévesque would occupy the hot seat, and
Trudeau would ask all the tough questions about Lévesque's treason to Quebec and to Canada. I, the Winnipeg Jew, was to play the
Nice Guy in the interview. I would reassure Lévesque and the
viewers that, despite Trudeau's brutal questions, I and the English
Canada I spoke for loved Lévesque and hoped he would become
prime minister some day—perhaps after he tired of being prime
minister of a sovereign Quebec. If necessary, I was to rebuke
Trudeau for his heavy-handedness and ask: "But you do agree,
Pierre, that we English Canadians have been barbaric to Quebec
and now must pay the price?"

Watson asked for a run-through of my new role as Canadian
WASP spokesman. I was thrilled at last to be a hot-seat interviewer
for the greatest television show in Canadian history, and I ran
through my scenario with an exaggerated bit of lusty bravado.
Watson laughed heartily, but Trudeau smiled benignly and said absolutely nothing. I wondered if he were some kind of mute and
whether he would sit through the actual interview again saying
nothing, leaving me to run the show. At this point Watson brought
the meeting to a close and told us to be at the studio for makeup at
7:30. Trudeau escorted me to his two-seater green Porsche, and we
drove off for dinner to a private Montreal club that he frequented.

It was a strange place. The walls were covered with paintings of
the English countryside and Irish setters, and the famous photograph
of Churchill by Karsh hung in a prominent place. The menu consisted of variations on roast beef and Yorkshire pudding. It seemed
like a perfect English gentlemen's club. The first surprise was that everyone there spoke only French, and the second was the sound of two
coins—two quarters—that Trudeau plunked on the table as a tip.

■

The atmosphere in the Radio-Canada studio was distinctly unpleasant. The makeup lady made it clear that the studio was Lévesque's turf and that both Trudeau and I were mere interlopers. The studio director barely talked to us as he chatted up Lévesque and directed sardonic nods and winks in our direction every fifteen seconds or so.

The interview quickly became a disaster. Trudeau asked several questions about the forestry industry in Quebec and what Lévesque planned to do about it. Lévesque gave long, boring, tree-by-tree answers. The studio crew, once fearful that the beloved René would be hammered in the interview, was lulled to an early sleep. Suddenly Watson, from the control booth, signalled the reluctant studio director to pass a private message on to me. It was short and to the point: "DROP TRUDEAU. TAKE OVER THE INTERVIEW—COMPLETELY—NOW!"

I switched gears quickly, eager to show Lévesque the dark side of English Canada that I was now so nimbly representing. My sudden role reversal reduced Trudeau to virtual silence, especially when I asked Lévesque if he hated English Canadians, if he would drive non-Québécois out of his homeland, and why he and the Québécois were angry when we English Canadians had already made our dollar bills bilingual. Lévesque broke into raucous laughter and said: "I see you're really acting, playing a role, aren't you?" I refused to say yes or no, but inwardly I glowed at the star recognition Lévesque had given me by his on-air observation.

On the flight back to Toronto, I quaffed a half-dozen scotches to celebrate my triumphal debut as the television champion of English Canada. This interview with Lévesque I knew would be the making of me. As for Trudeau, he had said goodbye to me politely—and the scotches soon made me forget him completely.

Trudeau was the farthest thing from my mind when I checked into *Seven Days'* Toronto headquarters the day after the Lévesque interview. There I was greeted by producer Beryl Fox, a fellow North End Winnipeger, who hailed me as a great interviewer. "Christ," she said, "if it weren't for you, your mealy mouth of an interview partner would have put Lévesque and the whole country to sleep! Who is this guy Trudeau anyway, apart from being one of Watson's upper-class French buddies?"

I barely had time to sit down before I discovered that my next hot-seat assignment would be none other than Lévesque in Montreal that coming Saturday night. CBC brass insisted that the show be redone. Once again, Trudeau would be my partner. Again, he would be the heavy, and I would be Mr. Nice Guy.

■

For Round Two of Réne Lévesque versus *Seven Days* featuring Pierre Elliott Trudeau and Larry Zolf, Watson did not accompany me to Montreal. I knew he had engaged in a private chat with Trudeau, trying to get him to drop his long-winded questions for shorter, punchier approaches. He hoped the new Trudeau would be able to carry the second Lévesque interview, while my Good Guy Canada stuff would provide needed filler and contrast.

Oddly enough, I met Trudeau in the same Montreal hotel room as the previous week. He, too, looked the same: serene, stoic, irritatingly calm, and dangerously bland. The only stylistic difference this time was that he was elegantly attired in a three-piece Harris tweed suit.

Trudeau and I were alone in the hotel room, but that was not the cause of the sense of foreboding that crept upon me. I began to sense jitters and uncertainty in the air—and not just mine. Perhaps I was overreacting to Trudeau's silence. Perhaps Trudeau had nothing to say. Perhaps, once again, I would have to dart into the fray. In my nervousness, I took a strange route trying to cut the ice with Trudeau. I decided to tell him about my sexual exploits and steamy adventures. This erotic performance drew a strange Cheshire cat smile from Trudeau that spread slowly from below his high cheekbones to the corners of his aristocratic mouth.

Thinking I was making headway, I told him about my pet hate—socialists who pretend to love the people but who are, in fact, hypocrites, misanthropes, and exploiters of the humble and weak. I worked myself up to a particular froth against a former professor of mine in Winnipeg who had marked me harshly after he found me drunk at a college function. This obscure bit of personal trivia got an even wider Cheshire cat response from Trudeau. I didn't know why then, but later on I learned that my professor was a close socialist friend of Trudeau. As prime minister, he appointed my prof to a senior government post.

Still, while I didn't really know Trudeau, I liked him. There was an aura of decency and conviction about him. He was well mannered and courteous and, although he was obviously a duck out of water on television, he was still determined to do his best to massage the medium.

Before the interview was to begin, Trudeau took me in his Porsche convertible for a short sightseeing tour of Montreal, his home town. During the ride, he spoke in short, punchy statements of his love for the city. It seemed to me that it was just these kinds of statements that would make our interview a success. For the first time, I really believed Trudeau could pull it off. I was as happy as I could possibly be—confined as I was to the secondary and far less exciting role of Mr. Seven Days Nice Guy.

Our arrival at the Radio-Canada studio at 7 that evening banished these reveries. Again, the makeup women were surly and unfriendly. The francophone technicians and crew were openly contemptuous of *le juif et le vendu*, the Jew and the sellout. Lévesque had not yet shown up, and panic calls to Watson soon followed.

An hour and a half passed. The tension in the studio was acute. Finally, at 9 p.m., Lévesque arrived with a entourage of aides and persuaders. A half hour later, he mounted the interviewee's dais. As he did so, he gave Trudeau a withering look of scorn and contempt. Trudeau did not flinch. My respect for Trudeau increased a bit more.

The studio director cued Trudeau. He proceeded to rattle off the major benefits federalism provided Quebeckers, followed by the economic problems that would beset Quebeckers if Canadian federalism were to disappear. Trudeau questioned whether Lévesque had fully considered the implications of Canadian federalism and the problems that the Quebec balance sheet would suffer if federalism collapsed.

Lévesque completely blew his cool. Pushing aside the shotgun mike, he shouted: "This is Montreal, Saturday night. I refuse to spend it in the company of jackasses!" Then he and his entire entourage marched briskly out of the studio.

Trudeau accepted all this negativity with complete equanimity. He gave me an idle shrug of the shoulders, the first of many to come in his long and remarkable political life. I shook his hand and said goodbye.

■

On my arrival in Toronto, I headed home for some well-earned sleep. In my absence, the CBC and *Seven Days* had one of their early major battles. *Seven Days* now wanted to air the first version, the original taping of Lévesque, Trudeau, and me. The program won that round. News that the first interview was running and in the key spot bowled me over. Once again, I would be Mr. Hot Seat, master of the leer, the sneer, the innuendo. Once again, I could wag fingers and shake jowls. Now for sure I would phone home to Winnipeg and exult: "LOOK MA, I'M A STAR!"

This Hour Has Seven Days was more a cult, a private religion, than a mere public affairs television show. On Sunday night, the weekly air date, staffers would gather to watch the show, providing cheers and boos, thumbs up or thumbs down, laurels or darts, to the items as they appeared on the screen. Their response to my Tough Guy Canada stance was extremely gratifying. They cheered every venom- and innuendo-loaded question I asked Lévesque. They booed lustily and voted thumbs down to Trudeau's few tiptoes into the fray. The odd "wimp," "sissy," "coward" greeted Trudeau's long question about Quebec's forests. Instead, the staffers shouted "Right on" to my remarks.

On Monday morning, *Seven Days* had its traditional postmortem meeting. Beryl Fox had just come back from risking her life in Mississippi, where she had finished "One More River" and "Summer in Mississippi," both soon to become Canadian classic documentaries. She launched into an attack on Trudeau. "He has no balls," she cried. "He let Larry carry the can on this one. He is a television disaster! I move that *Seven Days* never use Trudeau again!" Shouts of "yes, yes" filled the meeting room. A motion to bar Trudeau from *Seven Days* for life was made and duly carried. It was as if Trudeau had never been one of us at *Seven Days*. It was as if the Lévesque hot seat was a solo performance, done all by me alone.

I was a star at last. People all over Canada were now asking who that quiet little guy was, with high cheek-bones and an aristocratic mouth, who couldn't get a word in edgewise against real hot seaters like Réne Lévesque and Larry Zolf.

■

Two years later, when I was at home in Winnipeg watching the CBC with my mother, a familiar face appeared on the screen driving the familiar Porsche around Montreal's hot spots. The interviewer was Norman DePoe, and Pierre Elliott Trudeau, the newly appointed justice minister, was on the move. I snickered to myself and thought, Can a bad interviewer be a good minister?

My mother had no such doubts. When the program was over she turned to me and said: "That, my son, is the next prime minister of Canada." "Sure, Ma, sure," I replied sarcastically, wondering if an extended stay in the Jewish old folks home was, perhaps, not a bad idea for her. But I was forgetting that my mother had accurately predicted the outbreak of two world wars and, in the old country on November 7, 1918, had told the Jewish women in the Zastavia marketplace: "An armistice is coming any day now. Trust me on this one!"

There is a myth in Canada that the media made Trudeau and that he was their patron saint and protector. But the truth is far more complex. Beginning with Trudeaumania in 1968, the media really covered Trudeau only in a raw-meat fashion. Their ignorance of

Trudeau's true skills and intellectual clout was appalling. Their dislike of him was palpable. Some even said he hated the Québécois, his own people, or that he preferred the Elliotts to the Trudeaus. To these media types, Trudeau was the freak show to their Barnums and Baileys, and they would get the sucker readers and viewers into the tent. Many in the media felt sorry for or superior to Trudeau. They saw him as a spoiled rich boy who would soon get his comeuppance. Other media veterans grumbled about Trudeau's alleged physical cowardice and his chicken war record, draft-dodging during the Second World War. And so it remained. To my recollection, none of the media were ever close to Trudeau.

Trudeau's ignorance of the media was equally pathetic. He knew nothing about how a prime minister should charm the press and tickle its rump. Take the annual Parliamentary Press Gallery Dinner. Traditionally, prime ministers get funny on this occasion and laugh at the press and at themselves. Trudeau, the non-media man, hated this most sacred media ritual most of all. Several times as prime minister he refused to show up, unthinkable behaviour for an alleged media guru. In 1972, when Trudeau blew his majority and needed everyone to keep his marginal minority government afloat, he was told that he had to make the dinner appearance and deliver a satirical speech.

The Trudeau office commissioned me to write that speech. It was a funny speech, simply written and full of comic effect. I twitched in my seat at the dinner as Trudeau read my speech in a slow, unhappy cadence. When he at last got some laughs, he did not stop to take them in and respond. Instead, he kept reading, as the laughs from the audience drowned out the next laughs on the page. It was a disaster.

As far as Trudeau was concerned, the media were always on the make and the take, but they were not going to make and take him. Nor did they ever really cover him well. Rather, he covered them, wrapped them in a nice warm magic blanket of his making, and spun them out on the floor when he needed them. The media were always grateful for Trudeau's Oriental carpet treatment. Trudeau's favourite TV interviewer was shrill, rough, tough, no-nonsense Jack

Webster from Vancouver. Trudeau would appear with Webster any time, any place. He knew that Webster's feigned boorishness only made him look good. The rawer the interview, the better Trudeau liked it.

During the October Crisis in 1970, the anglo Press Gallery interpreted the War Measures Act as an example of Trudeau putting the frogs in their place. They loved him for that, and they also loved being at the centre of the world's biggest story of the day. Trudeau gave them preferential treatment over the likes of Robert McNeil, Peter Jennings, Tom Brokaw, Mike Wallace, and other stars of American TV who were trying to get into Canada. The media jumped into bed with Trudeau—for the first and last time—and found Trudeau already there, grinning.

■

Trudeau's handling of the media was enhanced by his rapidly acquired on-air skills with the electronic media. On the first day of the War Measures Act, Trudeau was confronted in Ottawa by a CBC TV News camera crew. Asked about the tanks in the street and how far he would go, Trudeau said: "JUST WATCH ME!" These three marvellous words fully expressed the smooth efficiency, the delicious ambiguity, and the unveiled threats that were the essence of Trudeau during the crisis.

I heard Trudeau pronounce these words as I stood beside Tim Ralfe of the CBC. Ralfe's bleeding-heart outrage at the soldiers in the street did not move me at all. The kidnapping of one innocent and the cold-blooded murder of another, plus the holding of a state to ransom, moved me far more. After he had answered Ralfe, Trudeau turned to me and asked if I had anything to say. "Yes, Prime Minister," I replied, "what took you so long?"

Few in the Press Gallery shared my view, but my respect for Trudeau rose dramatically. I still didn't like having my Canadian identity boiled away in a vat of multiculturalism, and I still felt bilingualism was for the élites, but all that criticism was forgotten in the October Crisis. Trudeau's TV speech invoking the War Measures

Act really hit home for me. It was the best TV performance ever by
a Canadian.

Just watching Trudeau deal with the War Measures was a treat.
The Platonic gowns had been put in mothballs, and the humble,
arrogant mask of Machiavelli now separated Trudeau from the
smug, haughty faces in the Trudeau lyceum. A wonderful opportunity soon presented itself to Trudeau as Machiavelli. The Red
Tories, led by student leader Hugh Segal, had come out against the
War Measures. To the former Conservative leader, John Diefenbaker, these Red Tories were akin to traitors. Trudeau sensed his
opportunity in this Tory division and wooed Dief without ever
asking him once to support War Measures. First, Trudeau moved
to secure Diefenbaker, who was high on the FLQ hit list, against
attack. When I went to Dief's house to bring him to the CBC for an
interview, his home was guarded by an armoured car and several
dozen Canadian soldiers. A soldier with an FN-C2 escorted us to the
taxi and climbed into the front seat. When the taxi driver made a
wrong turn, the soldier put the barrel of his gun against the man's
temple. It took Dief ten minutes to talk the young soldier down.
Dief loved "Fort Diefenbaker" and knew who had made all that
excitement possible. His love for the prime minister knew no
bounds when, some time later, Trudeau had a shower installed in
Diefenbaker's office, the first shower on the Hill.

During the October Crisis, my relationship with Trudeau became almost strategic. The Liberal Party held a policy convention
in the early days of War Measures, and Trudeau addressed the dele-
gates in an open session, fielding all kinds of tough questions. I
asked for an interview with Trudeau and got it, but it came with a
stern prohibition: "You're to confine your questions to the party
convention and its policies only." "Sure," I said, surprising Trudeau
with the speed with which I had accepted his castrating *diktat*.

The interview was to be a full half hour. My first question to
Trudeau was, "If I were a delegate to the Liberal Party convention,
I would ask you this"—and I fired off a tough War Measures question. Trudeau stared at me with a flinty eye. He wanted to see how
far I would go. I repeated my "if I were" preamble for the next

four questions. He was now hopping mad and knew he had been had by Winnipeg's gift to the media. He tapped me on the shoulder and said, "You can drop the preamble. Just ask your question." "Are you sure, Prime Minister? I don't mind doing the preamble at all." "Yes, but I do," he retorted. I dropped the preamble and the interview went so well that the *Toronto Star* called it "deft but refreshingly undeferential."

■

Ottawa in Trudeau's time was a small town full of secrcts, which everyone knew. The favourite secret about Trudeau whispered to me by some of the most intelligent members of the Press Gallery was that Trudeau was either gay or bisexual or both. According to gallery gossip, Trudeau was madly in love with a senior Ottawa bureaucrat. Several gallery members swore they had seen him and his "friend" strolling hand in hand down Ottawa's corridors of power. Bizarrely, Trudeau's alleged love companion was anything but handsome and possessed the charisma of a spent firecracker. Nevertheless, his wife and children loved him, as did the hundreds of civil servants who served under him.

None of this deterred the rumour mongers. Nor were they discouraged by the array of beautiful women Trudeau squired around town. One of his all-time favourites would go to 24 Sussex for alleged intimacies while her boyfriend waited in the car outside to take her home,

Another Trudeau favourite was a neighbour of mine. Extraordinarily beautiful, she was the sex fantasy of all Ottawa, including those gallery members peddling the "Pierre is gay" line. One day, as I left the CBC parking lot, the attendant yelled: "Did you know Pierre got married today?" I forgot all this as I drove home. There the Trudeau beauty, her husband, and her children were our guests. After dinner, I remembered and blurted out the news. My neighbour broke down, locked herself in a closet, and wouldn't come out for hours. This married woman, it seems, was weeping at the loss of the one real man in her life. All I could think of was, if the rumour mongers could see this scene, they'd have to wonder how an alleged gay like Trudeau could have such a hold over so many beautiful women.

■

Shortly after I left Ottawa and the Press Gallery, I returned to Toronto. There I decided to write a shrivelled opus on Trudeau and the press. It was called *Dance of the Dialetic*.

The *Dance* attracted a great deal of attention. In honour of my book, the Parliamentary Press Gallery decided to hold a party and invited the prime minister and all the party leaders. I felt fine until I saw that Trudeau had shown up and I realized there would be speeches. Public speaking is my number one phobia. I went white with terror. A good friend dragged me off to a private cubicle and poured a bottle of gin down my throat.

I now felt fine, but I couldn't walk well. I staggered to the podium. Trudeau stuck out his hand in congratulations. I, right out of my skull, retorted: "You look familiar! Who the fuck are you, anyway?" Trudeau slapped his chest in total surprise and said, "Why, I'm Pierre Elliott Trudeau!" Everybody laughed, thinking Trudeau and I were part of a vaudeville act. Incredibly, the event went on, with Trudeau making regular checkups to see if I was okay.

■

These days Trudeau and I have a lot of fun talking on the phone, having lunches, writing bizarre letters to each other, dissecting idiots, displaying our prejudices, and getting our dossiers ready. Occasionally I read him satiric material I have written. There is nothing like the sound of convulsive laughter coming from Trudeau at the other end of the phone.

It's hard to be objective and analytic when writing about a friend. It's easier when you're younger and your friends are younger —and can take it in stride. Suffice it to say, in all objectivity and honesty, that Trudeau was once a bit of a prig, a callow and insensitive person, a too-decisive person, a person who may have gone too far with the War Measures Act. Trudeau, of course, denies any such criticism. As Trudeau's friend, so do I.

As a friend, Pierre, let me say I miss you at the helm. I want an end to government by Sales Team Canada. I want an end to "I'm sorry" leadership and government by apology. I want an end to deficit reduction as the official weight-loss mantra of the fat cat Chrétien-Martin government.

Here is my idea, Pierre. You come back as prime minister, but this time you will not have to stand alone as the second-guessed *Seven Days* hot seater, the northern magus, the philosopher king. This time the Canadian people will give you three fresh cabinet ministers you can always count on: Justin, Michel, and Sacha. Trudeau's Gang of Four or the Four Wise Trudeau Men has a nice media ring to it. Add Sheila Copps to this mix for gender balance, Pierre, and you can govern safely at least until the millennium.

Now that's an offer only a cranky, cantankerous old man with too much time and too many beautiful women on his hands could possibly refuse.

A Child of Nature:
Trudeau and the Canoe

■

JAMES RAFFAN

James Raffan, *professor of education at Queen's University in Kingston, is also a canoeist and writer. His books include* Wildwaters, Summer North of Sixty, *and the best-selling biography of Canadian paddler and filmmaker Bill Mason*, Fire in the Bones.

As an iconographically loaded image, Canada could not have asked for a more potent one than Pierre Trudeau as he floated through the mist in a canoe, gliding like a phantom across the glassy surface of a northern lake, resplendently adorned in fringed buckskin, his chiselled features as inscrutably handsome at 73 years as they were at 40. Collectively, a riveted nation gasped. The greatest media star it had ever produced was back, leaving Canadians with no choice but to do what we'd always done when the effortlessly charismatic Pierre Trudeau deigned to cross our perceptual field: just watch him.

– Geoff Pevere and Greg Dymond, *Mondo Canuck*, 1996

H ACKNEYED though it may be, the image of a paddler in a red canoe evokes essential Canadian values: ruggedness, independence, technical prowess, balance, freedom, possibility, echoes of English, French, and aboriginal heritage, and more than a little nostalgic schmaltz. It has been used to sell everything from libations to life insurance, and even the odd politician. And there he was, Pierre Elliott Trudeau, confidently dipping his way across our television screens, leading viewers into his cinematic biography. For some, the image was a cynically shallow and clichéd attention-grabber; for others, especially those who share Trudeau's passion for canoes, the sequence may have signified something more substantial. It could be that, at the root of Trudeau's gunslinger stance—"Just watch me!"—there is a guiding metaphor, a certain confidence, and a deep and abiding sense of truth derived from his wilderness experiences *en canot*.

Throughout his tenure as prime minister, Trudeau, by serendipity or design, always maintained his image as a committed canoeist. During visits to Thailand and Brazil, on Canada Day in Ottawa, and elsewhere, he would jump into a canoe with the least provocation and provide excellent photo opportunities for the waiting photographers. When Charles and Diana were married, he sent them a handmade canoe as a wedding gift. And when opportunities presented themselves, he would hie off to the wilds, always in relative secret but rarely escaping notice of the press. In the case of the well-known photo of Trudeau paddling on the Amazon, former press secretary Patrick Gossage reports in *Close to the Charisma* that paddling alone in a Brazilian canoe was "a pleasant way to put some distance between himself and the travelling press corps." To those who watched these canoeing images of our prime minister, there was never any doubt that he took great delight in engineering such opportunities, partly for personal pleasure but also to put on a good show for the crowd. There was no question about it: Trudeau was and is a skilled paddler and a delightful performer in a canoe.

Trudeau's unceremonious 1979 exit from office was marked by political cartoonist Frank Edwards of the *Kingston Whig Standard* with an image of the prime minister from behind, striding off into the sunset with a canoe on his head, pitching a rose over his shoulder, as if leaving office with a cavalier shrug and a sure step towards the water, where he really belonged. When he left office for good in 1984 the canoe mystique only grew. Stories emerged of a Canadian filmmaker who was trying to cast Pierre Trudeau to play the part of Grey Owl in a feature movie, and of an actor checking in from Newfoundland to CBC Radio's *Morningside* who confided to host Peter Gzowski that she was burdened by a recurring dream about paddling in a canoe with Trudeau. Little wonder that when the time came to film his memoirs, the canoe scene came to mind: It fits; it sells.

Whatever political marketing value the sculpted PM-as-paddler image may have had for Trudeau, it is clear that his love for the craft and for the places it took him was genuine. The white-water paddling sequences in his television memoirs, for example, though less elegant than the misty Meech Lake sequences that so captivated the authors of *Mondo Canuck*, took him back to the foot of Mont Tremblant, where his family spent summers cottaging in the Canadian Shield north of Montreal. It was here that he learned the rudiments of canoeing, that he made the association between fictional and historical literature and the centrality of the canoe in the Canadian historical and cultural landscape. "Those summers," he recounts in his *Memoirs*, "kindled my great love for the outdoors and canoeing." From Lac Tremblant and experiences as a Boy Scout in Montreal, he graduated for two summers to Camp Ahmek in Algonquin Park, where, according to Stephen Clarkson and Christina McCall in *Trudeau and Our Time*, "the private school boys gathered there were astonished by this thin kid from Montreal who vied with them at diving and canoeing while quoting Baudelaire at the same time."

In the rich mix of experiences that was his coming of age, added to these halcyon days of independence at school and camp, were travels with his family across Canada, through Europe, and to other parts of the globe. He learned a classical quest view of adventure, one where preparation leads to separation and to tribulation from dragons unknown, but always returning home to tell the tale, wiser and perhaps even more ready to begin again another heroic cycle. Likewise, at Collège Jean-de-Brébeuf, where he skied, paddled, and studied among the Jesuits and the sons of the Outremont élite, Trudeau found friends, a love of the wild, and a certain confidence in his ability to excel physically, intellectually, and spiritually, especially on the trail.

By the time Trudeau graduated from Brébeuf and moved on to study law at Université de Montréal, the yen for learning from experience and the pattern of periodic travel for challenge, respite, and reflection was well established. He had found, almost by default, the classically Canadian cycle of forays to the spartan *pays d'en haut* followed by return to the garrison comforts of home and school. He learned to crave that blend of rough and smooth, crooked and straight, nature and human nature. After his first year of law, at twenty-one years of age, still reeling from his father's death five years earlier and puzzled by his ambivalence to the Second World War, Trudeau teamed up in the summer of 1941 with Guy Viau, a classmate from Brébeuf, and two others to travel in the spirit of Radisson and Des Groseillers from Montreal to James Bay—up the Ottawa River, over the elevated land mass, and down the Harricanaw River. It was during this outing that he clarified his thinking on many fronts. In an article about this trip published three years later in *Jeunesse étudiante catholique*, he explained what he had found: "A canoeing expedition . . . involves a starting rather than a parting. Although it assumes the breaking of ties, its purpose is not to destroy the past, but to lay a foundation for the future. From now on, every living act will be built on this step, which will serve as a base long after the return of the expedition . . . and until the next one."

In his enthusiasm to emphasize the grand scope of the experience on which this wisdom is based, he recounts that he and his friends "were obliged, on pain of death, to do more than a thousand miles by canoe, from Montreal to Hudson Bay." In truth, the trip went from Lac des Deux Montagnes to James Bay (which flows into Hudson Bay), a distance of about a half a thousand miles. Despite the exaggeration, the article remains one of the most cogent expositions of the canoeing experienced ever published. On the lighter side, one gets a glimmer of Trudeau as canoe partner, and it has a decidedly magisterial cast to it. He describes sitting in the canoe while his partner hauls him, and the canoe, up a rapid:

> You watch your friend stumbling over logs, sliding on rocks, sticking in gumbo, tearing the skin on his legs and drinking water for which he does not thirst, yet never letting go of the rope; meanwhile, safely in the middle of the cataract, you spray your hauler with a stream of derision. When this same man has

also fed you exactly half of his catch, and has made a double portage because of your injury, you can boast of having a friend for life, and one who knows you well.

Friend for life, indeed!

Throughout his university career, Trudeau travelled widely, often by canoe. With Viau he toured the Gaspé on foot and the Maritimes by motorcycle. He summered with his sister in Mexico. He retraced, by canoe, the route taken by François Paradis, hero of *Maria Chapdelaine*, from La Tuque, near Quebec City, north to Péribonka on the shores of Lac St-Jean. At one point he even concocted a canoe-related device in which he tried, unsuccessfully, to row from Florida to Cuba. And as part of his studies in political economy at Harvard, he decided to research the interplay between Christianity and Marxism by going walkabout in the Far East. Of this journey, he wrote in his *Memoirs*: "This trip was basically a challenge I set myself, as I had done with sports, with canoeing expeditions, and with intellectual explorations. I wanted to know whether I could survive in a Chinese province without knowing a word of Chinese, or would be able to travel across a war-torn country without ever succumbing to panic."

These journeys had many layers, many dimensions. On the surface, they satisfied a young man's thirst for adventure. Trudeau had the time, the resources, the parental support, and, most significantly, the drive and inclination to act on his impulse to wander. And the trips taught him geography through the soles of his feet. Below the surface, these forays away from home, especially those by canoe, provided context to appreciate the cyclical action-reflection-reaction nature of the learning process. And at an archetypal level, in following his heroes from literature and his lessons at school, he was Radisson, Brébeuf, Paradis, or Gandhi, finding truth in the process of active and purposeful living. With a vagabond's pack full of travel lore growing with each mile, all it would take would be a quick paddle close to town or a walk in the snow to draw from these experiences the inner resolve needed to focus energies on puzzling matters of the day.

For many, the aphorism "education kills by degrees," holds true: The dawning of adult sensibilities eclipses dreams with the stuff of reason and logic. Trudeau, though, has always listened to his adventurer's heart and always found ways to liven book learning with the lessons of experience, engendering his trademark blend of humility, confidence, audacious verve, and authenticity. "How does the trip affect your personality?" he asks on his return from James Bay. "I would say that you return not so much a man who reasons more, but a more reasonable man."

Trudeau eventually finished his schooling and wound up in Ottawa as MP for Mount Royal, but he continued to cultivate his love of challenge in peripatetic ways. In the spring of 1966, when he was parliamentary assistant to Prime Minister Lester Pearson, Trudeau encountered Eric Morse, then national director of the Association of Canadian Clubs, who was organizing a speaking tour for the young parliamentarian. In meeting Morse, Trudeau affiliated with the pre-eminent wilderness canoeist of the time. When Morse and Trudeau met to discuss the tour, Morse mentioned that the details needed to be finalized soon because he would be "incommunicado up north" for much of July and August. Trudeau's eyes lit up. And when Morse told him that one of the original trip participants had been forced to withdraw, Trudeau was keen to take his place. Trudeau went to his friend and fellow canoeist Blair Fraser and said, "This man Morse, he's asked me to go on a canoe trip with him down the Coppermine. Do you think this would be an okay thing to do?" Fraser replied, "Oh, JUMP at it! It'll be terrific. I wish I could go myself." Unbeknownst to Trudeau, Morse also asked Fraser about Trudeau's suitability for a Coppermine trip. "A good bet," was the reply. And so began a lifelong association between Eric and Pamela Morse and Pierre Trudeau.

That summer on the Coppermine, Trudeau paddled with Angus Scott, headmaster of Trinity College School, who remembers him as a reasonably skilled paddler and a congenial companion. It was a grand and uneventful trip except for meeting up with a couple from the United States, Alice Wendt and Erwin Streisinger, who had capsized in Sandstone Rapids, damaged their kayak, and lost most of their gear. Trudeau joined in with the rest of the crew to help the beleaguered pair. In subsequent years, it was reported that Ms. Wendt took some delight in knowing that she'd been warmed on that frightening occasion with a sweater from the soon-to-be prime minister of Canada. In his account of this trip, detailed in *Freshwater Saga* (1987), Morse remembers Trudeau's petulance in finishing the trip: "The picture [of Bloody Falls, the last major rapid on the Coppermine] is more vivid in my memory for the sight of one canoe of our party containing Angus Scott and Pierre Trudeau passing us at great speed, its occupants paddling like mad. 'What's the hurry?' I asked. 'We have lots of time to reach Coppermine on schedule.' 'The river has become dull,' answered Pierre. 'Now that it has lost its life, I want to have done with it.'"

Morse was not the only legendary canoeist with whom Trudeau had a close personal association. Soon after becoming prime minister, he heard about a Meech Lake neighbour who was filming captive wolves in an enclosure in his back yard. Out for a stroll one weekend, Trudeau called at the wolf place and began a family friendship with Bill Mason, maker of the films *Paddle to the Sea, Rise and Fall of the Great Lakes, Path of the Paddle, Song of the Paddle,* and *Waterwalker.* Although the Trudeaus' children were about ten years younger than the Masons', various combinations of kids and parents played hockey and broomball through the winter and paddled white water in the spring and summer.

Mason and Trudeau were an unlikely duo—Mason the artist, Trudeau the politician—but they united around their passion for canoes and wilderness, for the freedom and release of a good day on the rollicking spring rivers of the Ottawa Valley. As different as they were in disposition, they were similar in size and stature—short, compact, and, at least in Mason's case, eager to compensate in bravado and robust adventure for what may have been lacking in brute physical size and strength. Trudeau makes no secret in his *Memoirs* that he was "a frail child, endowed with neither strong health nor strong muscles," who grew up determined to overcome these weaknesses. In this sense, his love of the physical challenge of sports such as skiing, diving, and especially canoeing was at least partly compensatory. Paddling a canoe in the wilderness, or through the mists on Meech Lake, gave an impression of physical size and ability that belied his actual height and weight. Trudeau always said his diminutive friend Mason "made a good guest," and he always seemed proud to introduce his canoeing friends to visiting dignitaries, including Prince Philip and Queen Elizabeth.

Before his election to the highest office in the land, there was no need for more than ceremonial security for Canadian prime ministers—and certainly no call for mounting RCMP details to secure them on canoe expeditions. But as Trudeau came to power, things were changing. Robert Kennedy was assassinated during the US election in 1968, and the October Crisis of 1970 heightened the security need even more. There was no training régime in Mountie headquarters that would put a pair of gold-crossed paddles on the sleeve of any red serge tunic, so officials in the Prime Minister's Office had to work in concert with the RCMP to recruit officers for this unusual task. Things always worked out eventually, but there are several good stories about securees rescuing securers, and Mounties going missing on muddy Gatineau logging roads as they followed a white-watering prime minister from bridge to bridge down a river in spring flood. And there were occasional days when Trudeau would fire up his vintage Mercedes 300SL sportscar and head for the Gatineau Hills, with the RCMP in tow. Remembering thumb-travelling days, he would stop to pick up a hitchhiker on his way to Harrington Lake, giving the Mounties much to think about. But nothing compared with keeping in touch with canoe parties in the barrenlands of the Northwest Territories before the days of cell phones and satellite communication. This problem was finally surmounted by use of military aircraft, flying just out of sight, with which the paddling RCMP could communicate by radio at prescribed times and locations.

All these efforts to get away, nefarious and otherwise, point to the enduring significance of wilderness and canoe for Trudeau. The contemplative aspect of wilderness travel was and is something he craves. Getting away was critical to building personal confidence and capacity, and to finding a special kind of truth. Canadian political scientist Ned Franks, also a canoeist, suggests that this request or expectation of the wilderness canoeing experience may have arisen as much from Trudeau's French-Canadian Catholic roots as from anywhere else:

> It might well be that semi-Jesuit soul of his—that [drove his] personal quest to seek new vision. There's a huge literature in French Canada, far greater than English Canada . . . that ties very closely with the role of the Catholic Church in the search for spiritual truth and enlightenment in the wilderness . . The act of being in a canoe IN the wilderness resonates with the French Catholic sense of the contemplative life, and thinking about your relationship with yourself and with the Almighty . . . How else could he have done what he did in the constitutional amendment and sacrificed what he did, including the assent of Quebec, to get a Charter of Rights and Freedoms, without having a deep, deep internal vision of order and coherence in the world, stemming from some basic principles?

Trudeau shares with English romantic poets such as Samuel Taylor Coleridge or William Wordsworth, or even Victorian wilderness writers such as John Muir or Henry David Thoreau, that sense of secular renewal derived from escape to and identification with the countryside. Yet somehow these notions do not fully explain Trudeau's zeal for paddling, nor his grounding in the paddling experience. In the context of his influential Jesuit teachers at Collège Jean-de-Brébeuf, however, or of authors of France and French Canada such as Louis Hémon, it may well be that, as a result of this distinctive cultural perspective, Trudeau sought and found something divine and perhaps absolute in the truths teased from the interior and exterior scapes he travelled by canoe. As he wrote in his account of his first long canoe trip:

> What fabulous and undeveloped mines are to be found in nature, friendship and oneself! The paddler has no choice but to draw everything from them. Later, forgetting that this habit

was adopted under duress, he will be astonished to find so many resources within himself.

Nevertheless, he will have returned a more ardent believer from a time when religion, like everything else, became simple. This impossibility of scandal creates a new morality, and prayer becomes a friendly chiding of the divinity, who has again become part of our everyday affairs. (My friend, Guy Viau, could say about our adventure, "We got along very well with God, who is a damn good sport. Only once did we threaten to break off diplomatic relations if he continued to rain on us. But we were joking. We would never have done so, and well he knew it. So he continued to rain on us.")

The test for the claim that canoe trips gave Trudeau access to a particular clarity of vision and a particular acuity of truth would be to find a trip, besides the 1941 adventure on the Harricanaw, in which a crisis was turned or a momentous decision made. Nowhere is this better illustrated, still only by proxy, than in the summer of 1979. Having lost the election and been relegated to the opposition benches, where did he go? To the North in a canoe to contemplate his future.

A quirky record of this journey is a hand-written note from the expedition placed in a cairn on the Hanbury River. In the tradition of everyone who passed that way, one of Trudeau's compatriots on his Hanbury-Thelon trip wrote a note that was duly signed by everyone in the party. It reads:

4 August 1979

This sturdy group of eight *hail* fellows is travelling from Sifton Lake to Hornby's Cabin. Poor Hornby, we keep reflecting, as we munch our way through baked stuffed fish, lamb kebob, cheese fondue (complete with two bottles of Mouton Cadet) and Mom Kotcheff's All Bulgarian Bannock. Let this diary record that our last member may well expire from overeating. *La qrande bouffe en canot.*

But enough of this idle chit-chat. No, we are not going to offer you metaphysical reflections on the mysteries of male bonding, or the Great Outdoors as Salvation of the Human Soul. For this the reader would be well advised to turn to other notes in this can, or David Silcox's book *The Silence and the Storm* (not yet available in paperback).

Down to the nitty-gritty. First, who are we? Well, we certainly are gritty (make that Gritty).

Peter Stollery, M.P., Toronto Spadina
Pierre Trudeau, M.P., ETC., Ottawa
John Gow, Vice President, Sunshine Village, Banff
Craig Oliver, CTV News, Ottawa
Jean Pelletier, *La Presse*, Montreal
Tim Kotcheff, CTV News, Toronto
David Silcox, Arts Magnate, Toronto
John Godfrey, Kings College, Halifax

The weather was cold and blowy until to-day, the bugs were minimal (one of Mother Nature's little trade-offs) the coffee was always excellent, thanks to P. Stollery, Esq., and nobody dumped. For further documentation you may consult *The Hanbury: Fat City* (in press, with recipes, meals, and photos by Silcox and Kotcheff) or see John Gow's forthcoming cine-epic *Rocks!* The more literary-minded may care to turn to Godfrey, *The Diaries*, vol. 5.

Your Humble Scribe, John Godfrey (*Canoeists' Arctic Cairn Notes*, 1997)

Beneath the "male bonding" and "hail fellow, well met" lustre to this account there was, for Trudeau, much to think about with respect to his future. He describes this juncture in his career in the *Memoirs*:

I think a lot of people want to go back to the basics sometimes, to find their bearings. For me a good way to do that is to get into nature by canoe—to take myself as far away as possible from everyday life, from its complications and from the artificial wants created by civilization. Canoeing forces you to make a distinction between your needs and your wants. When you are canoeing, you have to deal with your needs: survival, food, sleep, protection from the weather. These are all things that you tend to take for granted when you arc living in so-called civilization, with its constant pressures on you to do this or that for social reasons created by others, or to satisfy artificial wants created by advertising. Canoeing gets you back close to nature, using a method of travel that does not even call for roads or paths. You are following nature's roads; you are choosing the road less travelled, as Robert Frost once wrote in another context, and that makes all the difference. You discover a sort of simplifying of your values, a distinction between values artificially created and those that are necessary to your spiritual and human development.

In conversation about this trip, a member of the expedition paints a portrait of a "thoughtful" even pensive Trudeau—"He's standing there staring off into space and I'm hunkered down doing the dishes!"—but, as always, an image of a man in his element. "There is no doubt," reports the tripmate, "that Pierre Trudeau loves wilderness and connects with it in a very deep way." It was a particularly tough time for Trudeau in his career. Friends had chided him for what he had and had not done. Others urged him to quit politics altogether. There was much to be considered that summer on the Hanbury-Thelon. Besides the bonhommerie of the cairn note, a glimmer of the nature of those musings came one day on the shores of the Thelon River when, for some reason, a bush plane flew low over their camp. It is reported that Trudeau was exultant: "The Conservatives have defeated themselves and they've come to get me!" Within months, he was back in government.

At a policy level, it is difficult to make direct connections between Trudeau's love of canoes and wilderness and his governmental decisions. Clearly, his inclusive sense of the country as a whole was informed by his first-hand encounters with rivers and portage trails. Nahanni National Park was created during his tenure as prime minister, and this was a river he did travel from Virginia Falls to Nahanni Butte in 1970; however, this event might have happened as a result of bureaucratic momentum regardless of, or in spite of, political direction. Under Trudeau's leadership, however, with a young Jean Chrétien as minister responsible, the National Parks Branch in Ottawa prepared a National Parks System Plan in the early years of the Trudeau administration which called for representative parks in each of thirty-nine natural regions across Canada. Forward-thinking bureaucrats suggested that the National Parks Act might be amended, as had been done in the United States, to add special-purpose preservation areas, such as river corridors, to the Canadian network of protected lands. Guided by this new plan, and driven by the need to find jobs for graduating baby boomers, a few dozen young men and women, all canoeists, were employed during the summers of 1971 to 1974 to carry out the Canadian Wild River Survey. A summary report, produced in 1974, identified various rivers for conservation in a national wild rivers system. And although this recommendation languished for four years, even with Trudeau at the helm, when his friend and fellow avid canoeist Hugh Faulkner became the minister responsible for Parks Canada in 1978, a conference of paddlers and river enthusiasts was convened in Jasper, Alberta, and the Canadian Heritage Rivers System was born. Although there were many people—ministers, bureaucrats, and others—who helped with the establishment of these two initiatives, Trent University historian and canoeist Bruce Hodgins ties them both, particularly the Wild River Survey, to Trudeau and his love of canoeing: "I happen to think that the Wild River Survey was positively HIS initiative, despite what minister happened to be doing it . . . his commitment to canoeing and to wilderness is something that transcends everything else, and there's an element of tremendous genuineness in this idea."

As important as any policy initiatives taken during his reign as prime minister, Trudeau's public presence as a canoeist did much to raise the profile of wilderness canoeing as a sport. Images and mention of Trudeau have occurred frequently in *Kanawa* magazine, published by the Canadian Recreational Canoeing Association, the only national canoeing publication in Canada. And in a collaboration benefitting both men, Trudeau-as-canoeist emerged in the foreword to Bill Mason's best-selling canoe book, *Path of the Paddle*. Here, placing himself unequivocally in the canoeing ethos as a participant with and crony of the master, Trudeau writes: "I have known Bill Mason for many years. I have paddled with him, traded outrageous stories with him about past canoeing expeditions, and listened for hours as he shared his rich experience of nature." Peter Milliken, Liberal MP for Kingston, and himself a committed canoeist, summed it up this way: "Pierre Trudeau raised awareness and made canoeing respectable. He inspired people to do remote trips. People said, 'if Pierre Trudeau can do it, then I can do it too.'"

Through his canoeing, Trudeau was, and is, grounded in the Canadian landscape. Whatever truths he holds from that experience, he believes to be genuine and authentic. The underlying legacy of his paddling is a metaphor through which to interpret the rest of his world. This is a man who would collect his writings under the title *Against the Current*; who would look across the table at 24 Sussex Drive and wonder what kind of a canoe partner a visiting head of state might make; or who would say "Just watch me!" knowing he's met and surpassed the challenges of the trail. This is a man who persists with his passion; who paddled Blair Fraser's Petawawa River as recently as 1996; and who capsized with his guide at Crooked Chute and carried on, soaking wet, unfazed, and ready for further travail. This is a paddler-politician who, in his late seventies, continues to affirm with thought and deed, as he has done throughout his public and private life, the essential Canadian truth he described in his youth: "What sets a canoeing expedition apart is that it purifies you more rapidly and inescapably than any other. Travel a thousand miles by train and you are a brute; pedal five hundred on a bicycle and you remain basically a bourgeois; paddle a hundred in a canoe and you are already a child of nature."

Six Scenes of Separation: Confessions of a Post-Facto Trudeaumaniac in Pursuit of the Personality Cult

∎

MARK KINGWELL

Mark Kingwell, a philosophy professor at the University of Toronto, is also a popular and prolific writer. He is the author of Better Living: In Pursuit of Happiness from Plato to Prozac, Dreams of Millennium: Report from a Culture on the Brink, *and* A Civil Tongue: Justice, Dialogue, and the Politics of Pluralism *and a contributing editor of* Saturday Night, Shift, *and* Descant *magazines. His essays, columns, reviews, and scholarly articles have appeared in more than forty publications, including* Harper's *and* Utne Reader.

Summerside, Prince Edward Island, 1973

S HE COULD TOUCH her nose with the tip of her tongue, this girl. She didn't like to do it because she felt like a freak, but now and then she would, to impress a boy or a crowd. Her name was Alison Gaudet. They were all called Gaudet or Arsenault or Beamon or McIntosh, it seemed. She was a bit cross-eyed, her face covered in freckles, her hair a hand-cut brown helmet. Like the rest of us, she always wore baggy sweaters and worn corduroys to school. It was grade five, we were ten or eleven, and we lived on a grubby air force base. We had good clothes for church—I had my First Communion outfit, a purple leisure suit in itchy polyester, tight bell-bottom trousers, and a sleeveless tunic that went over a matching purple-and-white paisley shirt with huge wing collar and five snap buttons at each wrist—but on the whole we dressed like slobs. This was before ski clothes went neon, before the NFL and NBA annexed the playgrounds of the continent, before clothes became billboards. We were genderless, indiscriminate, anonymous.

One day Alison showed up wearing *it*. The bright red oblong popped out of the brown and grey visual field of the concrete schoolyard, otherwise brightened only by the twined-together rubber bands we used to jump over in a modified hopscotch game. It felt like the whole playground suddenly went into glacial stop action, zooming in frame by frame to the dab of colour she sported with studied casualness. The patch was made of thin, shiny fabric with a sticky back, and it adorned Alison's brown jacket like a gaudy military decoration or badge of rank. In the middle there was a stylized *L* and a small maple leaf. Alison had joined the Great Man's army. She was a Liberal.

Alison brought more patches to school the next day and she was, without warning, the most popular girl in grade five. We all wanted the L-patch for ourselves, craved the obscure identification with great events, and especially the Great Man, whose talisman it was. We knew his face well enough, the famously simian features, the curved lips of that slight smile. Vaguely we recalled the tossed frisbee, the trampoline escapade, the screaming crowds, the flashy sports jackets—images imprinted not from television, as they would be now, but from black-and-white stills of newspapers left on the living-room floor, glimpsed as we lay on our stomachs looking at the cartoons. He was the first media icon, the first Personality I ingested almost entirely by osmosis, soaking up the snapshots and judgments and alleged character traits without full consciousness. I had seen cartoons and T-shirts of him saying "Fuddle Duddle" and I thought that was funny, though I didn't know what it meant. I heard people talking about the rose in his lapel, the rumours of sexual escapades, the ability to make young women swoon, and the subtle promise of sexual and political liberation from our bleak northern lives. He seemed sophisticated, urban, impossibly far away—yet somehow mine too, my leader, my beacon. I was ten.

Before long there was a war on the playground because somebody's brother had obtained a small supply of Conservative patches —red, blue, and white rivals for our attention. Running battles broke out, with little gangs of us ostracizing each other for wearing the wrong patch, or making sudden runs at one unlucky girl to tear the sticky thing from her jacket. We had debates about the relative merits of the two parties: which looked friendlier or cooler. The Conservative patches appeared to fly the American colours (very bad), while the Liberal ones were reminiscent of Team Canada (very good), which we had watched beat the Russians the year before on a big cabinet-style TV rolled into the portable. The word "Conservative" sounded dull, boring, parental. "Liberal" seemed, by contrast, full of possibility, a tiny squeak of adolescent rebellious-ness still audible in its etymology.

I decided to expand the scope of my enthusiasm. I asked my mother about the leader, the Liberal, the Great Man, the Personal-ity. She twisted her mouth in disapproval. "Arrogant," she said. It was the first time I had heard this word. "What does that mean?" I replied. "Ask your father."

But my father was non-committal, contenting himself with hinting darkly at past sins and future punishments, all beyond my ken. The Great Man, he suggested, was on the verge of something disastrous. "Pride comes before a fall," he said, like a fire-and-brimstone preacher. The grisly and incongruous events of 1970—the James Cross abduction, the Pierre Laporte murder, the military occupation—were still fresh in many minds, though not my own. My father, who had grown up on hard-scrabble streets in Quebec City, entered a religious order, left to join the Air Force, and stud-ied political science in Ontario, perhaps felt some proprietary in-terest in the case: the deep pull of righteous political violence in general and Quebec nationalism in particular, the countervailing prickly dangers of statism, the sick logic of the crackdown. On the whole, he seemed to think that the Great Man had done more harm than good with his treatment of the October Crisis. The journalist Walter Stewart was of the same mind; already, in 1971, he had written a book called *Shrug: Trudeau in Power*, the first sus-tained critique of the Great Man's loose-cannon approach to polit-ical leadership.

Understanding came to me only later. At the time, the sugges-tion of these big events, all this passion and violence, just made me wish, as no Grand Funk Railroad or Edgar Winter record in my brother's collection could, that I had been born a few years earlier, so I would be old enough to understand the pull of the shadowy Great Man, this political magician who had such power to inspire strong feeling. So I could make sense of the excitement. So I would know why people found the phrase Fuddle Duddle worthy of wearing on a T-shirt. What could it mean?

Winnipeg, 1977

It meant he *was* arrogant, I realized, from the relative wisdom and worldliness of high school. In February 1971, it turned out, the Great Man had, in a stormy Commons debate on unemployment rates, told two Conservative MPs to *fuck off*, mouthing the words to keep them out of Hansard. Challenged by opposition backbencher Lincoln Alexander to repeat the words, the Great Man did so— silently again. "Mr. Speaker," he then said to the House, "I challenge any member opposite to say that they heard me utter a single sound." Asked by the press scrum later what he had said, he uttered the immortal phrase, the keynote words of early 1970s Canadian politics. South of the border, at around the same time, the Americans were having their own encounter with a troubling leader with aspirations beyond democratic accountability—Richard Nixon's downfall was a process we all watched unfold between doses of Saturday morning cartoons—but here we had made a joke of it: Fuddle Duddle, for God's sake. It was ridiculous.

But the Great Man loved the absurdity of it all, and now, looking back at it from the perspective of high school, I was impressed, though not entirely in a good way. I found it tempting to read Fuddle Duddle as a kind of mythical midnight for Canada's celebrated civility, the old culture of diplomatic politeness I associated as much with Lester Pearson as with my parents' moral strictures. This seemed exciting, daring, even counter-cultural. It was easy for me to imagine the Great Man swearing with inventiveness and abandon, and indulging in other profane pleasures like sex and strong drink—things that appealed to me at a pretty deep (if unrealized) level in grade nine. He was a man; more than that, he was a mensch.

In fact, this judgment of the Fuddle Duddle episode's cultural weight was entirely in keeping with the new image of the Great Man that I now began to construct. This version of the Personality had been there all along, but it was new to me, distilled not from the overheated chemicals of late-1960s mania but from older materials, nostalgia about the heady days at *Cité libre* (which I had never

read), intense discussions on the streets of Quebec City (which I
had never visited). This new Great Man was more intellectual, less
frivolous than the leader of the red-L playground faction: brainy,
reflective, more *il penseroso* than *l'allegro*.

I often found myself looking through one of Don Harron's
satirical Charlie Farquharson books, somebody's Christmas present
to my father, which featured pictures of the Great Man in compromising poses under captions that mocked him and his carefully
maintained Personality as the philosopher king. It was meant to be
dismissive, but somehow, though I did not know anything about
Plato, I found myself thinking: Yes, that's it. The mythical leader,
the politician as worldly sage—the ruler greater than the man,
the leader larger than life. I read the biographies, soaked up the
details of his bicultural upbringing, his Jesuit education, his sense of
manifest destiny, especially his celebrated citizen-of-the-world
period in which he travelled the globe, deciding at leisure where
he would make his historical mark. I was, let it be said, in a Jesuit
school myself.

Arrogant—I knew exactly what it meant now, the twin edges of
a personality admirably certain of itself and distressingly convinced
of its own superiority to everyone else. I also knew that nobody was
more arrogant than Trudeau, that he was a genius with it, a virtu-
oso, especially when you factored in the false modesty, the boyish
charm, with which he had fended off suggestions of design on the
highest elected office in the land. "I just want to go on being justice
minister," he had said, smiling bashfully, not looking at the cameras.
The same way he had said a year before that, with a sense of knowing what he was talking about, "the state has no place in the bedrooms of the nation."

What did it all add up to, what did it mean? It meant he was a
star, maybe the first and last one Canadian politics has produced,
his status as Personality stronger by the year despite the realities of
policy or budget plan. Things had moved on even in the Personality, of course, and the mania was fading quickly, all but gone. But I
was looking backward and there were facts that could not be denied, even if they could be obscured. Bedrooms, roses, intellectual

passion, wiry athleticism—still all there. And then there was Margaret, the hippie the Great Man had wed in 1971 when she was just twenty-two—her own mother two years younger than the groom himself. Even when they split apart, even when she was spotted partying with Mick Jagger and the Rolling Stones at Studio 54 in New York, it somehow reflected well on the Great Man. "If this gorgeous, free-spirited flower child could go for the PM—despite the chasm of age, experience, intellect, and inclination that yawned between them," one spectator wrote, "then we must indeed have the coolest and sexiest leader on the face of God's earth." Oh yeah, baby.

"Just watch me!" he had said of his decision to invoke the War Measures Act in 1970. Who could resist watching his every move? Not I, looking wilfully backwards, at fourteen.

St. Michael's College, University of Toronto, 1980

I learned what a philosopher king really was in my first semester, in a philosophy class taught with truly extraordinary ineptness. In a year-long course that was supposed to span the centuries of the Western tradition, we barely made it past the pre-Socratic philosophers Heraclitus and Parmenides. But we did read *The Republic* cover to cover, or I did, and it is still the most illuminating book I have ever read on the snaky temptations of political power, the harsh demands and occasionally soul-destroying imperatives of ruling. Only those who had glimpsed the Form of the Good, the ultimate truth, says Plato, were suitable to rule, because only they could be trusted to guide the state to proper ends with the necessary mixture of wisdom and deft deception of the philosophically less able. The philosophers would not want to get their hands dirty in this fashion, of course, preferring the tidy pleasures of abstract contemplation of geometrical figures, mathematical axioms, and philosophical essences. But devotion to wisdom would demand it of them: reluctant kings, condescending to lead the rest of us out of our dark ignorance. "Cities will have no respite from evil, my dear

Glaucon," Socrates says to his young friend at the crucial point in this argument, "nor will the human race, I think, unless philosophers rule as kings in the cities, or those we now call kings and rulers genuinely and adequately study philosophy—until, that is, political power and philosophy coalesce, and the various natures of those who now pursue the one to the exclusion of the other are forcibly debarred from doing so."

That's an inspirational thought to some, a terrifying one to others. But it seemed to me that the Great Man was not quite what Plato had in mind. For one thing, his reluctance to rule—a paradoxical sign, Plato suggests, of someone's suitability to take up the job—was always more feigned than real. The Great Man actually craved power, felt the need for it in every bone of his small frame. In Platonic terms, he was not so much philosopher as timocrat, the honour-lover or guru who seeks self-aggrandizement in the form of political power; the man devoted not so much to wisdom as to himself. And there was, of course, no mention in *The Republic* of the singular portentous talent for siring children born on Christmas Day. At the same time, the haughty style of the philosopher king, the unwillingness to suffer fools, the sense of superior knowledge were all there.

As was much else, too, always depending on the moment and the audience. That same year, on New Year's Eve, Marshall McLuhan, the college's resident sage and media darling, died at the age of sixty-nine. There was a long obituary of him in the college newspaper. McLuhan, I discovered later, had been a fan of the Great Man, or of his media phenomenon, of his Personality; they had corresponded and dined together regularly. McLuhan had famously called the Great Man a pure creation of the television age, a persona-projecting actor admirably suited to the demands of media-saturated politics. A politician who expertly practised the truncated discipline of the sound bite, before the term was invented, and made his personality more important than his policies. A prime minister who thrusted and parried with the press, mocking their inadequacies, demolishing their lines of reasoning with an alchemical compound of witty deflection, exaggerated Gallic shrugs, and shrewd insult. "The medium can't take a real face," McLuhan had said of the Great Man's televisual triumphs. "It has to have a mask."

Also that fall I heard, for the first time, the phrase "cult of personality." It was used, pejoratively, to describe an editor of the main undergraduate newspaper who possessed qualities of wit and bravado sufficient to motivate his sceptical peers. He made himself and his moods the subject of editorials, wrote incessantly in a style borrowed from comic books and tabloid newspapers, and did wickedly accurate imitations of everyone he knew. His merest utterance was listened to with a mixture of devotion, fear, and dislike. He was hated, respected, and—in an odd way—loved. You felt you wanted to resist the influence of that carefully crafted persona, but you were drawn to it anyway. So with the Great Man, and for the same reasons. He was, still at this comparatively late date, an obscure object of our love: a complicated and much-scored devotion that prized, even while mistrusting, the fact that he could be charming or statesmanlike or cool, whenever the occasion demanded it. Robert Fulford has said, accurately enough, that Canada was a much less provincial place in the late 1960s and early 1970s than it became in the 1980s, when we bogged down in constitutional bickering and intramural dither. In 1969, for instance, John Lennon and Yoko Ono came north to visit both McLuhan and the Great Man, a pilgrimage of almost unmeasurable cool. The meeting with Trudeau in Ottawa has been sagely described by one analyst as "the politician as pop star welcoming the pop star as politician." Yes, indeed.

But by 1980, with McLuhan dead and the Great Man apparently not long for the political world, Fulford's judgment seemed all too accurate—and depressing. Once again I felt deprived of something dangerous and challenging but highly desirable, like a boy who turns eighteen the day before armistice is declared. Trudeaumania had by this time become almost a joke word, as diminished and tarnished with time as the word "groovy," as risible as platform shoes or bell bottoms. People who had been drawn into politics by the mania, seduced by the madness and aura of the 1968 campaign, the

Great Man's pop-star ascension to the highest elected office in the land, now looked back on their youthful foolishness with a kind of detached disapproval. How very young we were! How impressionable! How desperate in our longing for something sexy . . . modern . . . world-historical! But I didn't want to go to that middle-aged, self-abnegating place, that region of what I now recognize as Boomer revisionism. I was seventeen and I wanted the cool party, the celebration of the politician as hipper-than-thou Personality, to keep going and going. I wanted to keep my political optimism, my sense of Canada as a player on the world stage, my suspicion that power really is sexy—and I wanted them free of the cheap editorial cynicism of hindsight.

So in some quarters, notably among the newly politicized left-liberal university students of my acquaintance, the cult itself continued, even intensified—modulating now away from sheer pop-star hysteria and gradually taking on the quality of a religious or spiritual gathering, a focusing of hope and aspiration on a central point that seemed to possess position but not dimension. The very idea of the Great Man alone remained now, the politician as wise patriarch, dutifully supporting the three children Margaret had borne him, a father to us all. She was long gone, a dim reminder of the lesson of 1967—that Canada could be genuinely world class without having to resort to actually saying so. But the surface cool had deepened to a richer and more lustrous appeal, a mature charisma, and in this way, as Larry Zolf said in 1984, the Great Man became "our permanent Expo," aging patchily along with Habitat and the rest of the Montreal site, but reminding us, despite the cracks and stress spots, of future possibilities as well as former glories.

In 1982, finally, the Constitution Act patriated the founding documents of Canadian politics. The Great Man was fading, the mania a thing of the past, but his legacy was going to be glorious. I bought a copy of the act, which I still have somewhere. In my politics class the shadow that he cast over us all was long, if also rarely mentioned. We didn't bandy his name about because we didn't have to; it was in the very air, even if it was not on the cover of the act itself. We were his children, three hundred of us in a

giant lecture theatre every Monday, Wednesday, and Friday at ten,
the former patch-wearing kids from the playgrounds of the nation.
When we thought about what it meant to be Canadian—when I
think about it now—he inevitably comes to mind.

Convocation Hall, University of Toronto, 1984

It was his last speech as prime minister, part of what can only be
called the farewell tour. Like an ageing rock musician or fading
tenor, he took to the road to thank the little people, one last time,
for the glory days of old, the bright promises and high hopes of two
decades of public service. There was no mania, only a muted hint
of that madness, a willing suspension of the accreted disbelief and
misgivings, for the sake of the moment. The 1983–84 global peace
initiative had been a bust, the scope of the Great Man's ambition
for the first time openly mocked: Here, after all, was the same man
who, in 1970, had sent tanks into the streets of Montreal with a dismissive shrug. But still we could not resist watching him, cheering
him. As editor of the university newspaper, I had a ticket. With a
mixture of awe and irony I joined the expectant crowd, aware that
my younger selves—and those I had not been, but only imagined—were all along for the ride.

There was, too, a mythological aspect to the Great Man's stepping down—his famous midnight walk in an Ottawa snowstorm, his
striking out on foot, game as always for exercise even at sixty-four,
to ponder his future and his calling: A piece of self-dramatization so
perfect, so Byronesque in its romanticism, that we would have had
to invent it if it had not happened. The dark sky, the falling snow,
the hard choices: it was a scene from a dream or a film. It was both
fake and utterly right, and why not? On such moments as this the
Great Man's entire image depended, a cult that had been artfully,
lovingly constructed.

I saw him, before the speech, striding manfully around King's
College Circle with the president of the university. The Great Man
was wearing a big fur hat to keep the cold away from the famous

bald head, now considered thoroughly chic, a sign of mature viril-
ity. The two of them, swinging their arms and taking bold steps
through the scattered, awestruck undergraduates, looked as though
they were having some kind of race. The Great Man, smiling imp-
ishly, was, of course, winning. I came within perhaps ten feet of
them. He seemed happy, enjoying himself thoroughly, making
even this little convivial stroll into a fierce competition. That spoke
easily of the man's mercurial personality, the ingrained vigour and
charisma, but I saw, too, an eerie analogue of the midnight walk,
a kind of Russian-poet-turned-double-agent effect now, a low-
pitched John le Carré echo.

The speech itself was not memorable. He was going. He was
gone. And all those who followed him must be, by comparison, as
dwarfs milling round the legs of a titan. Looking on benignly, from
above, he would watch them bury themselves. Some acts really are
too hard to follow, he said, without having to shape the words. I sat
in the stuffy hall, slush melting off my boots, and believed him.

Bora Laskin Law Library, University of Toronto, 1987

The last time I saw the Great Man in the flesh was in the fall of
1987, when I returned to Toronto for a visit from Yale. I was
twenty-four, in graduate school, and had just started to grapple
with the idea of justice and the philosopher king. By a delicious
coincidence, the October edition of *Saturday Night* magazine
placed a reprinted 1960 profile of Pearson, written by pundit-on-
the-rise and future Trudeau biographer Richard Gwyn, next to a
subtle new analysis of the Great Man's legacy by the historian and
novelist Michael Ignatieff, the son of George, a diplomatic colleague of Pearson. "He lacks a capacity for ruthlessness," Gwyn
wrote of Smiling Mike, then leader of the opposition, "and will go
out of his way not to hurt people's feelings . . . His success at the UN
did not come about through grandstand plays but through patient
negotiations in back rooms to bring about commonsense compromises." In contrast, Ignatieff had a different take on the northern

magus: "In political warfare he never had any patience for niceties. No-one played harder or rougher than he, and he would claim that the constitutional issues at stake demanded the knockout punch rather than the polite rebuke."

The more I thought about it, the more I was convinced that Fuddle Duddle had indeed been the death knell for the old Canadian culture. It signalled the beginning of a long decline into political manipulation and braggadocio, the unquestioned preference among subsequent generations of politicians for hardball and, on the flip side, the voters' penchant for cynicism about lawmakers. Fuddle Duddle was Canada's Watergate, the first significant breach in the old bargain of good faith between governors and governed. The Great Man had, perforce, been at the centre of it, cementing his status as the most notorious politician of his country's young existence. His arrogance had extended not only to his parliamentary colleagues but also to the conventions of parliament, even— taking the statism of the October Crisis into account—to the rule of law. Not even high stakes could justify such contempt for citizens' rights, I thought. The glow of adulation faded in me, as in so many others, though I have to admit to a certain delayed reaction. I saw it all, clearly, for the first time. And for me, the bloom was finally off the rose in his lapel.

Or was it? Once again I sat in Convocation Hall and listened to the Great Man speechify about the nature of politics. He did not give a firebrand address this time, nor even a wistful one, but, instead, he presented a reasoned legal brief, heavy with casebook references that I could not imagine he had chased down himself. He reviewed the growing body of Charter decisions, speaking dispassionately but still somehow like the proud father of that document. Carefully, and in detail, he assessed the judgments of Chief Justice Brian Dickson, who was sitting in the front row, gazing awkwardly up. It was eerie: a thoroughly academic performance, but set against a background of history and personality, a strangely moving drama of nation-building people pausing to reflect on their work.

The occasion was the opening of the Bora Laskin Law Library. The reception after the speech was picketed by striking library workers and, though I have never crossed a picket line before or since, I decided to squeeze through the gate to get closer to the Great Man, to feel the dying heat from the embers of his Personality. There was a crowd. I tried going to a smaller gate, reasoning, incorrectly as it turned out, that there would be no picketers there. With no other visitors around, I was singled out for special attention and called a scab. I didn't feel much better when, glass of wine in hand, I watched the Great Man stroll by. He swam through the crowd expertly, smiling and greeting like a Royal, and I caught his eye and smiled at him. His gaze didn't linger. I was left standing. I took a sip of my lukewarm wine.

The Annex, Toronto, 1997

I have never met him, certainly never had the opportunity to test the limits of the Personality, in its various forms, against the reality of the person. I have only been close, in spirit and in body, these few crucial times—close enough to reach out and touch him, close enough (in another mood) to spit on him. In 1993 the television series images of him slowly paddling across a glassy lake, resplendent in buckskin and seventy-three years of hard-won experience, struck me as ridiculous, especially when he J-stroked past the camera to reveal the cheesy "Canada" logo embroidered on his back. The famous arrogance was revealed again—Canada personified, no less, the philosopher king as a soulful combination of hardy woodsman and Emersonian nature poet. Less interesting, and less forgivable, was the cynical fact that the television series was aired to coincide with the publication of the Great Man's gruel-thin memoirs. Still, both the series and the book enjoyed great commercial success—proof of the Great Man's continuing hold on the Canadian people.

These days I live a few blocks from the home of the young love child, the product of a late-life romance, the celebrated case. The Great Man has been spotted in the neighbourhood, an unmistakably old man now, trundling the love child up and down the streets, pushing her idly on a swing in tiny Sibelius Park. I figure a meeting is only a matter of time.

I like to imagine it as I stroll through the neighbourhood on my way to class or to the bookstore. I will be cool, of course, because we are Canadians, and he is a private citizen now, and the child has enough burdens already without having to grow up as the object of prurient interest from fans (or otherwise) of her unlikely, aged father. But I will stop to pass the time of day, chat about the weather, compliment the child on her complexion. I might allow that I know who he is, that his Personality has had some impact on me, and that his presence has shaped my views both of politics and somehow of life itself. I might tell him the ups and downs I lived through as an heir of his vision, a fan, a critic, a disciple, in the original meaning of that word, which our Jesuit masters would have understood well.

He will be old, wizened, maybe a little world weary, his sharp eyes a bit bleary now, and too many lines of battle etched on the waxy skin of his face. He will be past it, in short, a cult leader without a following, living out this chosen retirement, an elder statesman with his incongruously young daughter, herself a kind of emblem of the old days, the Great Man's virile legacy.

I will ask him to shake my hand.

Of Wardrobe and Mask: Seven Takes on Stitching a Prime Minister

■

KAREN MULHALLEN

Karen Mulhallen is editor-in-chief of Descant *magazine and the author of five volumes of poetry and a travel-fiction memoir. For many years she was the arts features editor of the* Canadian Forum *and the Canadian columnist for the* Literary Review. *Her essays on literature and culture have appeared in magazines in Canada and abroad. She teaches English at Ryerson Polytechnic University.*

FOR ENGLISH CANADIANS of a certain age, Pierre Elliott Trudeau conjures up endless summer—summer in the air about him, even as he skis down another glamorous slope, in Gstaad or, closer to home, on Mont Tremblant, or south at Aspen. In his skiwear he reminds us that there are no impediments. It is all possible, not just in Canada but in the land to the south and in the mountains of Europe. He seems like one of the Olympians, one of those golden beings who soar. Yet also a father, not young, often accompanied by his three young sons.

There is no separating him from his aura. It's as if he had come to us from a story by F. Scott Fitzgerald, unspeakably glamorous, charmed, and, because he is ours, his story does not end in damnation but in an elegant city, where he continues to thrive and we continue to await his infrequent but important pronouncements. And there it is again. They are not just remarks, or even comments. When Trudeau speaks, it is still a pronouncement.

My diction suggests he is either a dictator or the Messiah, and there's a bit of both in views about him. In press photographs the year he became prime minister, the summer of 1968, he often appeared in sandals and kurta. If not Christ, he was at least one of G.I. Gurdjieff's Remarkable Men. He had been to India, and this was the era of the Mahareshi Mahesh Yogi, of the Beatles, of the West going to the East and the East coming West. Incense and the sound of sitars were everywhere. Not long after he managed a collaboration with the heavenly theatre director as he staged the births of two of his sons on Christmas Day—births already astonishing enough, given their father's age and rumoured earlier inclinations.

And the dictator? That aspect, too, was soon revealed in the October Crisis in 1970, the War Measures Act, and the arrests, detentions, and censorship that followed.

In that first run to office, Trudeau carried the spirit of the anti-Vietnam War era, of the student uprisings throughout the Western world. Although he was a wealthy internationalist by birth and training, and a law professor, he represented energy, youthfulness, optimism, and radicalism to those who were young in the late 1960s. Any comparison of a picture of Trudeau next to one of Lester Pearson, John Diefenbaker, or Louis St. Laurent provides proof ocular that Trudeau represented a new age. In hindsight, this image seems almost an error in judgment. Although Trudeau had supported the union in the Asbestos strike of 1949, and argued John Stuart Mill's philosophy that "a democracy is judged by the way the majority treats the minority," he still called in the Canadian army against a small group of Québécois separatists. Even if it is true that "martial law is preferable to civil war," a kind of papal authority has always been one of his personae.

When I look at the dates, I realize that Trudeau was only six years younger than my father, yet for Canadians of my generation (the pre-boomers and boomers who constituted the enormous voting power of the 1960s) he was a contemporary. He was the youthful dark horse, scarcely three years in parliament before he became prime minister. His first decade was marked by a series of cover-shots and fashion spreads: Trudeau as MP in the Commons, wearing sandals and sporting an ascot; Trudeau in the election campaign of 1968, bouncing on a trampoline, diving into swimming pools. Casual, athletic, youthful, we assumed these qualities meant he was sincere. And he was no ordinary Johnny Canuck. If the British comedies of the era characterized us as dim-witted, plaid-jacketed lumberjacks, there was our elegant prime minister giving them the finger. Sporting his habitual red boutonnière, he swings down a banister in England at the 1969 Commonwealth Conference in London or, evening-tails flying, he pirouettes behind the queen.

He was sexy. Before his marriage his name was attached to a string of glamorous young actresses, Louise Marleau and Barbra

Streisand among them, and he partied with his old school chum from the London School of Economics, the Jamaican prime minister Michael Manley, another man with a sexual and political charge. His marriage to a woman nearly thirty years his junior, while it seemed to be a blow to the women's movement, also confirmed the myth of his sexuality and, soon after, his potency. Press photos and fashion sketches from those early years show Trudeau in a leather trench coat with épaulettes, appropriately collaged with images from the Beatles' album *Sergeant Pepper's Lonely Hearts Club Band*. Fashion, New Music, World Culture, all capital-letter words. The only prime minister ever featured in the press for his clothes—and his footwear.

One of Trudeau's personae remind us of the influence in the period of Oriental thought and specifically of a popular form of Indian mysticism. Trudeau was born just as Hermann Hesse's books began to be published, and he came to prominence as my generation was discovering Hesse. In Hesse's works we can seen the subthemes of much of the debate over our enigmatic prime minister. If he caught our imagination by his mysteriousness, the nature of the mysteriousness seemed justified by the very literary texts we were absorbing: Eastern mysticism, search for the self, disregard for convention, denunciation of militarism, and opposition to narrow nationalism. Hesse's characters in *Siddhartha*, *Steppenwolf*, and *Magister Ludi* resonate as well. Middle-aged intellectuals, ascetics, sensualists, their journeying and their search for salvation highlight the tensions between the private and the public, the contemplative and the active life.

Trudeau, like Hesse, had been to the source. Wearing a Sikh turban, he had backpacked the Indian subcontinent. In Bedouin headdress, he had travelled in the Near East. He was both enlightenment and sexual liberation. "The state has no place in the bedrooms of the nation," he argued and, as minister of justice in 1967, he reformed Canada's draconian and destructive divorce laws and liberalized laws on homosexuality and abortion. He caught the women's movement and gay liberation, all at once, and made clear that his reforms would be significant, not just smoke and mirrors. His clothing might fuel Trudeaumania, but it was more than just appearance.

■

For, looking away from individual cases, and how a Man is by
the Tailor new-created into a Nobleman, and clothes not only
with Wool but with Dignity and a Mystic Dominion—is not
the fair fabric of Society itself . . . the creation of the Tailor
alone? (Thomas Carlyle, *Sartor Resartus*)

Trudeau's style echoed changes already afoot. In the June 1950
issue of *Cité libre*, the magazine he had helped to found, he wrote of
the need to "cast out the thousand prejudices where past encum-
bers the present" and of the "struggle for the New Man." That past
included narrow nationalism. In June 1964 he spoke of the "hope
that in advanced societies, the glue of nationalism will become as
obsolete as the divine right of kings." Four years later the London
Spectator saw his advent as Canada's coming of age, as if Trudeau,
singlehandedly, "would catapult it into the brilliant sunshine of the
late twentieth century from the stagnant swamp of traditionalism
and mediocrity in which Canadian politics had been bogged down
for years." The sense of change was perceived at home and abroad.

The first article devoted to Trudeau's clothes seems to have been
in 1968, where he insisted that he bought clothes "for comfort, not
effect." Fatuous as articles on his clothing might have seemed to a
man who had Petro-Canada, an Offical Languages Act, a Charter of
Rights, a Constitution, and an Opportunities for Youth project on
his plate, Trudeau still played to the crowd. Photographed dancing
beside the campaign bus, his physical vitality captured the public
imagination to the point where the hijinks and animal magnetism became the stuff of crowd expectations. In his *Memoirs*, a caption for a
photograph of him sniffing a carnation during the leadership convention reads: "In my box at the convention pretending nonchalance
with the aid of a carnation, not a rose." Colleagues commented on
how quickly the "egghead" had become the political professional.
From the beginning, he was recreating himself for the public gaze.

Commentators agree that fashion is a material culture, regulated
by capitalism and commodification. The reading of fashion is a

study of the relations of power and persuasion. Even anti-fashion, in its challenge to accepted norms and sensibilities, is self-conscious and hierarchical. Sartorial extravagance has always been a mark of aristocratic power and privilege, first among men, but, since the eighteenth century, among women, as it became a wife's responsibility to display her husband's wealth through her clothing. And, as cultural critic Kaja Silverman explains in *Fragments of a Fashionable Discourse*, imaginative dress in the second half of the twentieth century has become a way of challenging not only dominant values but traditional class and gender demarcations.

Trudeau turned the last hundred years of Western male vestimentary sobriety on its ear. Flowers and capes demanded the limelight. And he continued to outmanoeuvre in the grace with which he sported the *vêtements* of power, wonderfully evoked and mirrored in a December 1969 Ottawa photograph with John Lennon and Yoko Ono on their Give Peace a Chance mission. All three are garbed in the homogeneous uniform of the power élite. If we didn't know otherwise, we'd swear they were stockbrokers or General Motors executives.

Trudeau's shape-shifting was catalytic. My own family, for example, was highly political and deeply divided. My father was a Tory organizer who ran rural campaigns from the family library and worked for a time as Dalton Camp's assistant. My mother had been a newspaper editor and printed the *Canadian Forum* on her presses in Belleville. My eldest brother was a Marxist, and I had worked for the Young Conservatives at the University of Toronto. Trudeau's style spoke directly to the divisions in my own family— its agrarian conservatism, its urban socialism, its Canadian nationalism. In the 1960s, like many of my generation, I turned left. Trudeau was the emblem and liberalization of our whole social contract, not just of Liberal Party Politics. He symbolized the shifts from Tory to Red Tory, from the moderate New Democrats to the Waffle, from a dormant to an active Canadian nationalism.

In the summer of 1968 Canadians felt they had leapt from the nineteenth to the late twentieth century in one vault. The great release had already been signalled by the World Exposition in

Montreal the year before. It was carried forward by Trudeau's affiliations with that city. As a bilingual Montrealer, his background was
both English and French, his culture international *à la mode*.

The real Birth of the Nation, then, was one hundred years after
Confederation, beginning with Expo and including the patriation
of the Constitution and the creation of the Charter of Rights and
Freedoms. As an equal on the world stage, Trudeau defended his
dream of Canada abroad and at home. In its way, it is a nationalist
dream, historical, romantic, and contemporary. Canoeing in his
Memoirs, he reminds us of one of the *coureurs des bois*. Garbed in
buckskins, his skin is brown, his cheek-bones high. And yet, as our
first prime minister born in the twentieth century, he also seemed
to carry the century with him. Winning the 1980 election, he welcomed us to the 1980s. The body's map is society's fabric.

■

> For neither in tailoring nor in legislating does man proceed by
> mere Accident, but the hand is ever guided on by mysterious
> operations of the mind . . . Body and the Cloth are the site and
> materials whereon and whereby his beautified edifice, of a Per
> son, is to be built. Whether he flow gracefully out in folded
> mantles, based on light sandals . . . or girth himself into separate
> sections . . . will depend on the nature of such an Architectural
> Idea: whether Grecian, Gothic, Later Gothic, or altogether
> Modern, and Parisian or Anglo-Dandiacal . . . In all which,
> among nations as among individuals, there is an incessant, in
> dubitable, though infinitely complex working of Cause and
> Effect: every snip of the Scissors has been regulated and pre
> scribed by ever-active Influences, which doubtless to Intelli
> gences of a superior order are neither invisible nor illegible.
> (Thomas Carlyle, *Sartor Resartus*)

Two texts by the nineteenth-century English writer Thomas
Carlyle provide an interesting sidelight on fashion and public office.
In *Sartor Resartus* [The Tailor Restitched] (1836), Carlyle insisted on

the utility of clothes, by which he meant literature and art, government and social machinery, philosophies and creeds. Clothes make us human, but they must be sacrificed or changed according to the ideal behind them. "The beginning of all wisdom" argued Carlyle, "is to look fixedly on clothes . . . till they become transparent." Five years later in *Heroes and Hero-Worship*, writing very much against the democratic, scientific, and evolutionary trends of his time, Carlyle presented his great-man theory of history: history is the history of what man has accomplished.

There is a connection between the raging prophet Carlyle and the cool analytic Trudeau. Carlyle demonstrated that heroic biography goes hand in hand with the conscious presentation of the self in public life. Apply this union of idea, social rituals, and tailoring to photographs of Trudeau descending the steps of the bleachers in Toronto at the Grey Cup Game in November 1970. He seems the very model of a dandy, a Beau Brummel. His hat is set at a jaunty angle, he holds a cape over his shoulders, and his trousers are cut from cloth of a brash checkered pattern. In his buttonhole is his trademark boutonnière. On his right, a man in a Stetson hat gazes at him as he descends. The steps become a runway. The prime minister becomes for that moment a vedette, a model existing in the gaze of the gazing man.

■

Any reflection on Trudeau and Fashion moves effortlessly into Trudeau and Style. He was the first of our prime ministers to aim the F-word at reporters and hecklers and critics—along with the F-finger. This diction and this body language confirmed earlier public projections and mythologies about Trudeau—observations that mimic the life pattern of the culture hero as outlined by both Joseph Campbell and Northrop Frye. Both critics write of the perilous journey, the conflict, the crucial struggle, the pathos, and the exaltation of the hero. Each also charts the social relation to the mob, and human society's search for a ritual scapegoat. And each discusses the tearing apart of the sacrificial body.

The periodical indexes immediately make clear the intense tracking of Trudeau's fortunes by the media and the public, with such article titles as "Quebec's new face in Ottawa," "Trudeau up front," "Chains of office bind PET to loner's role," "Trudeau can afford to be cool to the press," "M. Trudeau: nouveau Messie," "Who says Pierre Trudeau is all that hot," "Whom should he marry?" "man of moods," "Pierre's hush-hush soirées," and "Why they can't burst the Trudeau balloon." He was the new Messiah, cool, distant, a loner. Imaging also began early in his political career, and they never let up. He was portrayed, photographed, and drawn, in eveything from the *Financial Post* to the *Last Post*, from *World Affairs* to *Chatelaine* to *Weekend* magazine.

Certain Canadian journalists seem to have staked Trudeau as their special territory, in a way that went beyond their function as parliamentary reporter or whatever. They became interesting barometers, their opinion of him waxing and waning with his pop-ularity: Alan Fotheringham, Peter Newman, Denis Smith, Walter Stewart—and there were many more.

Intriguing subtexts begin to emerge. By mid-career, there were complaints about his lack of decorum, his autocratic behaviour, the way he made people edgy. People began to call him the president of Canada, suggesting that he saw himself above parliament. He was no longer the "philosopher king," just the "king." He was a dilettante, a priest with a catechism. There were also frequent ascriptions of aloneness, solitariness, isolation, an exotic mindscape. He was a boxer, and the press had a ringside seat at his matches. He was Machiavelli, a Napoleon IV in the making. He was a fugitive from reality, a prince of darkness, a prince of light, a wizard in Ottawa who wowed the élite.

As silly as all this labelling seems, it was deadly earnest, a real sociopolitical indicator. In his last few years in office, when many commentators argued that his idealism had changed to cynicism, the analogies continued, and they focused on his shape-shifting and his enigmatic personality: the Phantom, the Man in the Iron Mask, the master-manipulator, the betrayer of family and marriage, Big Brother, Houdini, the Shadow. Yet the portrait photographs, many in colour, continued. Only one writer, Anthony Westell in *Canadian Business* in April 1981, attempted to blow the whistle on the mythologizing: "Mysterious evil genius of the North?" he asked. "Nonsense. Trudeau's magic is of our own making." But the fact that we are the makers of the myth is exactly the point.

The descriptions were larded with biblical analogies to both the Old and the New Testament: to the Messiah; to a negative version of the God portrayed in the Psalms, one who does not deliver us from evil; to the three wise men (the magi) from Quebec, not Iran; to the biblical Samson, as in Milton's *Samson Agonistes*. Later, Trudeau fell from Grace. He was the healer whose recipe of Reason over Passion had failed. Biblical analogues were counterpointed, and occasionally reinforced, by extensive references to the characters and life stories of American culture heroes, from Frank Sinatra (Old Blue Eyes is back, 1977) to the Lone Ranger, and to narratives in American popular songs: "Some echanted evenings," "After the ball was over," "Shall we dance?"

Virulent but engaged, the press was unrelenting: his "shrug is beyond compare": he is a master with minions; he is "lip-deep Pierre" who lays a "New Year's egg," going through a male menopause, cranky and costly. And yet, when he left, there was a profound sense of loss: Peter C. Newman bid farewell to a "man of mystery," *Maclean's* extolled "The man in the mask who was true to himself," and the *Financial Post* called him "Marathon Man." The *Alberta Report* asked rhetorically if he was "Hip-Shooter or Analyst," knowing he was both. Cast by the media as the leader "with a thousand faces," "the new Ulysses" making his "journey of destiny," the guru who aspired to Olympus, Trudeau's mythic allure has survived his resignation.

■

In 1993 Trudeau published his *Memoirs*, accompanied by 253 photographs, 106 of them in full colour. The dust-jacket photograph is a head and shoulders shot of Trudeau wearing a buckskin jacket and an open-neck shirt. At the end of the book that informal shot appears again, only now Trudeau is full-bodied, in jeans and buck-skin, striding through a forest. And the text itself is framed by two portraits, Trudeau elegant and serious, looking off to the left, red rose in his lapel, the Canadian flag behind him. The publisher's blurb estimates that, in his sixteen years in office, Trudeau was snapped, posed, or ambushed, hundreds of thousands of times. In one Trudeau file alone in the National Archives of Canada there are 160,000 photographs. And to such figures can be added news photos, amateur snapshots, and family photos. Together they create the public man, a man of many faces: Trudeau smiling, Trudeau arrogant, Trudeau enraged, Trudeau laughing with friends, Trudeau athletic (on a trampoline, skin-diving in Cuba, swimming, doing handstands, skiing, canoeing, doing judo), Trudeau as elegant bachelor, Trudeau in love, Trudeau as husband, Trudeau as father—a national single parent, the New Male.

The *Memoirs* themselves are words for pictures, for this was our first television prime minister. The project began as a film, and the book is a kind of "novelization." Reading the *Memoirs* is picturing the *Memoirs*. The real text is the pictures; the words are the shadow reality. The *Memoirs* result as responses to interviewers' questions. Trudeau does not initiate the view: the frame is created for him, and he enters to fulfil the frame.

The *Memoirs* are intimate, and yet they are somehow unsatisfying. They might leave the reader/viewer craving more, craving deeper knowledge, yearning to be trusted. A foolish desire, perhaps, but a yearning nonetheless. The informality of many of the pictures, and the casualness and apparent candour of the captions, leave us wondering what we are missing. Is he really just a "beautiful guy," as his ex-wife was given to saying? We believe he is sincere, we believe in his integrity, we know he is intelligent, but this is the crux of the enigma. Somehow the northern magus eludes the text and the photographs. What appears, instead, is an all-round nice guy. The moments of rage, even of obscenity, seem to be justified, even irrelevant, and what emerges is *almost* the ideal "man next door," whose priority is his children, who juggles parenthood with an important job, who loves his country, who is curious and adventurous. In every way he appears as a role model—impossible to imitate, but an inspiration.

We are left feeling there is no secret behind the mask, the personae. The facial features are not eloquent. Do they just appear to be masklike, to allow us a ground for projection? It is a face that lends itself well to cameras and to events. It is handsome, but not offensively so. The trim body maps an active world. The simulacrum is rich in friends and family. Is all this enigmatic? Not apparently, except in the sense that each human being is ultimately unknowable.

In the preface, Trudeau asserts that the *Memoirs* are his version of the events in which he was involved. On the dust-jacket, the McClelland & Stewart marketing department gives them an alliterative half-dozen characteristics: personal, philosophical, political, personality-filled, patriotic, and pertinent. But what underlies the document and gives it its shape is its governing idea—passion. Robertson Davies once said that in his works he had tried to chart the secret, passionate life of Canadians. These fabricated *Memoirs* provide a similar map. Trudeau speaks of his national dream of a unified, peaceable, proud, vibrantly individualized, free, and just society. Whatever moment we focus on, we find passion. How appropriate, too, that they are *Memoirs* that were first oral, then transcribed, for Trudeau's own best speeches were those that seemed extempore, impassioned.

■

Trudeau is our only prime minister who made his retirements glamorous international events. For his first retirement, which many political commentators characterized as a signal defeat, he was photographed in triumph, scarf flying, driving away from Parliament Hill in one of the most beautiful sportscars ever created, a late 1950s gull-wing Mercedes. For his second retirement, he acquired an elegant art-deco house by architect Ernest Cormier in one of Montreal's most attractive, historic, and expensive neighbourhoods. These images would fit easily into the Hollywood of Nathaniel West's *Day of the Locusts*, and the international press was quick to catch the aura. Trudeau's physical charm, wealth, sexual appeal, and taste in cars added to his pop-star glamour. He was seen quite simply as "one of the most charismatic leaders on the world stage." That image has not changed.

In *World Leaders Past & Present*, Thomas Butson and Arthur M. Schlesinger Jr. comment that "he created passion where there was dullness, elegance where there was drabness, spontaneity where there was artifice, mystique where there was ordinariness." Although Trudeau's politics and personality angered many people, he was adored by the very media he affected to dislike for its intrusiveness. Much of the language in which the media clothed him carried with it an American pop aura. On his retirement, a Canadian MP from Alberta seemed to echo these Hollywood western myths: "After almost sixteen years of riding tall in the saddle, our Prime Minister has decided to hang up his spurs. He leaves us his footprints all over the nation."

■

One cold winter evening in Toronto I was flipping through a few days of accumulated newsprint on my kitchen table. As so often happens, I came upon photographs and caricatures of our ex–prime minister. Once again, I was struck by his ongoing presence. A large advertisement in *Now* magazine, showed an actor dressed in buckskins, sitting in a canoe, wielding a feather paddle. The copy was instructive: "Trudeau returns to political stage. Trudeau and the FLQ return to the Toronto theatre scene . . . This spectacular *comedy noir* features the VideoCabaret Ensemble playing everyone who was anyone between 1963 and 1970." The cut line under the photograph read: "Monty Python meets Pierre Trudeau, says *Toronto Life*."

I turned next to the *University of Toronto Bulletin*, where I found a picture of Trudeau himself, pen in hand. The caption noted that he was in Toronto to attend the inaugural Senator Keith Davey Lecture hosted by Victoria University. The address had been given by the renowned Canadian economist John Kenneth Galbraith, an Emeritus Professor at Harvard University. Although Galbraith's speech was featured in the *Bulletin*, it was Trudeau's photograph that appeared.

The Smart and Determined S.O.B.: Trudeau and the West

■

ROBERT MASON LEE

Robert Mason Lee is a journalist whose articles have earned him many honours, including three National Magazine Awards, the University of Western Ontario President's Medal, two National Newspaper Awards for investigative and spot news reporting, the Southam President's Award, and an Asia-Pacific Foundation of Canada Fellowship. He is the author of Death and Deliverance: The Haunting True Story of the Hercules Crash *and* One Hundred Monkeys: The Triumph of Popular Wisdom in Canadian Politics. *Formerly the West's columnist for the* Globe and Mail, *Mason Lee is now the host of "Mason Lee: On The Edge," a current affairs panel program on the CTV national network. He lives in Vancouver with his Vespa, Rainbow.*

WHAT I LIKED BEST about Trudeau was how angry he made my father.

Trudeau's name first came up as we were visiting. In the Badlands of southern Alberta, where I was raised three or four decades ago, a "visit" meant a road trip of several hours with relatives packed in our car. As a child, I found these road excursions as unavoidable and tedious as Sunday school. The men would sit in the front seat, women and children in the back. I would stare out the window and half-listen to the adults' parallel conversations about their parallel lives, as the lines of telephone wires and highway paint smoothed past.

I was sprung from the talcum prison of my aunts about the age of nine, when I was deemed worthy of the company of the men in the front seat. Although I wasn't allowed to say anything, the move permitted me to see the road ahead, admire the chrome-plated instrument panel, and listen to the man-talk of crops and politics. I soon learned you could carry a sensible conversation about both simply by repeating the words "drought" and "son-of-a-bitch."

"What do you make of that god-damn Trudeau?" my father asked one day. "He's a son-of-a-bitch," said Uncle Allen. "But he's no worse than the other sons-o'-bitches." I could tell my father did not agree. His lips were sunken, but nothing came out. His reaction reminded me of the time the rogue grizzly killed our cattle.

We had heard the cattle bawling in the middle of the night and had grabbed our rifles, but by the time we got to the fields it was too late. Those cattle that were not dead were mutilated beyond help.

My father raised his rifle. We needed the meat, so we butchered the carcasses in the field, covered in blood and guts and moonlight. My father kept his disappointment behind closed lips, for which I was grateful. That herd of Aberdeen Angus breeding stock had been his dream of a better life.

In the end, we hunted down the grizzly. But the way my father looked that night was the same as the way he looked when Trudeau's name came up.

■

I recall seeing my first photo of Trudeau in the summer of 1967, when I was ten years old and realized I would never get to see Expo. I might as well have asked to go to the moon, since Expo, like Trudeau, was so remarkably advanced, so unimaginably sophisticated, so impossibly remote.

Our town had celebrated the year by stencilling the maple leaf pattern above the Centennial Pool, but as an Albertan I had never seen a maple tree in my life. My flag's symbol was a foreign plant symbolic of Ontario and Quebec, but this did not strike me as odd. In a colonial economy, one quickly learns not to expect too much in the way of the explicable. One learns, instead, to accept and to trust, while remaining as suspicious as hell.

My dad said they had a different language in Montreal, but Uncle Allen said that wasn't a problem; you could get along fine with your English. This reassurance did not convince my father because Uncle Allen had also told him he could get rich on Aberdeen Angus cattle. No one in our family had ever been to Montreal— none, in fact, had been off the Prairies other than in wartime.

I could not even see Expo on the television because we had no TV set. No one in our town did. For a few hours on Saturday nights the local CBC broadcast recordings of the previous week's hockey game, and some people bought sets just for that. But there was nothing else to watch; the rest of the week, TV sets were plant stands.

So it was from a Canadian magazine that I first caught a glimpse of Trudeau and saw why he riled my Mountie father.

The prime minister at the time was Lester Pearson. As I understood it, Pearson was sworn into office to replace the slain John Kennedy; I never thought there might have been prime ministers before him. But I knew that Trudeau would come next, because a child could see he was anointed. Pearson was a kindly and thoughtful figure who appeared to be lifted from a daguerreotype, but he was as expressive as a cow and made no impression on me whatsoever. It was all the more reason to be transfixed by this photograph of Trudeau, who was wearing long hair and sandals and appearing to have a good time.

Alarmed by the Beatles' arrival a few years before, my father had taken to shearing off my hair with horse clippers. He intended either to reinforce his dreams of raising cops and astronauts, or to thwart my own ambitions of becoming John, Paul, George, and Che Guevara. Because my romantic childhood fantasies were filled with Che, Trudeau's flirtations with Red China and Cuba never bothered me as much as they did my father. I understood Marxism, then and now, to be largely a matter of attitude and style. Trudeau liked to dress up in Mao suits, whereas for me it was jungle chic.

The media talked about Trudeaumania as though they were its collaborators, as though it were an invention, a trick of the lights and the camera. They didn't understand charisma, not in the way a shaven-headed ten-year-old boy understands it, with a longing for sandals and curls.

Charisma is the rendering of unvoiced cravings in the form of human flesh. Viewed from the Jurassic Park of Alberta politics, Trudeau met the craving for some fun—Robin, the colourful Boy Wonder, played against Social Credit's dark and driven Batman. I wanted to hop a Batbike with him and ride, first to Expo, then to the jungles of Bolivia.

My father picked up the magazine and saw the picture of Trudeau. To his trained Mountie eyes, Trudeau was evidently a deviant, and some damn fool had put him in charge of the Justice Department. He stared at the picture for a long while, considering what to say. He looked as though he was chewing someone else's spit. "Nothing but a God-damn hippie," he said.

That was all I knew about Trudeau. For the time being, it was all I needed to know. I was his.

■

I was listening intently to a transistor radio propped against a trapper's cabin by the river bank. My brother was trying to catch his stupid horse, a high-strung thoroughbred. He was waving a wooden plank at the horse to herd it into a chute. I told him to be quiet because Neil Armstrong was walking on the moon. I was excited, but aware that everyone else in the world was watching on television, which left me feeling a wallflower at the dance of history. Even then, I knew there was a gap separating the rocketship from the old wooden plank.

The river that flowed past the cabin was the Athabasca, which feeds into the Arctic Ocean. We had left the southern plains for Fort McMurray, then a frontier town of a few hundred people located north of Alberta's great divide, which separates the waters which flow into the Arctic from the rivers that flow into Hudson Bay.

There were no paved streets in town, and I was the fourteenth white child registered in the school system. On my first day walking to school, I sank up to my thighs in muskeg and needed to be uncorked by heavy machinery. But there was a perverse pride in living under such conditions, and we all knew its reason and purpose: oil, locked in the tar sands under our feet. On hot days, the oil melted out of the earth and people needed to pause frequently to scrape away the heavy clumps of tar stuck to their shoes.

"For 70 mi. along the Athabasca river in northern Alberta there are great reserves of oil in oil-impregnated tar sands, and these are now going to be exploited," said the 1969 edition of *Encyclopedia Britannica*. "The undeveloped Athabasca oil sands have reserves estimated in excess of 100,000,000,000 bbl." The encyclopedia was an expensive compensation for the family move. It was well thumbed because there were no other books in town until a provincial "bookmobile" began a 300-mile journey over gravel roads with its precious cargo of ink.

It was an isolated existence, but oil was our ace in the hole, our ringer, our ticket to ride. That astonishing figure of 100 billion barrels—fifteen times the amount of the known reserves of Canadian crude oil—was our pride and joy. We never tired of ways to express it: "There's enough oil here to keep the world going for thirty years after the world runs out," my father would say. "It's expensive to get at now, but they will come for it when they need it."

It was only in the mid-1960s that the Alberta petroleum industry grew to supply 85 percent of Canadian production. The boom caused a Bacchanalian riot of consumption, but its psychic effect was more uplifting: It meant the world had a purpose for us. We were part of the modern age. We had the fuel for the rocketships.

No longer were we dustbowl farmers and gullible cowpokes belonging to a previous century. We had come some distance from the two-room sod houses where both my parents were raised, a dozen sleeping in a single room, the boys with dad in one bed, the girls with mom in the other. Now we were the blue-eyed sheiks, the custodians of the keys to tomorrow. The oil was safely in the ground, it belonged to us, and no one could take our birthright away.

Or so we were told. It did not explain why, whenever the Toronto bosses landed in their private jets and came to my home for cocktails, my mother fussed so much over her dated skirts and my father laughed too hard at their jokes.

■

The Front de Libération du Québec I could understand fine. Their communiques were nifty and the knitted toque, I thought, was a nice Canadian accessory to the terrorist fashions of the day. I understood what they meant, if not what they wanted, when the FLQ kidnapped and killed people. It meant Canada was world class. We had our own revolution, and it was all most exciting.

The revolt had to be put down, of course. I understood that in a cowboys-and-Indians sort of way. What I could not understand was all the fuss. It seemed perfectly logical for terrorists to kidnap and kill people as part of their revolution, and for the state to kidnap and kill in turn. You take your best shot and accept your lumps. This I could understand; the anguishing over the decision I could not.

It was similar to the confusion I felt during Expo, when Charles de Gaulle had delivered his "Vive le Québec libre" speech. I now understand this line was an act of contempt, an interference in Canadian affairs, and the fomenting of sedition, and that any self-respecting country would have declared war on France, or at least assassinated de Gaulle, before the afternoon was out. But I did not then have the foggiest idea what de Gaulle was going on about, nor the faintest suspicion that Canada was not a self-respecting country. The political euphemisms of the day, as always, prevented me from seeing the situation clearly.

Ever since Expo, I had been noticing the terms "national identity" and "national unity" being used to describe Canada by the people who defined Canada for us, which is to say the Privy Council Office and the CBC. The FLQ I could understand; federal doublespeak I could not. I had no idea these terms described fears, not aspirations. "National identity" referred to the efforts to have me read books by Ontario authors instead of Oregon ones. "National unity" had to do with "Quebec separatism." As a means of walking through a cow pasture and calling it a flower bed, these poetics would still be in use thirty years later. Then it appeared to be some kind of Ottawa code, lost on those of us in the hinterland. Unity. Identity. What did they mean by that?

I had no problem with my identity. I was a plainsman of Scots-Anglo-Norse-Iroquois descent, loyal to Her Majesty the Queen and the *Wonderful World of Disney*. I occupied that corner of *Dent's Canadian School Atlas* illustrated with oil derricks, cattle, and sheaves of wheat. The other corner, where the FLQ was acting up, was occupied by voyageurs in canoes. It was never intended for the twain to meet, except once or twice a century when Britain went to war. These incidents were terribly divisive, and so were milestones of "national unity." The two solitudes seemed a sensible arrangement, something like Queen Elizabeth and Prince Philip keeping separate beds.

We shared Quebec's sense of exclusion and lack of control over our lives. We knew, and did our best to disregard, the lack of control over our own existence; the fact that we had no bank presidents or company headquarters, that we had no representation in the federal government, that the decisions that affected us were made on presumption. We knew, and did our best to disregard, that Alberta was a possession wrapped in a dominion inside an area of influence. But in the euphemisms of the day—then and now—western complaints were called "grievances" while Quebec complaints were called "aspirations." It is petty to grieve, but noble to aspire. Where Trudeau responded to Quebec's complaints with an invitation to share his power, his response to Albertans was to give them a taste of it.

I blame ourselves. Quebeckers had responded collectively with the cult and myth of ethnic nationalism; Albertans had responded with the cult and myth of the individual. In either case, the myth served to ease the shame of dependency, to calm the psychological whipsaw of obsequiousness and aggression.

The colonial response depends on two conflicting beliefs to maintain self-respect and sanity: one, that the foreign ruler is wise, beneficent, and all-powerful; two, that the foreign ruler is neglectful, arrogant, and illegitimate. These beliefs must be held firmly and at once, or the subject will fall either to fear or to self-loathing.

It was at this crossroads that my father and I came together over Trudeau on the implementation of the War Measures Act. I liked the bang-bang, but for my father Trudeau's decisiveness made instant amends for the Official Languages Act, legalized sodomy, and the scandalous reality that abortion and divorce had become easier to obtain than a carton of milk, or a *litre* of *lait*.

Trudeau's forcefulness made the difference: He was still hated, but he had earned deference. As Machiavelli taught, it is better to be feared than loved, since men can withdraw their love, but not their fear. My father still despised Trudeau, but he was much happier being able to respect him at the same time. After the tanks of national unity rolled through Montreal, Trudeau was still a son-of-a-bitch in my father's eyes, but a smart and determined son-of-a-bitch. You'd have to keep your eye on him.

■

When Peter Lougheed arrived at the Alberta legislature in 1971 with his forty-eight-member caucus in tow, not one of whom had ever set foot inside the building before, he decided to sprint up the stairs. A newspaper photographer caught the moment, and my political iconography—which then consisted of Trudeau and Che —grew by one. I had never before seen an Alberta politician on the move. Ernest Manning had been premier since God was a pup, and he moved with the speed of the Rock of Ages. The Social Credit caucus were farmers who washed with lye soap and whose idea of progressive social legislation was daylight time. The Conservative Lougheed was surrounded by lawyers and oilmen who had read something other than the Bible—even though they might still have insisted that no other book was necessary.

Lougheed was young, athletic, intelligent, driven by ideas and purpose. He was, in many ways, a companion to Trudeau. Both shared a classical liberal sense of the sovereignty of the individual, both had a modern liberal belief in state intervention and social goals, and both were patriots and federalists. Although Lougheed was a regionalist and Trudeau a centralist, none of this mattered a damn to anyone in Alberta in 1971. The thing that mattered was that Alberta had found a match: one not only to equal the New West's own aspirations but to equal Trudeau. While Trudeau possessed the Apollonian gifts of the sun, intellect and reason, Lougheed held the Plutonian secrets of the underworld, wealth and oil. Both men were of Titanic rank.

Lougheed was sophisticated enough to impress most Albertans, but earthy enough to approach them. He had regular guy hair, not a Roman cut. He quoted the *Edmonton Journal*, not Proust. He drove a Chevrolet Caprice, not a Mercedes gull-wing convertible. And because he did not paint himself over with the mystique of power, there was no need to dislike him.

Nor could any dislike have lasted for long. The province was awash with oil money and I, too, got my share. The Alberta government gave me a small fortune and instructions to get a proper education overseas.

It was an early lesson in federal-provincial relations. Trudeau spoke of the just society and the equality of opportunity of all Canadians. Lougheed simply put cash in my jeans and wings on my back.

■

A global perspective on the Canadian identity: a pub, anywhere in Europe. Sodden beer mats, overflowing ashtrays, a tongue bitten with curls of tobacco and the sour taste of hops. Old men and women want to talk about Canadians in the war. Young men and women don't care; their interest in Canada is different. "Your prime minister is Trudeau," they say, in pubs from London to Paris, from Stockholm to Milan. "His wife had an affair with the Rolling Stones."

■

I returned from my schooling to Alberta to live in Red Deer, the dead centre of the oil patch. I arrived at the insane, insufferable, insupportable height of it all. Lougheed had put the oil money in the Heritage Trust Fund, and Albertans acted as though they had fallen into a personal line of credit worth $13 billion. The Heritage Trust Fund was wise government but bad psychology. People behaved with the temperance and prudence of lottery winners.

I returned to find that three of my old schoolmates had died of drug overdoses and that another was working on it, living in a welfare hotel in Edmonton. At one point he had it all—journeyman's ticket, a steady job, the most money he had seen in his life. When I met him for a pint of draft at the Strathcona Hotel tavern, his shaking hands spilled his lager on the terry-cloth table. I asked him why things had gone wrong. "I couldn't handle having so much to lose," he said.

Everyone else had a job and a new truck. Few had stayed in school longer than the legal leaving age of sixteen; wages were so high in the oil patch that dropouts could earn as much as professionals. They bought houses, speedboats, Birks silver, and reptile-skin Tony Lama cowboy boots for $3000 a pair. They bought strip clubs and hookers and affairs with their neighbours' wives.

Once again, Alberta was out of step with the outside world. The first oil price shock of 1973 had sliced the growth rate of the Canadian economy by two-thirds, and stagflation had severed the cables of monetary controls. Governments everywhere were attempting to cope with inflation and unemployment, while confronted with their first deficits in a generation. Times were tough, and government had lost hold of the basics. But in Alberta, government stuffed the mattresses with cash, and the novelty of being rich insulated the people from such faroff concerns as the Joe Clark comet and René Lévesque. The OPEC cartel and the election of separatists in Quebec were worrisome, but amounted to little more than a nuisance. Lougheed had the oil situation covered, and Trudeau could handle Quebec.

Riding in the front seat as before, but now in a much larger Lincoln Continental, I adopted a snottily federalist—which was to say, Liberal—point of view, reflecting my worldly sophistication and spiritual affinity with Trudeau. I was the one who explained that the Parti Québécois was more than the political action wing of the FLQ. I defended the right of its sympathizers not to be imprisoned on Baffin Island. I counselled accommodation, moderation, and appeasement.

It was modern and progressive to take the centralist view. To preach the Trudeau doctrine was to be sprinkled with the Expo fairy dust of limitless expansion and fathomless reason, bottomless patience and endless goodwill. The pan-Canadian view required much in the way of book learning, regarded warily by my kin. I convinced my Uncle Allen not at all, and myself less and less as the years went on.

We were growing thin on the ground, those of us with a wild rose in one lapel and a red rose in the other. Trudeau likened western discontent to Quebec separatism, but he didn't know what he was talking about because so few in his caucus came from the West.

Western separatism never made much of an inroad beyond the hairy old men alarmed by world Jewry's imposition of the metric system. They were always far outnumbered by Liberals, who formed the dotty class of academics, museum curators, and folk festival organizers and whose core political beliefs were still exemplified by John Lennon's song "Imagine." They were loyal to Trudeau because they shared his anxiety over the eclipse of love and the waning of the Just Society. But they had not read Machiavelli on love. Trudeau had.

■

"The OPEC oil price shocks of 1973 and 1979 had destabilized the world economy, sent inflation through the roof, and increased social and political tensions," Trudeau wrote in his *Memoirs*. "People are more optimistic, generous and confident when incomes rise. When incomes stagnate, fear starts to take over. As faith in government declined, the pursuit of personal gain became the driving force not only in the economy, but in society as a whole. The Love Generation of the sixties was moving towards the Me Generation of the eighties."

In one short and uninterrupted burst of thought, Trudeau connects the rise of oil power with the decline of love. I have to believe this link had more to do with his approval of the National Energy Program than any of the official reasons. The decline of love, after all, is another way of saying the decline of Trudeau's own potency. "The Love Generation" is a code name for Trudeaumania, while the "Me Generation" stands for the Thatcherism, Reaganism, and Mulroneyism he despises. And he was indeed growing impotent, as his actions on energy and the Constitution were to prove, since unilateral action is contemplated only after politics have been surrendered.

There is little point in arguing who was right and who was wrong over the National Energy Program. Debating it now is like harping on marital complaints long after the courts have disposed of the property. There is no point in bringing up the Borden Line or Alberta's $50 billion subsidy to central Canadian industry; little purpose in arguing the merits of the NEP's putative goals of self-sufficiency and Canadianization. There was a marriage and it ended; there was a growing power base in the West and it was put down, though not for long.

Did the eastern bastards, at the end of the day, ever freeze to death in the dark? Did the Alberta oil taps remain closed? Did the US industry forever abandon Alberta's sedimentary basin? Did the "Canada lands" ever turn an honest dime? Do we now have Canadian control over the oil industry? Are our resources protected from the cupidity and avarice of the world markets? Of course not. Everything about the NEP as a policy instrument was ephemeral and illusory, but this much was real: My house dropped in value by one-third overnight; my brother lost his job; my father, who had put his money into real estate at Uncle Allen's urging, saw his last chance of a comfortable retirement fly away like cinders. Whatever other objectives it might have claimed, the NEP was cruelly efficient at economic assassination.

Alberta's response to the oil and constitutional wars, to Trudeau, and to Quebec was based largely on an emotional hangover from the NEP. There were no longer any illusions about Ottawa's beneficence. The NEP had turned Albertans into a village in revolt. Lougheed, in his own words, had removed the federal government from the living room and tossed it from the front porch. It would never again be allowed on the property.

It wasn't long after that fiasco that I met with Preston Manning for the first time. He was staying at a cinder-block motel owned by a born-again Christian who gave him the room free. We sat on the bed and he laid out a map of Canada for me, explaining his plans to conquer Canada through its hinterland. I thought he was ambitious, but not at all deranged. More ambitious plans had been successfully launched by Fidel and Che, in more unlikely settings. Manning carried other colours, but relied for local forage on the same resentment against the ruling classes.

That night, I drove to a bluff that afforded a view of the Rocky Mountains and the highway to the United States. The highway consisted of a long line of drilling platforms laid flat on their side, the whole machinery of Alberta's oil industry headed south. The scene reminded me of a refugee column.

The sun was setting on the summer of love. I decided, when placing your faith in those sons-o'-bitches in Ottawa, it was best to be suspicious as hell. I claimed a birthright of sorts that night and thereafter sat more comfortably in the front seat. Trudeau made me.

3

———

THE
CARTOONIST'S
TRUDEAU

Trudeau: A Portfolio

■

DUNCAN MACPHERSON

JANUARY 30, 1968

APRIL 25, 1969

It's Tommy this an' Tommy that, an''Chuch 'im out, the brute!' But it's 'saviour of 'is country,' when the guns begin to shoot. – *Kipling*

OCTOBER 15, 1970

SEPTEMBER 17, 1970

SEPTEMBER 29, 1971

APRIL 6, 1972

NOVEMBER 30, 1973

"NOW, AS FOR PRESS STATEMENTS ON OUR TALKS—HERE'S YOURS"

JUNE 14, 1974

OCTOBER 21, 1981

JUNE 29, 1976

NOVEMBER 13, 1976

JUNE 29, 1976

MARCH 21, 1978

4

TRUDEAU'S
POLITICS
& POLICIES

Trudeau in Power: A View from Inside the Prime Minister's Office

■

JIM COUTTS

Jim Coutts is a Toronto businessman who was born and raised in Alberta. He practised law in Calgary and from an early age was active in Liberal politics in Southern Alberta. He was private secretary to Prime Minister Lester Pearson from 1963 until 1966. Coutts left Ottawa to attend The Harvard Business School, following which he joined the international consulting firm of McKinsey and Company. In 1970 he co-founded The Canada Consulting Group.

In 1975 Coutts returned to Ottawa where for seven years he was principal secretary to Prime Minister Pierre Trudeau. In 1981 he returned to business, creating a financial holding company (CIC — Canadian Investment Capital Limited), which has acquired manufacturing companies throughout North America.

I T HAS BEEN FOURTEEN YEARS since Pierre Elliott Trudeau
stepped down as prime minister. During his sixteen years in
office, he made politics and government meaningful and exciting for thousands of Canadians who had never before been interested in public life. The period stands in stark contrast to the last
dozen years, when many Canadians have become cynical about
and even given up on politics. I worked closely with Trudeau during eight of his years in power. Because Canadians continue to
identify with him, no week has passed since 1984 without someone, somewhere, asking me about him. "Do you ever see him?"
"What is he doing?" People who inquire after him often say, "He
made us so proud to be Canadians." And many add, "He had such
charisma!"

There is no doubt that Trudeau was a charismatic leader. His
charisma enabled him, a newcomer to the national political scene,
to win the Liberal Party leadership over seasoned veterans who had
spent decades preparing themselves. And as prime minister, at least
initially, his charisma often allowed him to bypass powerful interest
groups with whom most leaders have had to compromise.

This same charisma also hindered Trudeau in achieving one of
his main goals: to change the way Canadians participated in politics. Trudeau and his early advisers envisioned a new era in which
the traditional system of power brokers would end. Rather than
be manipulated by political bosses, citizens would debate directly
with their elected representatives, putting forward new ideas to
reshape the country. Politics would become "participatory" and a
victory of "reason over passion." But reason does not motivate the

followers of the charismatic figure. They want the leader to pass down the message and show the path. They do not want to participate in a national debate in which they have to find their own way. Though Trudeau talked of "participatory democracy," he had little idea how it would work.

Even when the effect of his charisma ebbed and flowed, other aspects of Trudeau's personality helped make him a formidable politician, able to retain power and work at his reforms. A wide range of skills and qualities, developed during his youth, contributed to his political style and helped shape his political views. As his attitude evolved towards the Liberal Party, the parliamentary caucus, and the cabinet, he managed to communicate his story through the media—and often in spite of them.

Much has been written about the formation of leaders with charismatic personalities. Typically they are lonely and rejected youngsters. Trudeau was no exception. He talked, at times, of his father, whom he greatly admired, but who was too busy to understand his son's interests or spend much time with him. His father's death was a devastating blow to the sixteen-year-old boy. Charismatics battle endlessly to compensate for the attention they failed to receive or the weaknesses they struggled with as adolescents. They try to create a stronger personality to compensate for the missing pieces. The athletic hiking, diving, and skiing outdoorsman we saw in Trudeau at the age of fifty was a striking contrast with the puny and shy boy who was easily brought to tears. With doggedness, Trudeau gained physical strength and intellectual agility. The youthful motivations that shaped the man also helped to create the charismatic personality that electrified Canadians in 1968.

Trudeau's greatest political asset, and one he worked hard to develop, was his searching intellect. He was, and still is, a consummate student with an extraordinary curiosity for the widest range of subjects. I once told him that I had purchased a reproduction of the first three-volume edition of the *Encyclopedia Britannica*. Trudeau promptly named most of its authors and asked if I was going to stop there. He went on to name all the publication dates of later editions, remarking that the 1911 edition was the most interesting. It became clear that he had read and absorbed great parts of many *Britannica* editions.

Though he benefited from a rigorous Jesuit training, Trudeau was primarily self-taught. He learned most by talking at length with those who had special knowledge of a subject, spending hours with a farmer, teacher, craftsman, athlete, or musician who knew his subject and was prepared to share insights with him. Even as prime minister, he would return after one of these encounters and say, "That guy I just talked to told me some very interesting things." In contrast with his love of informative discussion was his thorough dislike of small talk. His disdain for the superficial was a perennial political problem, for it frightened and annoyed political colleagues and alienated would-be supporters, especially those who had little of interest to say. On many occasions, Trudeau simply walked away from a person who bored him or to whom he had nothing to say.

Trudeau was excited by the use of words. He wrote well and precisely in both English and French, admired the skilful use of language by others, and was highly impatient with staff and ministers who were sloppy in their diction or grammar. His obsession with the written and spoken word caused him endless frustration. Every leader is inundated with correspondence, often from citizens writing with great passion and creative ideas or sound criticism. Trudeau was always perplexed that he could read only a small fraction of the hundreds of letters that arrived each day, and he was highly uncomfortable when the letters were acknowledged without him seeing the replies. His greatest exasperation came when staff-writtten letters of reply in "final" form arrived for his signature. He spent hours redrafting many of them, because he felt that the substance was inadequate or that a limp phrase had been used— not one that *he* would ever use.

Trudeau was equally uncomfortable using speech writers. He much preferred to deliver speeches without a text from notes he mapped out himself in advance. No prime minister has the time to write his own speeches, so this was one reason why he was often reluctant to deliver formal speeches. His marginal notes to speech writers were filled with both encouragement and rebuke: "This is a wonderful phrase" and, just as often, "This paragraph means nothing." On one occasion he wrote: "This is crap—where is the speech I asked for?" He got deeply involved in editing, and sometimes extensively redrafted his speeches. Alan Grossman, his speech writer, who had written for leading magazine and newspaper editors in both Canada and the United States, told me that Trudeau was "the best editor I ever worked for."

He instinctively disliked standard political rhetoric. Senator Keith Davey, the Liberal campaign chairman, once urged Trudeau to end a speech on national unity with the phrase "Canada, Canada, Canada." "Why on earth would you repeat a word three times?" asked Trudeau. On another occasion, he was required to read a dull speech text on a dull subject in the House of Commons. Characteristically, he made his feelings clear to his audience. As he droned on and saw MPs paying little attention, he ostentatiously turned a page, glanced up, and said: "My speech writer goes on to say . . ."

Trudeau developed a powerful capacity to concentrate and an unusually long attention span. With crises raging in the halls and meeting rooms around him, he could sit at his desk for hours and concentrate on one letter, one speech, one book, or one file. He also remembered with near-photographic accuracy the details of a subject he had studied or a letter he had prepared. He once asked me, "Do you remember that letter I wrote to [Peter] Lougheed two years ago in April? I'm sure that in the first paragraph on the second page I said . . ." I found the two-year-old letter. The sentence was precisely as he remembered it.

His concentration gave him great political advantage. He often knew more about a cabinet item than the minister who put it forward, and he knew a lobbyist's brief better that those who came to lobby. His memory enabled him to savage questioners in the House of Commons or journalists at a press conference. He especially loved to rip into badly prepared premiers at First Ministers' meetings. It was satisfying, but not always politic. Capacity to reason and to recall enabled him to deliver a powerfully logical and convincing forty-minute speech without a single note. He relished debate and was seldom outdone. Argument was his game. He loved it, and he loved to win at it.

But Trudeau was not a storyteller; he could not tell jokes or recount funny incidents. The good storytellers—ministers like Don Jamieson or Gene Whelan who excelled in bizarre or folksy anecdotes that they recalled or made up—would delight Trudeau. But theirs was not a technique he could imitate. I once tried to insert several jokes into his speaking notes and to explain to him how the jokes worked. I said that humour depended on the timing of the punch line and that the punch line worked because it was out of kilter with an otherwise logical sequence of events or statements. "But why would you want to mix up the sequence?" he asked. I decided to drop the subject.

Politics is usually a profession for the gregarious, but, throughout his political career, Trudeau's power to concentrate was honed in hours spent alone. He enjoyed and required solitude to read, think, and write. More surprisingly, he also used his time alone to rehearse—for he was an actor.

The public saw Trudeau as a quick-witted, almost insouciant man who tossed off casual remarks, slid down royal banisters, or made faces and gestures on whim. But he did and said little publicly that was not carefully rehearsed in advance. Before one press conference he asked an aide to describe how a particular journalist looked and where he would sit, so he could pretend not to know his name and ignore his questions. Most people assumed that the notorious pirouette Trudeau enacted at Buckingham Palace, in the presence of Queen Elizabeth, was simply a spontaneously rude and impulsive gesture. In fact, he planned it hours before because he strongly opposed the palace protocol that separated heads of state from heads of government. The well-rehearsed pirouette was a way of showing his objection without saying a word.

Trudeau's little-known need to rehearse created an interesting political problem. Most of his colleagues never understood why he refused to invite people into his car while he drove to a political event. Local politicians who expected to accompany him during his once-only visit to their town were often deeply insulted, and some were even asked to get out of the car. US president Lyndon Johnson, in contrast, would invite six local officials to ride in his limousine, and he also knew three flattering facts about each one. Not Trudeau, who rode alone simply because he wanted the time to rehearse the logic, words, mood, and gestures for the next event.

An aspect of Trudeau's early life that eventually became a political asset was his passion for travel. As a young man, he spent much time travelling widely through Europe, Africa, Asia, and the Middle East—alone, with no baggage and very little money. Finding odd jobs and learning the local language were tests he set for himself. Years later, I accompanied him on official visits to countries where he had travelled in his youth. He could create immediate empathy with local leaders by talking of their geography, of weeks spent on their desert, or of conflicts he had witnessed on their home turf. Cedric Ritchie, chairman of the Bank of Nova Scotia, told me he learned more about countries where he conducted business from a one-hour conversation with Trudeau than from two full days of briefings by local managers and international economists.

Trudeau's views on individual freedom, minority rights, and the need for a strong nation-state were partly shaped by his observations as a traveller. In contrast to his predecessor, Lester Pearson, who had met many world leaders while both he and they held more junior positions, Trudeau was far more likely to have met his counterpart in jail or during a demonstration. He was a student of history, but he had also personally witnessed outbreaks of aggression, civil war, and political turmoil. The passion he brought to North-South development initiatives, for example, was rooted in early travels where he saw the horrors suffered by "the wretched of the earth."

Another characteristic of Trudeau was his apparently complete lack of physical or emotional fear—a product, I believe, of the physical and mental discipline he had set himself. In the eight years I worked with him I saw no occasion when he held back in fear. Most politicians feel emotionally threatened by certain antagonists, whom they avoid or dread meeting and debating. Trudeau was different, as though he had made peace with himself and his maker and was prepared to face any storm, heckler, bully, or adversary. He urged his followers on, "Come on, let's get at them." This stance was not an act: He was a brave man who loved to ski the black runs, canoe the fastest waters, or challenge the local bully. On one occasion he was provoked by three young toughs in a bar in British Columbia. He challenged them to arm wrestle and bested them all.

But Trudeau could also be reduced to tears by an act of kindness or the sight of children with disabilities who were trying to do their best. To those who were in trouble, alone, or bereaved, he was capable of extraordinary gestures of kindness, heartfelt and always private. He refused to sign "political" letters of sympathy to people he didn't know, but sometimes spent hours crafting a handwritten note to someone he cared about who was in distress. He was also most considerate of others. One Sunday he phoned his speech writer and said, "What a beautiful spring day. I'm sorry you have to be inside working on that speech."

■

Just as Trudeau's youth shaped his personality, it also helped to shape his political views. There are only two kinds of political leaders—those who want to be somebody, and those who want to do something. To the former, the challenge is to get to the top and to stay there; to the latter, the challenge is to bring about reform. Trudeau's agenda of reform was shaped years before he entered parliament in 1965. His early life in an isolated Quebec under Duplessis and his travels in a troubled world both fed his determination to help carve out a new role for francophones in Canada and to expand the individual rights of all Canadians.

Trudeau's general goals often sounded similar to those of earlier prime ministers, typified by what Mackenzie King said in his 1948 farewell address to the Liberal Party: "My goal has been to advance the cause of unity, security and freedom for Canadians." The critical difference lay in how Trudeau sought to achieve those ends. Most federal leaders formed coalitions of strong regional representatives to act and speak for the local citizens. Mackenzie King, for example, depended on ministers like James Gardiner, C.D. Howe, James Ilsley, Ernest Lapointe, and Louis St. Laurent to represent the regional interests. By contrast, Trudeau thought that every citizen should have his own stake in the country's politics and play a role in his own right, not through an agent. While previous prime ministers had to master the art of negotiating with regional ministers and provincial premiers, Trudeau said the regional baron system diminished the rights of the citizen. He believed that the central power must remain strong, and that citizens' access to that power should be direct. He was not saying, "Follow me and I will protect your rights." Rather, he was advocating, "Demand your own rights."

Trudeau never achieved this new political understanding between the federal government and its electors. First, provincial activists felt threatened by a strong central power and were able to appeal to local fears and myths. Second, the task of involving citizens directly in politics was bigger than Trudeau and his team had anticipated. Finally, many Canadians were turned off when they became convinced that his government was too preoccupied with the French-English language issue.

Though Trudeau seemed less clear and certain about other items on his political agenda, he actively championed many policies and programs that were not related to language. For example, he was personally active in native affairs for a time, deeply involved in the anti-inflation and National Energy programs, and he played a leading role in the North-South initiatives in foreign affairs. To a large extent, he operated by choosing strong and effective ministers to take the lead in policy areas where he shared their reform agendas. In this way he backed Marc Lalonde in health-care reform and major increases in old age security; Jean Marchand, Allan Mac-Eachen, and Romeo LeBlanc in measures that diminished regional income disparities; and Otto Lang in programs to overcome the damaging cyclical variation of farmers' incomes. He actively also backed ministers who moved to ensure Canadian ownership in basic industries ranging from energy and aerospace to the cultural sector. Few of these initiatives were on Trudeau's agenda when he first came to office. But many succeeded because of his interest, coaching, and support. By contrast, other prime ministers have ducked ministerial program failures, only to step forward at critical junctures to take personal credit for successes.

Trudeau had two major failings in how he dealt with the domestic agenda. First, he spent far too much time re-examining entire systems. Especially in the administration's early years, endless study groups examined subjects from top to bottom, only to write reports many months later that produced few initiatives and frustrated everyone. This exercise was repeated on everything from foreign policy, inflation, and youth unemployment to energy and corporate concentration. One review even devoted more than two full years to determining the government's "priorities," without ever really deciding what they were. Most of these studies were counterproductive, squandering government resources and sapping the creative energies of both elected politicians and the public service.

Second, Trudeau ignored the trusted political rule that a reformer must come to office with four or five very specific ideas to implement and concentrate on those. With luck, he will succeed in two or three. Apart from keeping Quebeckers in Canada and expanding individual rights, Trudeau was not focused and determined on a few initiatives. As a result, he achieved less than he could have. Of course, not all initiatives can be planned. Crises arise and must be addressed, and Trudeau was notably successful in dealing with three major ones: The Front de libération du Québec crisis of 1970, the anti-inflation fight of the mid-1970s, and the 1980 Quebec referendum.

■

The political events of 1968 represented one of those special convergences between one man's personal history and one country's public events, to use historian and psychiatrist Erik Erikson's terminology. In that year, Canada felt exuberant coming out of its one hundredth birthday celebrations and confident enough to gamble on the unorthodox. In Trudeau, Canada had a leader who broke all the political rules.

Although he had many other qualities required of a national leader, Trudeau knew little about party politics and had spent barely two years in parliament when he became prime minister. Indeed, his pre-1965 speeches and essays were punctuated with sharp criticism of "cynical" political parties and their "mindless" election machines. Rather than fighting his way into office, Trudeau had been recruited by the Liberal Party. Key members of Pearson's entourage who were seeking to put a new reform face on Liberalism had found Trudeau a safe seat in 1965, and a small band of Ottawa insiders initiated his party leadership campaign in 1968.

Trudeau made little secret of his view that a political party was simply an instrument to implement his agenda. He once told an unfriendly Edmonton audience that he and his friends had taken over the Liberal Party "because for Quebeckers it was the easiest to take over. If you don't like what we've done, take over some other party and go put your ideas to work."

These were shocking concepts for those who had faithfully attended Liberal Party conventions for two decades, worshipped the icon-posters of Laurier, King, St. Laurent, and Pearson, and applauded speeches that told of their exploits. Many long-time Liberals deeply resented a new leader who appeared to belittle party loyalties. Especially hurt were Pearson Liberals, who saw themselves as reformers who had introduced national medicare, better pensions, enlightened immigration laws, and the beginnings of official bilingualism. Senator John Connolly, for example, said to his son Peter as they walked home from the 1968 convention, "This is a disaster. They have stolen the party from us." Next morning, Connolly, who had been both party president and national campaign chairman, sat in silence over breakfast with his family. Finally he said, "This fellow Trudeau could be all right. In fact, he could be the greatest leader we've had. We're all going to work for him."

Like Connolly, traditional Liberal core members held their tongues, stayed loyal, and waited in the wings to go to work. In the months after the leadership convention there were really two separate Liberal election campaigns. In the background, traditional Grits pulled together the different leadership camps into a unified national party apparatus. Senator John Nichol, the party president, knew that the "Old Liberals" were not crucial for the 1968 election, but that the convention wounds had to be healed and the team kept together for the future. In the foreground, a second election campaign was waged by Trudeau's "new guys with new ideas." Many were extremely able; certainly they were keen. Most were young, drawn partly from among university students and faculty. They fashioned a campaign that hailed a new politics and a new Canada, one that Trudeau was more than willing to lead.

Inevitably, perhaps, their post-election hopes for a new utopia were dashed. While the government assembled elaborate study groups instead of action teams, those who simply wanted to get on with the old way of governing by solving problems were frustrated. The country also faced recession. By the 1972 election, the government was reduced to a minority.

I recall meeting Trudeau on New Year's Day 1973 at the official reception after Pearson's funeral. Trudeau was sitting alone on the stairs and I sat down beside him. "We're in a bit of trouble," he said. "You're in more than a bit of trouble," I replied. "You're in deep trouble. But there are hundreds of Liberals who will help if you ask." "How can I do that?" he asked. "Just pick up the phone and ask them to come and help," I said. I was not sure he believed me, but in the weeks that followed he began to call on the old pros. Those he drew together began to work on the 1974 election campaign. I'm not sure whether Trudeau had the most fun getting to know the "old hacks" or whether the old pros had more fun getting to know Trudeau. In any event, there was an amazing marriage between the two. Trudeau was determined to keep control of the party to achieve his goals, and the professionals wanted to be wanted. In the process of being "used," many older Liberals became more ardent followers of Trudeau and his agenda than the young gurus who had helped elect him in the first place.

My views on Trudeau's way of dealing with parliament and the cabinet are based on my experience, over six years, of working daily with parliamentarians and regularly sitting in on cabinet meetings. Trudeau's approach to these institutions was quite different from the public impression, characterized by his infamous remark that when they leave Parliament Hill, MPs are "nobodies." In fact, Trudeau's work with MPs attempted to enhance their role as parliamentary "somebodies." He constantly took a keen interest in backbench Liberals who showed leadership in parliamentary committees and he often invited them to his office to discuss their work, which he had followed by reading committee transcripts. Trudeau greatly increased research budgets for all MPs to ensure they had the resources they needed to do a better job.

Trudeau's method of leading cabinet was to encourage discussion and to be notably patient while listening to debate. Of course, not every minister was satisfied with every decision, but I don't know any who felt he or she was not heard out. At the end of debate Trudeau almost always sided with the sponsoring minister's proposal as long as it was well developed, though he often intervened to find compromises that satisfied all the ministers. He could, however, be bitingly impatient with sloppy presentations or illogical proposals. He simply took them off the agenda and rescheduled them later when they were better prepared. He did not tolerate tactical emotional outbursts by ministers. I recall a cabinet meeting where a minister, losing an argument, dramatically slammed shut his cabinet book and headed out of the room. Trudeau said, "You can stay and make your case again, or you can leave. If you leave, don't come back."

■

Because they are democratically elected, prime ministers often feel that they are entitled to try to implement the national agenda and that the media should simply tell the story of their plans and programs. The media's view, in contrast, is that the government agenda is only one part of the story, which also includes the views of the opposition, interest groups, and others. In effect, the media says, "We'll interpret the agenda—you, the government, are only a piece of the story."

The initial "honeymoon" lasts for only a few months or, on rare occasions, a year or two. Trudeau recognized this scenario as early as 1968, when he told his staff and friends: "All of this will end. Trudeaumania will become Trudeauphobia." Just possibly, Trudeau may even have looked forward to the end of the honeymoon, for he believed he had the skill to go over the media's heads. Certainly he enjoyed punching them figuratively in the nose.

Many of us argued with the prime minister that little was to be lost in working with the Ottawa press gallery, especially those who had long experience in national affairs. Trudeau seldom listened. As a crusading editor of *Cité libre*, he had seen a corrupt Quebec City press gallery bought off by Duplessis. He also thought many Ottawa journalists were lazy, uninformed, and lacking long-term political perspective. As a result, he treated many reporters' questions with scorn, ignoring or making fun of them. A favourite trick was to claim he had not read their articles, which was true only technically because staff always briefed him on press coverage of the government.

Trudeau took an equally jaundiced view of media owners. Earlier leaders had developed close relationships with publishers and editors, such as the working partnerships between Mackenzie King and Joe Atkinson of the *Toronto Star* or, at the provincial level, Alberta premier Ernest Manning and *Calgary Albertan* publisher Max Bell. The several attempts I made to recreate such publisher—prime minister relationships were inevitably disasters. I would look for areas of consensus. Trudeau would soon turn the conversation to differences and then promote a debate on what he considered some wrong-headed editorial policy. The most charitable view of these episodes was that Trudeau was refusing to be hypocritical. Equally likely, as a seasoned polemicist, he was enjoying a good argument. Unfortunately, few publishers are used to the give and take of debate or like being challenged over editorial policy at a prime minister's dinner table.

An irony of Trudeau's increasingly bad relations with the media was that they themselves had largely created the powerful image that had helped to propel him into office and to override the increasingly "bad press" of the later years.

Trudeau thought deeply about the question of image, especially in the period leading up to his coming to office. Two prominent Canadians who began working with him at that time were Fernand Cadieux and Marshall McLuhan. Trudeau was especially intrigued by McLuhan's view that the public sees prominent figures as if they are wearing masks. As in an ancient stage drama, the public identifies with the character of the mask, not with the person behind it. McLuhan had interpreted the masks of several leaders: John Diefenbaker's, he felt, was that of a clown, and Trudeau's was that of a proud native warrior chief. When Trudeau projected a warrior image of calm, courage, wisdom, and self-sufficiency, it was the mask that held the magic.

Trudeau consciously exploited visual images. Just as his speeches were carefully rehearsed, he acted quite deliberately in striking the several memorable photographic poses that became icons of the man. An early symbol of his physical and political courage were news photos of Trudeau facing the hecklers and bottle-throwers at the Montreal St.-Jean-Baptiste parade on the eve of the 1968 election. As separatists began to jeer and throw objects at the reviewing platform, all the dignitaries except Trudeau scurried out of range to the back. Only Trudeau remained defiantly in his place, leaning forward in scorn of the demonstrators. This picture of Trudeau, "standing up for Canada," swept the front pages and TV screens, helping to catapult him to a majority victory.

A second iconic image was from a series of photos showing Trudeau as the lone athlete or outdoorsman, diving into a swimming pool from a high board or standing alone in the Canadian North, clad in a buckskin jacket and gazing out over the tundra. The latter image allowed Canadians to see this vast land through Trudeau's eyes and to better understand his message about our need to keep the country together.

A third image, featured in later election campaigns, was the "gunslinger"—Trudeau standing alone, feet apart, thumbs hooked under his belt, with no podium or speaker's text, appearing to think on his feet and ready to take on all comers. While other party leaders would be surrounded by local politicos and campaign paraphenalia, this man was seen standing alone, a fighter.

■

In the end, one must judge a Liberal political leader by the extent to which he comes to office with a reform agenda and is able to achieve it. Pierre Trudeau had one overriding goal as prime minister: He wanted to keep Quebec within Canada, showing francophones they could participate with the full rights of citizenship, and leading English-speaking Canadians to accept Canada as a bilingual and multicultural nation. By the time he left office, minority educational and other language rights were enshrined in the Constitution, most federal government services were widely available in both French and English, and francophones were more equitably represented in the federal public service. In cities like Calgary, anglophones continued to enrol their children in French immersion classes, underlining how Trudeau's policies and personal example helped to create a new generation more supportive of a bilingual Canada. And, however controversial it is now, his multiculturalism policy provided an important stepping stone for the new multi-ethnic urban Canada.

Trudeau paid a political price for being identified so completely with the language issue. He and his ministers pursued numerous other economic, social, and foreign policy goals—sometimes with considerable success. But the perception of Trudeau's concentration on the national unity question too often made him an easy target for those who did not share this agenda. The single-minded way he conducted his political battle also allowed Trudeau to be cast as a leader who failed to recognize regional identities, when in fact he understood the complexity of the country better than most.

The premiers often made Trudeau look inflexible in the media, but the reverse was usually the truth. I attended countless meetings where he indicated that the federal-provincial division of powers was entirely negotiable, as long as individual rights were enhanced in the final result. I recall a long conversation between him and a prairie premier who claimed to share the goal of advancing individual rights, but held out because the proposed changes, he said, would allow the Senate to block action by the provinces. Trudeau retorted, "Fine, let's get rid of the Senate. I'll lead the initiative. Will you go along?" The premier kept silent and did not go along.

Trudeau's constitutional argument was not that the provinces should be denied powers, but that all government powers should be limited so that individual and minority rights could be enhanced. Along with keeping Quebec in Canada, his other major goal as prime minister was individual rights. He partly achieved it through the historic entrenchment of the Charter of Rights in a patriated Canadian Constitution. The Charter will continue to strongly influence Canadian life in countless ways for many generations to come.

Trudeau knew that no federal-provincial "deal," no palliative phrase meaning different things to different Canadians—such as "distinct society" or "equality of provinces"—was an alternative to greater individual rights and more opportunity for all Canadians to participate in the life of their nation. Particularly during his later years in office, he failed to continue teaching that message and recruiting like-minded reformers to preserve and develop it. Partly as a result, he was followed in office by those who saw the deal or the palliative phrase as alternatives to a national vision, so that much of what he brought to Canada would not endure.

That said, however, Trudeau's insight into Canada, his vision of what Canada could become, and his charismatic ability to personify that vision, have secured his place in history as one of the most dynamic and distinctive leaders Canada has ever had.

The Trudeau Cabinet:
A Memoir

■

DONALD S. MACDONALD

Donald S. Macdonald is a lawyer at the Toronto office of McCarthy Tétrault. From 1962 to 1978 he was member of parliament for Toronto Rosedale and from 1968 to 1977 a member of Trudeau's cabinet, successively as president of the Privy Council and government house leader, minister of national defence, minister of energy, mines & resources, and minister of finance. He was chairman of the Royal Commission on the Economic Union and Development Prospects for Canada, 1982-85, and high commissioner for Canada to the United Kingdom, 1988-91.

ON APRIL 20, 1968, Pierre Elliott Trudeau formed what would become the twentieth ministry of the government of Canada. Although the swearing in occurred on that day, it was a temporary cabinet only. Some of the most senior portfolios were filled, but many of the other ministers were appointed as ministers without portfolio, or as acting ministers in certain departments. These were temporary assignments until the electors could decide which party would form the next government. The election on June 25 returned the Trudeau Liberals to power.

The first meeting of the full cabinet took place on July 6, 1968. For the nine years I was a member, this group of ministers constituted the core of the cabinet, although there were changes and additions as time went on. Two of the twenty-nine ministers had been members of the cabinet of Louis St. Laurent, and they, plus fifteen others, had been in the ministry of Lester Pearson. Of the remainder, nine of us had been members of parliament, but not ministers, in the previous parliament. Three new cabinet members had been elected to parliament for the first time in the recent election.

As often happens in the Canadian parliament, those ministers who had studied law, eleven in all, had the largest single vocation. It was noted at the time that there was a higher than usual percentage of ministers who had taken advanced degrees, particularly at foreign universities, and who had held professorial positions. In retrospect I can say, however, while higher education was no bar to success as a minister, it was no guarantee. Several of my colleagues whose judgment around the cabinet table and performance in parliament and in the country I most admired had only high school education. Good political judgment and the ability to win the confidence of the public are partly a gift and partly the dividend of hard-won experience.

Seven of the ministers had been candidates in the Liberal leadership race in the spring of 1968. They were different from the rest of us, for they had tasted the "royal jelly" of leadership. Each of these men had believed he had a special fitness, or "call," for leading the country. Each one had a mission or an agenda that he felt he could carry out as leader; and each believed he had the particular skills to persuade Canadian voters. There must have been some feeling of disappointment, but these aspirants were consoled by the invitation to re-enter cabinet and undertake new responsibilities.

For those of us who had not experienced higher aspirations, the opportunity of serving as a minister was similar to that of any new job: anticipation of new challenges and experiences mixed with nervousness at undertaking something not done before. For those who had been private members, some as parliamentary secretaries, we all had thought, as we sat behind the ministerial rows in the House of Commons or faced the ministerial row in caucus: "I can do that job," or, in some cases, "I can do that job better than the current minister." Now the moment had come; now was the opportunity to prove it.

Members from the Pearson days confirmed that there was a sharp contrast in mode of operation between the Pearson and the Trudeau cabinets. In Pearson's ministry, the discussion was much less highly organized, the documentation not as substantial, and the discourse not as disciplined. At times, several conversations had been going on in the room concurrently.

In the Trudeau ministry, much advance thought had been given to the structure of the cabinet process and its committees. Matters for discussion had to be preceded by carefully prepared documents. Except on emergency occasions, an oral briefing by the minister would not be an acceptable way of putting facts before the cabinet, and the documents and the issues to which they related would receive extensive advance discussion in one or more cabinet committees before coming on to the full cabinet's agenda for final decision.

The cabinet committees were of two kinds: central control committees such as Priorities and Planning or Treasury Board, and functional committees, organized according to departmental subject matters. The prime minister chaired and regularly participated in the Priorities and Planning Committee, but he rarely participated in any other. Rather, he waited until the discussion in the full cabinet.

The controlled and intellectual approach to cabinet discussion was closely reflective of Trudeau's own style. Highly disciplined in his own thinking processes and accustomed to examining with great care all available evidence before arriving at a conclusion, the process worked well and, apparently, effortlessly for him. Although I have always been a quick reader, I found absorption of all the material for each week's cabinet meeting very demanding. I particularly admired Trudeau's ability to ingest all this information and organize it in a way that would lead to cabinet decisions. I even adapted a line from a well-known hymn to describe Trudeau's ability to absorb information: "A thousand pages in his sight are but an evening gone."

A humble measure of the growing volume of documentation was the ever increasing size of the binders in which I carried my cabinet documents. Initially all the documents fit into a slim ring binder about the size of an ordinary portfolio. By the time I left cabinet in September 1977, I required a four-ring binder eighteen inches high by three inches thick—and even then I could barely accommodate the papers I needed.

When and how did we meet as a cabinet? When parliament was sitting, the House met from Mondays to Fridays, commencing each day with Question Period at 2:00 p.m., except on Friday, when the sitting began in the morning and was over in the afternoon. The full cabinet met on Thursday morning. Cabinet committees met Tuesday mornings and Tuesday and Wednesday afternoons after the Question Period, and sometimes on Thursday afternoons after Question Period if there were matters to deal with as a result of the morning's cabinet meeting, or if there was such a volume that it could not be dealt with earlier in the week. Wednesday morning was reserved for the party caucuses and, on the government side, the cabinet, the MPs, and the Liberal senators would all attend. For the ministers, it was an opportunity to persuade the government's own supporters to endorse courses of action that they were advocating, and for the prime minister it was an important occasion to pull together his parliamentary team and lay the groundwork for further actions. For the members of parliament, it was the best occasion during the week to make an impression on other MPs, ministers, and especially the prime minister. Caucus is the private member's opportunity to shine, and if this shining takes some of the lustre off a minister, so be it.

The first meetings of the Trudeau ministry took place in the East Block of the Parliament Buildings, in the historic cabinet room where Sir John A. met with his cabinet. It is a pleasant room looking out onto the green lawns behind, and to the point where W.H. Bartlett must have set up his easel to do his sketch of the Rideau Canal locks and the Gatineau Hills beyond. But there was not enough room around the table to accommodate all the ministers; the symbolism of some ministers at the table and others in the second row was simply not acceptable. Meetings were therefore shifted to much more pedestrian premises on the third floor of the Centre Block at the opposite end of the corridor from the prime minister's suite of offices. This room could accommodate a large green-baize table. The prime minister sat in a chair at the centre, with the ministers stationed around him in a pattern reflecting their seniority as privy councillors. Each was furnished with a water glass, a tablet of writing paper, and an ashtray. Many of the ministers smoked, although on occasion Trudeau would lead a silent protest by moving away from a cigar smoker to a more remote chair. Two telephone booths were recessed into the rear wall of the room, and on the opposite side was a table at which, in full cabinet, sat the Clerk of the Privy Council and a member of his staff to take the minutes.

As time went on, the cabinet meetings stretched into the luncheon period, and sandwiches, cold drinks, and coffee were sent in for the ministers. Access to the room came through two doors that led directly into the corridor. One time, an enterprising member of the press gallery, in the guise of being helpful, carried a tray of sandwiches into the room just to find out what the cabinet was talking about. It couldn't have been very interesting because no one else tried it again!

In the same way that the prime minister occupies the dominant position among elected officials, so the Clerk of the Privy Council is first among public servants. The Clerk, along with deputy ministers and other senior officials of deputy minister rank, is appointed by order in council and is outside the bounds of the Public Service Commission. It is a post that is normally occupied by someone who has made a career of the public service and who has risen by ability and good political instinct to this senior position. In some sense, the Clerk is the prime minister's deputy minister, but he or she is also the de facto head of the Public Service, playing an important role in senior appointments. The Clerk has a significant policy role, too, maintaining a careful balance between serving the government of the day but being available to serve its political opponents should the electorate make a change. The clerk is selected primarily for qualities of policy judgment. In the October 1970 kidnapping crisis, for example, a solution suggested by Gordon Robertson, who was then Clerk, was ultimately followed.

The devolution under Trudeau of the discussion of cabinet papers to cabinet committees had one important effect on the mode of cabinet government. Traditionally, no public official other than the Clerk of the Privy Council would appear in full cabinet. In the Trudeau government, it came to be accepted that a minister's senior officials could appear with him in committee, and soon the officials themselves began to participate fully in the discussions. In the Ottawa in which I grew up in the 1940s and 1950s, the senior public servants, particularly in economic departments and in External Affairs, were much admired, and many of the officials who advised us had been selected and trained by that earlier cadre of deputy ministers. Contrary to the image of the British permanent undersecretary portrayed in the television series *Yes, Minister* as an oily and obsequious character, some of the deputies I remember were outspoken; they backed away from no one except, perhaps, the prime minister when discussion became animated.

From the beginning to the end of my time in cabinet, Trudeau was incontestably the man in charge. The dramatic political events of the first half of 1968 in which he had risen to the leadership of the Liberal Party, and then won the election, gave him incomparable political prestige and strength. In the years that followed, although there would be criticisms in the country and in caucus of particular policies or actions, there was never any doubt that, as leader, he was essential for the government's continued success.

One of the press clichés about Trudeau's leadership was that he was dictatorial in Cabinet. That was never a just allegation. He recognized that cabinet ultimately has to make decisions on important questions, and that one of the roles of the prime minister in moments of cabinet division is to declare that decision. But on most questions he would not force his own views on the meeting or cut short those who disagreed with him. If anything, several of us considered that he was too patient, rather than too domineering, in letting protagonists with different points of view continue to fight it out around the cabinet table even after lengthy debates in committee. When the direction was clear and the time for a decision had arrived, Trudeau was still prepared to hear the arguments rehearsed once again. Some ministers were more prone than others to take advantage of his forbearance, and after one such occasion a cabinet colleague asked Trudeau why he had not stepped in much earlier to announce a decision. He responded that the subject was not one he knew from experience or on which he had firm opinions. He was prepared to learn as much as he could from a prolonged debate before having to make choices among the alternatives.

Of course, cabinet meetings were not always marked by statesmanlike serenity. Opinions were held strongly, and, like everyone else, ministers have their bad days. I had a number of sharp exchanges with Trudeau which temporarily soured our relations, and Don Jamieson recounted one of these episodes in his memoirs, *A World Unto Itself*. On a visit to the Soviet Union in May 1971, Trudeau had signed a Protocol on Consultations even though the cabinet had not discussed the matter. As minister of national defence, I asked that the minutes record my displeasure that we had been committed to a policy without prior consideration. On his return, Trudeau offered no explanation, but Jamieson remarked that a certain *froideur* continued between the prime minister and me for some time. Jamieson's explanation for the fuss was that I was unhappy because the prime minister had been holding up publication of the white paper on defence, for which, as minister of national defence, I was responsible. At the time, I thought my problem was with the prime minister's staff rather than with Trudeau himself. In the event, the white paper, called "Defence in the Seventies," was published and remained the statement of defence policy not only for that decade but well into the 1980s. The Moscow foreign policy initiative has long since been forgotten, much like the Soviet Union itself.

While Trudeau was normally magisterial in chairing the cabinet, he could on occasion be very rude. One of my experiences came in 1969, again on the subject of defence, but before I was minister. My predecessor, Léo Cadieux, had been going through the agonizing experience of downsizing both the department and the number of uniformed personnel. One morning he brought into cabinet a proposal to eliminate two of the regular force infantry regiments (each of three battalions), one of which was the Highland regiment, the Black Watch of Canada. I pointed out that the Highland tradition was long and honourably established in the Canadian army and, indeed, in the broader Canadian community. In anglophone Canada, it is associated with everything from ceremonial civilian dinners to country ploughing matches. Downgrading the Black Watch would be unpopular not just in the Maritimes, but in other parts of Canada. Trudeau exploded. He would have no discussion, the matter had been agreed upon by the generals, and that was that. I would like to say that I had a rapier-like riposte, but I was so stunned at the rudeness that I said nothing more.

On reflecting on the incident, I am left in no doubt what the reaction would have been if the roles had been reversed. What if I, an Ontario minister, had proposed downgrading the Royal 22e

Régiment, the Vandoos? The wails would have been anguished and the discussion lengthy. This was an example of the occasional insensitivity of Quebec ministers to attitudes and customs in other parts of Canada.

If there were many subjects on which Trudeau was prepared to defer to others, there were others that had been a matter of lifelong interest and study for him and on which he felt no want of confidence—the Constitution, the intricate politics of Quebec, the organization of modern government, and many fields of law. He was prepared to listen to and debate opposing views, but ministers were wise to make a good case, for he could effectively and quickly demolish a bad one. On many of these issues, he would give short shrift to irrelevant arguments that might becloud thinking. In time, in dealing with those areas that were of special interest to Trudeau, ministers learned to tread with caution, and with consideration about the direction the debate might take.

In October 1970 I had the opportunity of observing at close hand not only Trudeau's grasp of the issues of modern government but also his strength of character in his response to the kidnappings and murder carried out by Quebec terrorists of the Front de libération du Québec. Just two weeks before James Cross, the British trade representative in Montreal, was kidnapped, I had become minister of national defence. When word reached me in mid-morning that the British official had been taken at gunpoint and with the demand that a separatist agenda be met if he was to be released unharmed, I had no clear idea what we should do next. From the first of the emergency meetings during that stressful period, Trudeau adhered to the fundamental proposition that democratically elected governments could not give in to terrorist movements attempting to govern the country at the point of a gun. To flinch in the face of illegal acts and to surrender to them would only ensure that they would be repeated on an escalating basis. In the weeks that followed, it became apparent that the police authorities in Quebec were incapable of providing protection from further acts of violence. Premier Robert Bourassa urged the federal government to send in the Canadian Armed Forces and to invoke the War Measures Act, both of which it did. Given Trudeau's personal stand against the regressive actions of the Duplessis government in the 1950s, these actions must have been particularly painful for him. But he did not flinch in the crisis. In the trichotomy of "life, liberty and the pursuit of happiness" as set out in the American Declaration of Independence, liberty had to be sacrificed temporarily if kidnappers and murder were not to succeed over time. In the end, liberty could be restored, as could the pursuit of happiness, but life, once taken, could not.

For the first Trudeau cabinet, the FLQ crisis was the most difficult period, but every government has to face major crises that are often unanticipated. It is these crises that test the qualities of ministers. Most practical are the "all rounders" the ministers who are prepared to think about and speak to the difficult political questions to be resolved. A number of my colleagues fitted into this category, and, not coincidentally, they included those who had less formal education but good political judgment. On these kinds of questions, it was seldom a matter of being absolutely right or absolutely wrong. The critical contribution was to make an attempt to think through the problems. One or two "elder statesmen" were a subset of this group, men whose experience on political questions was respected. Habitually these senior members waited out the early stages of discussion, but they came in at a later point, either unbidden or when called upon.

The opposite of the "all rounder" was the "departmental" minister. These cabinet members intervened only in matters that were within their departmental responsibility. Although skilful ministerial exposition of a departmental brief might be respected, these ministers failed in their overall responsibility to contribute to major political questions that affected us all. Another group, the "buttinsky" ministers, though essential to good cabinet discussion, were a major irritant to the minister whose subject was under discussion. The minister responsible for a particular proposal, having worked hard on it with his departmental staff, would naturally acquire a proprietary feeling for both the substance and the form put forward. Still, debate is important on political matters, and the "buttinskys," who were well armed with opinions and prepared to sustain a contrary viewpoint, were frequently very useful.

As House leader, for example, I had the responsibility of putting to cabinet and then to parliament some substantial changes to the Rules of Procedure in the House of Commons. Some of the proposals were technical, but others were highly political in the sense that they would bring about sharp debate with the opposition. Now, every minister had experience sitting in the House and attempting to operate under the existing set of rules and, therefore, each one had an opinion. My proposal, the first I had ever submitted to cabinet, received a particularly bumpy ride from other ministers. At the end of the meeting, walking away from the room with one of my political mentors, I commented on the strenuous session I had experienced. My friend commented that, for two reasons, I should regard myself as fortunate that other ministers had intervened. First, there were ministers around the table who had much more experience in the House and with politics than I had and from whose experience I could learn. Far better to be given a corrective lesson in cabinet than to endure it publicly in the House or in the country. Second, a full cabinet discussion of any ministerial proposal, especially when changes are offered to and accepted by the sponsoring minister, transforms the proposal from that of the minister alone to that of the full cabinet. If ministerial acquiescence was won by full cabinet discussion, it ceased to be *my* proposal alone and became a cabinet decision on which I could expect full support. Moreover, he commented wryly, there was some poetic justice in my proposals being attacked by other cabinet members. I was a frequent "buttinsky" on substantive policy questions from other departments, and it was only just that I should get some of my own back!

My recollection is that, through my nine years' experience as minister, personal relations among cabinet members were good. There may have been individual rivalries and antipathies, but they did not adversely affect the atmosphere of good relations among ministers. The time taken on the job, both in parliament and in the department, was such that we would not have many social occasions together. But firm friendships were founded, particularly among those who were living full time in Ottawa and who met occasionally on evenings and holidays. There were few days off. If House or cabinet business did not demand, ministers were on the road, either on the political business of the department or to tend their constituencies.

Trudeau always remained in a class apart from the other ministers. Perhaps every prime minister is in that situation, but I think it must have been particularly so with him because of his personal style. Although he had a range of interests stretching from the ascetic to the exotic, he treated everyone, except for a few old and close friends, with patrician reserve. He was a very private person, and he assumed that others sought that same level of privacy. When ministers were going through difficult moments in their personal lives, no word of support or reassurance was forthcoming. But when unhappiness came into his own life with the breakdown of his marriage, he, in turn, did not seek any support or encouragement. These were private matters for each one of us and, in his mind, no one else's business.

At the working level, in contrast, he was supportive, he was good company, and he stimulated the best from his ministers. I created more than my share of problems for the government, but he always gave full support. After briefing him on the current disaster, his response would be: "Okay, what are *we* going to do about it?" The first person plural was a very important reassurance.

I served in parliament with three prime ministers, John Diefenbaker, Lester Pearson, and Pierre Trudeau, each one different, each with his own particular strengths. My relations with Diefenbaker were different from those with the other two because he was the leader of the opposing party, one against which I campaigned. But I came to understand the things he stood for and the fact that he stood strongly for them, even though most of the time I disagreed with him. Along with all the other Liberals, I smarted from the skill with which he attacked us in debate. Diefenbaker very much represented the Canada of my parents' generation, a country substantially rural, devoted to the British connection, and still in the process of coming to terms with the French fact, multiculturalism, and the changed place of Canada in the world. He was a skilled trial lawyer and, of the three prime ministers, the most accomplished "House of Commons man." On political issues on which he was totally in the wrong, he could put forth a defence of his position that would skilfully interweave his strong points, the misstatements of his opponents, and contested material. On such occasions we felt not that he was right, but that he had done a better job of showing how we were wrong than we had in championing our position. What seemed like a formidable defence from him at the time, however, would not look so strong in the media, detached from his oratorical skills. His timing was superb, his dramatic sense effective. Like Churchill, he had read extensively in history and political biography, and he had a formidable memory for the telling phrase. One could understand after hearing him in the House why he had been one of the most effective jury lawyers of his time.

The skills of a jury lawyer, however, are not those of a political leader who, day in, day out, must guide and coordinate a cabinet. On substantive issues he was true to the desires of his Canada, but many other Canadians had changed the subject. In the three elections in which I campaigned against him, he consistently won the support of rural Canada, in Ontario and the Maritimes as well as in the West. But in the changing Canada of the 1960s, with the shift in population to the urban areas, with Canada's wider involvement in the world, with voting Canadians who had come to maturity after the emergence of the dominion as a sovereign nation and major player in Second World War, his issues were often irrelevant.

Pearson's strengths were very different. Unlike Diefenbaker, Pearson did not enjoy the House of Commons or the hustings; they were places he had to be to do his job, but they were not his locales of choice. His political skills were in personal dealings with cabinet colleagues, caucus, and a group of friends in the media and the business world. His was a sunny personality with a quick humour that could ease tension. He was a team leader.

He had a policy agenda attuned to urban Canada of the 1960s. With the economic success of the North American economy, he was concerned to overcome the deprivation of ordinary Canadians that he had witnessed during the Depression. The Canada Pension Plan, better housing, and medicare were all on his agenda, and in his five years as prime minister he carried them all into legislation. In retrospect, his ministry achieved a remarkable legislative record—always without a parliamentary majority. The "great men" of the press gallery, including Charles Lynch and Arthur Blakely, used to write that Pearson was not a good politician. He was a much better politician than they were political analysts.

As a soldier and aviator in the First World War and as a diplomat in the 1930s and 1940s, Pearson had the opportunity to reflect on the questions of Canada's evolving national identity and role in the world. He guided Canadian policy on this second issue, first as undersecretary and then as secretary of state for external affairs. He took on the political fight to establish symbols of Canadian identity, the Order of Canada, the Maple Leaf flag, and the national anthem. It was on the flag that Pearson and Diefenbaker clashed most directly and Pearson prevailed, both in parliament in 1964 and with Canadians ever since.

I was not a member of Pearson's cabinet and cannot compare styles of management, but as a member of caucus I formed an opinion of his technique. He used to say that one of his preferred vocations would have been as manager of a major league baseball team. He also remarked that in every crisis there is an opportunity. The baseball manager has to respond to crises on the field which are unpredictable and unstructured, but which provide opportunity, and it was in dealing deftly with crisis as a diplomat, minister, and prime minister that Pearson excelled.

I have already commented on the style and qualities of Pierre Trudeau, so I will close by comparing him with his two predecessors. His intelligence and education prepared him to deal with most public policy questions, but his lifelong convictions about the importance of good relations between French- and English-speaking Canadians and the importance of a united country lifted him to another plane in national leadership. In his career before politics, he had been free to espouse positions without the necessity, fundamental for politicians, of persuading his countrymen to support the goals he advanced. Over the eleven years that he and I were colleagues, I witnessed the development of his formidable skills in public persuasion. Many times since I have been greeted by strangers who say: "I didn't support him, but Trudeau was what a prime minister should be!"

Trudeau and the Left: Violence, Sex, Culture, etc.

■

RICK SALUTIN

Rick Salutin returned home to Canada, after a decade of study in the United States, on the day Pierre Trudeau declared martial law in October 1970. He has been a writer ever since. His many plays include 1837, *on the movement for independence from the British Empire, and* Les Canadiens, *about the famed hockey team and its relation to the spirit of Quebec nationalism, which received the Chalmers Award for best Canadian play. He has written biography and history as well as two novels, one of which,* A Man of Little Faith, *was awarded the Books in Canada prize for best first novel. In 1993 he won the National Newspaper Award for best columnist for his* Globe and Mail *column on media, and he held the Maclean Hunter chair in ethics in communication at Ryerson Polytechnic University from 1993 to 1995.*

L ET ME START with a personal connection. My political formation occurred in the new left of the 1960s, particularly its American version, since I spent that decade in the United States as a student, first in Boston, then in New York. I was moved by the civil rights movement in the early years of the decade, then shaken by the rise of the anti-war movement in its middle years, then swept up by the new left in full roar, in the final years. Among the main features of this new left were reverence and even adulation for the national liberation movements of the Third World such as Cuba, China and Vietnam; and its revival of what it saw as the revolutionary marxist tradition—as opposed to the social democracies of Europe or the bureaucratic, repressive regimes of the Soviet realm, along with the Soviet-oriented communist parties of the west. Even at the time many of us knew there was a lot of rhetoric posing as theory in the new left, as well as much theatre masquerading as genuine political action. But these were internal blemishes—"contradictions"—to be faced and overcome as the movement matured.

My political view of Canada in those years was fundamentally contemptuous. Canada as I recalled it had room for neither a radical nationalism which aimed to sever its remaining colonial bonds; nor for revolutionary radicalism. The US had both, in deep if perverted forms: it had after all been born from a revolution for national independence. In this state of mind I heard distantly about the rise of a politician named Pierre Trudeau, first as candidate for leadership of the Liberal party, then as newly elected prime minister. I got this news through nothing more weighty than *Time* magazine and the occasional report in the *New York Times*. There were Canadians in New York like artists Joyce Wieland and Michael Snow who formed a pro-Trudeau group but I wasn't part of their milieu. Yet somehow—and I still find this odd—I took Trudeau's appearance as a sign I should consider going home to Canada, during a time when I felt far more *at home* in New York City than I ever had in Canada. I announced this . . . presentiment to my maoist comrades, who found it peculiar.

Now for me in those years, what has since become a great icon of Canadian potential—Expo 67—signified nothing. I had attended Expo but it didn't make me think even fleetingly about going home. Perhaps it meant more for those already in Canada for the duration and who were seeking proof that things in the country could change. But Trudeau—mere news reports about him—moved me. I don't mean I returned to Canada because of Trudeau. My return had more to do with the fact I'd run out of money to live on and burned my bridges in the philosophy department at the New School for Social Research—plus a desire to try writing, which for me seemed to require the sense of place I felt in Toronto. Besides, whatever role Trudeau has as my impetus for return- well, I arrived back the same day in October 1970 that he imposed military law on the country to stifle the revolutionary *indépendantistes* of Quebec. End of romance. Yet there had been that first response, as if there was a . . . consonance between my sense of Trudeau and the values and vocabulary of the new left.

Trudeau and Violence

Trudeau was a second North American coming of John F. Kennedy: young(ish), hip, sexy and, unlike their predecessors, Ike and Mike, products which seemed tailored to a new political marketplace, the first such items test-marketed into it. Both presented as liberals and progressives. Both behaved as if one of the first things a liberal must do in power is prove he isn't a weakling himself— despite, or because of, his sympathies for the weak and unequal etc.

As if they felt pressure to be manly, or at least prove they weren't unmanly. Kennedy unleashed the Bay of Pigs invasion of Cuba in his first months. Without that, it's unlikely there would have been a Cuban missile crisis two years later, when Kennedy seemed willing to take the planet into nuclear devastation, so long as he didn't look like the guy who blinked first. During his own first term, Trudeau icily declared the War Measures Act and imposed martial rule throughout Quebec. It's not just that he did it; he seemed to glory in it. When a reporter asked how far he'd go suppressing civil liberties which he'd long advocated, he spoke his famous "Just watch me!" I was working for a weekly satirical radio show then. I wrote a sketch in which Trudeau was a gunslinger à la Clint Eastwood: "They call me . . . the man with the War Measures Act." Max Ferguson did a superb Trudeau.

Now this kind of violent attitudinizing belonged not to the rightwing rhetoric of those years but to that of the left. Algerian psychiatrist Franz Fanon was a Marxist and national liberation advocate. He both theorized and eulogized the need for violence as part of the liberation process: it was therapy for colonial societies and individuals colonized in them. His theory was substantial but the language reached rhapsodic levels in some of Fanon's books, as if he was doing some therapy on himself. His texts were omnipresent among new leftists in those years, including Quebeckers. Author Pierre Vallières called his people *les nègres blancs de l'Amérique.* In the US, the Black Panthers advocated armed confrontation with the American state; and if you weren't part of the solution you were part of the problem. This was a conscious repudiation of the non-violence of the civil rights movement, and the Panthers paid a high price for it in numbers murdered or jailed by the police and FBI. The mood was also widespread among whites in the new left, who often took their cue from radical blacks. Mao's dictum that power comes from the barrel of a gun was quoted and approved. Left organizations like the Bay Area Revolutionary Union, to which some of my friends belonged, included arms training as part of their requirement for membership. By the early 1970s, a number of former student leftists, mainly white, had gone "underground" as the Weathermen to inspire a violent revolution in the United States on the model of "exemplary action," associated with Castro's victory in Cuba. (It vied for popularity with the "maoist model" of mass mobilization.) Were these young, mainly middle-class new leftists using violence to compensate for their radical idealism, in the way that Kennedy and Trudeau may have been trying to prove their liberalism hadn't made them squeamish? Did their fury imply an admission that the cause they embraced would probably not triumph? At Columbia University in 1968, young women at Barnard College screamed down from their dorms, "Up against the wall, motherfuckers," at New York police who'd broken student heads to end the anti-war protest there. Was it middle-class rage against parental and other authority—a rage all the stronger when authority hides beneath "tolerant" verbiage—the "repressive tolerance" that new left guru Herbert Marcuse critiqued? At any rate, acceptance of violence was common across race, class, and gender lines on the new left. It showed in the popularity of the term "revolution," strictly the property of the left in those years, though since appropriated by the right and by every form of merchandising. "By any means necessary," said the Panthers. "Violent" was more or less assumed within "revolution." It was necessary to be unafraid of violence, because "the ruling class" would use every means available to sustain their power, as had every such class in history etc.

An aspect of the new left that continues to perplex me is the way it mattered to us that "history was on our side": as Castro said, that history would "absolve" us. It's true this was marxist theory: proletarian revolution was, if not inevitable, at least smiled on by history. But that implies that simply fighting the good fight for justice was insufficient. There had to be a seriousness about results, about being hardheaded and "realistic." One didn't want to feel involved in quixotic idealism. We wanted to make clear we were not only committed and—in a phrase of the time, usually used ironically—politically correct; we wanted it known that we meant to achieve what we set out to do, to be winners rather than losers, you might say. This kind of "realism" also echoes in Trudeau's attitude.

He personally avoided membership in the CCF/NDP, even though he urged friends to join. In the early 1960s, he abandoned his previous "anti-capitalism" stance in favour of, as Stephen Clarkson and Christine McCall write, a "more impersonal and technocratic, less populist and democratic" position on social and economic issues. By 1964 he joined in issuing a federalist "Manifeste pour une politique fonctionelle" and "An Appeal for Realism in Politics." This kind of "realism," which privileges results over principles, is a plausible prelude to a willingness to use violence once in power, as Trudeau did in the FLQ crisis.

I'd like to cite as a sample of this realism in the Trudeau-new left era a conversation I had with Sidney Newman, named by Trudeau as head of the National Film Board from 1970 to 1975. Newman began his career in Canada but worked at the BBC for many years, doing successful dramas and series, including the action-adventure show *The Avengers*. When he took the NFB post, one of his actions was to kill support for Denys Arcand's documentary history of exploitation in Quebec's textile industry, *On est au coton*. (Arcand released the film underground, then used the experience as a plot hinge in his feature *Gina*.) When I asked Newman about this blatant censorship, he was unapologetic. "Those guys actually think you can use a government agency to do propaganda for class war," he snapped. It had the sound of "Just watch me!" But it also had the sound of someone who had firsthand experience with naive idealists. Newman, like many young Canadians, got his start in film at the left-leaning NFB created by John Grierson in the 1940s. Newman told me he hadn't actually been a member of the Communist Party in those days but said, proudly I thought, that he'd been "very close" to it. The Canadian Communist Party of those years, the Stalin years, with its strong Soviet tilt, was also "realistic" about its idealistic enemies, whether they were dissident workers or dissident Marxist intellectuals. Stalinists and redbaiters in the early Cold War years would have agreed: what mattered was knowing you were right, then doing whatever was necessary.

So Trudeau the gunslinger, thumbs tucked into his belt, feet astride, unapologetic about imposing the War Measures Act in

peacetime, shared a romance with decisiveness and righteous violence, that characterized the new left. Each delighted in the rawness
of power and was bent on being hardheaded and realistic. Showing
beneath this posture like a slip was a striking absence of democratic
scruples. In a crisis, it didn't really matter what "the people" said or
how they voted because they were victims of false consciousness, of
separatist propaganda etc. It seems to me Trudeau's espousal, early
in his political career, of "participatory democracy" rings as hollow
as that of the (old and new) left for "people's democracy." Beneath
each lurked a disrespect for the capacities of "the people" to determine what's in their own interest. As for how realistic such realism
really is: it seems to me Trudeau's unprecedented peacetime use of
state violence engendered a deep despair about the "Quebec problem" which is still with us: for nationalists in Quebec, a sense of the
impossibility of working within Canada; for those outside Quebec,
a sense that, in the end, only heavy-handedness will work, or nothing will.

Trudeau and National Liberation

I returned to Canada after ten years in the US by way of Quebec
City. I made my way back to Canadian politics, after the American
new left, by way of discovering Quebec as the Canadian version of
a national liberation struggle. That's how the world made sense in
the era of Vietnam, Cuba, or Portugal's African colonies. Canadian
poet Milton Acorn had published his poem *Where is Ché Guevara*,
about the spectre of an itinerant South American revolutionary
who haunts the bloody and complacent days of western leaders
("President Johnson busy breaking a treaty/ As his forebears used
to do on the Indians,/ And now he does on the entire world/ . . .
pauses just an instant in the middle of/ handing out a souvenir pen/
to think/ 'Where is Ché Guevara?'") Like many notions that look
limited in retrospect, the national liberation take on reality had a
lot of limited truth in it. (Almost everything looks quaint after

some passage of time. Think how clunky our computers will look a short while from now—or the gobs of naked wiring in our houses and streets.)

National liberation was the model on which many of those on the left in Quebec perceived their situation. They identified with anti-colonial struggles. (Another quaint-sounding term now. But think how quaint today's self-help argot about survivors of abuse, recovering victims etc. will some day sound.) They identified with Vietnamese or Cubans or—to some degree especially—Palestinians. Vallières published his *Nègres blancs*. Michèle Lalonde's poem *Speak White* carried the identification far beyond anything narrow or parochial: "Speak white/ tell us again about freedom and democracy/ We know that liberty is a black word/ as misery is Black/ as blood is muddied with the dust of Algiers or Little Rock/ . . . We know now/ that we are not alone." Even in less subtle versions, there was something vital and imaginative in this approach. It was a nationalism built not on European models but on those from the colonized Third World. It was at the very least an *interesting* way to be an *indépendantiste*. Compare that élan with the doughy, hectoring visages of Jacques Parizeau or Lucien Bouchard today and try to decide which was the more dynamic, or maybe just more human, approach to the Quebec "problem."

But when Trudeau became a national leader, he remained mired in the notion of Quebec nationalism as the conservative, backward force he'd fought as an intellectual in the 1950s—the Quebec nationalism of the Catholic church and Duplessis. He had no ear for the élan or idealism the new version involved—though he himself helped spawn it by his critiques of the old nationalism. ("*Cité libre* and Trudeau," said the late Gérald Godin, poet and Parti Québecois cabinet minister, when I asked how he overcame the martyr-soaked version of Quebec history he'd received as a child in church schools. "Trudeau?" I asked in surprise, since Godin and his partner, singer Pauline Julien, had both been imprisoned in the roundup of *all* nationalists during the FLQ crisis. "*Surtout Trudeau*," said Godin, unwilling to disavow the importance Trudeau once had for him.) But for Trudeau, there was no change in his valuation of the new nationalism as against the old. Lévesque might as well have been Duplessis.

It's hard to know whether this intellectual obstinacy on Trudeau's part is the sign of a grand obsession and *idée fixe* or just shows he grew intellectually lazy—and stopped examining his ideas, despite a reputation as an intellectual giant among Canadian politicians. The reputation may be an effect of context. It was possible to view him as the best mind in the country whereas he may have been just the best mind in the Liberal party—not the same thing. I don't believe you can find a serious issue on which his thought developed after he entered politics—and certainly not this, the great passion that drew him into the public arena and with which he stayed preoccupied to the end of his career as prime minister and beyond.

An enduring myth about Trudeau is that he was a Canadian nationalist. But he was above all an *anti*-nationalist, focussed obsessively on nationalism in Quebec. To the extent he acted as a Canadian nationalist at all, it was mainly in response to Quebec nationalism: the nationalism that is the enemy of my enemy is my friend. This is nationalism by default, without any root or heart; a device manipulated without passion for the sake of extirpating that other nationalism he so ardently loathed.

By contrast, the kind of Canadian (as opposed to merely Quebec) nationalism born in the new left years when Trudeau came to power also owed something to the national liberation model. In fact what the new Quebec nationalists were saying about Quebec in relation to English Canada could be said of Canada altogether— vis à vis the United States. So the new Canadian nationalism of the Trudeau years had an empathy for the aspirations of the new Quebec nationalism. The main vessel of the new Canadian nationalism in conventional politics at that time was the Waffle faction within the New Democratic Party; it urged an original and sympathetic approach to the possibility of an independent Quebec. Trudeau's Canadian nationalism, such as it was, looked far more like the traditional version, which always viewed the suppression of Quebec's national impulse as essential to Canada's success, and continues to do so.

The odd upshot of this situation in our own era is that the inheritors of Trudeau's position on Quebec *and* Canadian nationalism are not Jean Chrétien's Liberals but Preston Manning's Reform Party. They hold what Manning calls—claiming it's something new—the equality option, though that is pretty much what Trudeau implied whenever he insisted that while Quebec may be unique, so are Saskatchewan and Prince Edward Island. At least Trudeau spoke in conscious bad faith—knowing as he must that Quebec is unique in a far different sense than any province; that it is really a country within a country with its own language, history, culture, cuisine, legal and political institutions, etc. Whether Manning and his party know any better is a murky area. But they are also Trudeau's inheritors as tepid and contradictory Canadian nationalists, having discovered what Manning calls, in the words of his mentor David Frum, "the sleeping giant of Canadian nationalism." This, like the Trudeau version of Canadian nationalism, is a mainly anti-Quebec entity, largely lacking in positive economic, political or cultural content. To be sure there was *more* content in Trudeau's Canadian nationalism, in his loose foreign investment rules, for example. But Trudeau was trying to tempt Quebeckers to stay within Canada, and had to put something on offer. Manning is willing or possibly happy to see Quebec depart, and need *do* nothing to prove his "nationalist" position, besides attacking Quebec. So Reform *welcomes* foreign control of the Canadian economy and is uneasy at even mild signs of disrespect toward the US. Both however turn away from facing what seems to me the unresolved conundrum of Confederation: that Canada is a country composed of nine provinces and another country.

Trudeau and Sex

The most lasting, compelling component of the new left was feminism, though it arrived in the mix at a late point, well after, say, the rhetoric of revolution. Yet the language of leftwing revolution is almost entirely absent today, while feminism remains a preoccupation of our society. It didn't go away. Feminism in the new left began as a challenge to the movement's utopian and sanctimonious claims. The first time I heard the term "chauvinist," as in male chauvinist. I didn't know what it meant, but I knew a new and powerful weapon had been added to the arsenal of political discourse on every level, interpersonal to global.

Now I don't believe you could say anything like a feminist attitude marked Trudeau's time in power, with the possible exception of his last term. By conventional measurements like the number of women in his cabinet, both Diefenbaker and Pearson before and Clark and Mulroney after him, did more. His government did have to deal with the rise of the women's movement and feminist claims. But it did so in traditional Liberal fashion, attempting to set up institutions it could control, in order to accomodate or defuse the demands. The strength of Canada's women's movement, embodied in the National Action Committee on the Status of Women, owes more to Trudeau negatively: it was created in reaction to Liberal efforts at co-optation. Overall there is a strange lack of personal connection between Trudeau himself and the feminist environment which pervaded the social and political environment in those years. During his final term in the early 1980s, prominent women held prominent positions, not just in cabinet but as Speaker of the House and governor general, but by then that had become typical of the times. As for policy, the Trudeau years saw liberalization in areas like divorce and abortion rights that were high on the feminist agenda. But it's more plausible to locate these reforms within Trudeau's concern for individual rights, a concern that runs from his years as justice minister through the Charter of Rights and Freedoms in his final term, than to view it as a reaction to feminism.

What stands out about Trudeau's time in power, especially the earlier years, has more to do with sexuality than feminism. Sex was part of the ambience on the new left. There often didn't seem to be a gap between the political and sexual components of what was routinely referred to as just "the" revolution. During protest "occupations" of universities, having sex with random partners in the office of some professor seen as the mouthpiece of establishment ideology etc., was part of the anti-authoritarian nature of the event. A "liberated" sexuality seemed to be a natural part of liberated politics—though in truth the sexual revolution of the time owed as much to the pharmaceutical industry and the contraceptive pill, along with changes in the economy that led to economic self-sufficiency for many women, as it did to revolutionary theory.

Now Trudeau had this air of sexuality—you could even call it "new" sexuality—about him. It accrued partly as a result of his not being or having been married at the time he became prime minister. It had even more to do with his open sexual interests. This was enough to locate him within the adventurous, "revolutionary" spirit of the times, though his own sexual attitudes were basically traditional. He was more a rake, a playboy or a ladies' man than a new sexual being, an old-fashioned guy with an old-fashioned approach to sex, even prissy in his way—or so say some in a position to know—who took advantage of a situation in which he possessed the attractions of power and celebrity. He married a woman who hardly seemed his intellectual equal but who provided him with a family. I'm not judging that, just saying it conforms to traditional notions of partnering; and he beat her up when she humiliated him by having a good sexual time on her own and not concealing it. Perhaps he was bisexual; those rumours have circulated endlessly. If so, that, along with keeping it secret, hardly makes him unusual among members of his class, or gender. The fact he fathered a child outside of marriage at age 71 and acknowledged paternity, as well as maintaining a relationship with his daughter, stands as more unusual and admirable in my book. It's not pathbreaking in the last decade of the 20th century, but in the context of his life and practices, it looks good on Trudeau.

Trudeau and Youth

The generation of the new left was obsessed with its own youth.
This had to do with mere size and with a generational circumstance: those who returned from the Second World War were near
enough retirement that the young could foresee taking over from
them—unlike, say, the experience of the young in the 1950s or
1980s. "Never trust anyone over thirty," they said in the new left.
That they were obsessed with their *own* youth rather than youth
per se showed when they reached middle age and announced,
"Never trust anyone *under* thirty." They apotheosized their own
experience as if going on a protest march was as formative as riding
the rails during the Depression or slogging across Europe in a
world war. Some of them took to claiming that no good music had
been written after 1968, which in any other demographic would
have looked like traditional Old-fartism. Trudeau, who became
prime minister in 1968 at the age of 48, somehow became an hon-
ourary member of this cult of youth.

As John F. Kennedy had been. Kennedy was boyish, in contrast
to his predecessor, General Eisenhower. But Kennedy had also
been an officer during the Second World War, he was married and
a parent. There was no hint he used drugs or was a sexual hobby-
ist—that came years later and partly as a result of changes in sexual
attitudes that began at the time. Trudeau, though older than Kennedy when he came to power, was unmarried, hadn't fought in
some ancient war—and, above all, it was eight years later, *post*
sexual revolution, the era of flower power and the cult of youth.
He smoked grass and hash. Everyone knew. I don't know how
they knew but they knew. I guess some of them smoked with him.
And he was into sex, he said so, more or less. He seemed to scorn
authority and had a playful way.

In fact he was as ill-suited to the role of youth avatar as he was
to being a symbol of the new sexuality. He was middle-aged, self-
absorbed and intellectually rigid. He'd played an important and
principled role in the deep changes Quebec had gone through during the 1950s and early 1960s, something his privilege enabled him

to do. If the young gravitated to him—and they did—maybe they were covertly in search of a parental figure who looked as if that's just what he wasn't: in other words, a cool dad. For this task too, Trudeau was right guy in the right place at the right time. Like Chauncey Gardner in the movie, Trudeau was there. 90 percent of the job, as Woody Allen or someone said, is showing up.

Trudeau and Culture

The new left was, a friend of mine said at the time, a trip. It may not have accomplished much or left a lot by way of legacy and continuing influence—except for feminism—but it was a powerful, often joyous experience. By mid-1970 it was clear that this experiential quality was likely to characterize it more than any practical effects. One sensed this, like so much else, in the popular music of the time: the Beatles' quiescent "Let It Be" or Simon and Garfunkel's "Bridge over Troubled Water." It was only a few years but a long way from "The Times They Are A-Changing." When those anthems of resignation were on the jukeboxes at the same time, in the same bars where I'd seen patrons fling beer bottles at the TV screen as Nixon announced his "incursion" ("This is not an invasion, it is an incursion") into Cambodia, it felt as if any practical place for the new left in politics had drained away. The new left by then, perhaps all along, was more about culture than about politics. It had always placed culture—the music, drugs sex—at the very centre of its concerns, right beside the politics. By way of contrast, leftists of the 1930s would announce at their meetings, "We'll now have the cultural part of the evening," which true communists took as a sign to go out for a smoke.

Now setting aside the Charter of Rights as something not primarily "political," Trudeau has also left relatively little by way of continuing effect—aside perhaps from ongoing bitterness and incomprehension within English Canada of what Quebec "wants" and is about—and in this respect, I've argued, Preston Manning's Reform party, with its implicit preference to have Quebec just leave, is his true successor. Yet the presence of Trudeau remains strong. As Clarkson and McCall say at the outset of their work on Trudeau: *he haunts us still*—in books by and on him, TV series, curiosity, celebrity gossip, along with a sense that he remains the country's only political star. In fact, more or less, its only *star*.

But maybe this is what he always was. His impact and meaning were mainly cultural, not political. He was an iconic figure, a media presence, a star. This is the sense of Trudeau that Geoff Pevere and Greig Dymond caught by listing him in their book on pop culture, *Mondo Canuck*. His classification as pop culture icon rings truer to me than most historical or political analyses. It's where he belongs, where he endures. I believe you could see this during his interventions in the Meech and Charlottetown debates; he was less a part of the debate than the return of a beloved pop figure: the Beatles re-unite, the Stones tour again. Kids at a high school where he spoke clamoured for a look; they begged him to return to politics, far less for what he said than for the sake of the figure he cut.

In this respect I'd say his significance anticipated the politics of a later age, our own, in which politics has become mostly a show. I mean this in more than the sense that politics in Canada has always been partly entertainment; in 19th-century Canada, elections were often the best or only show in town. But back then politics was also more than show. Today, with the proliferation of culture and imagery in the society of the spectacle, you hardly need politics to fill cultural needs. But with the end of the Cold War and the disappearance of a socialist alternative to capitalism, along with the capitulation of most sources of opposition to the neoconservative economic agenda—from communist China to social democratic parties in the west—there is little left for politics to be about except show. This does not mean *pace* the rhetoric of the right, that *government* ceases to be important; it remains crucial to the maintenance and enhancement of the neoconservative agenda. But for the moment politics in the democratic, electoral sense, is no longer about making choices regarding social and economic direction, since all parties agree and no matter who you vote, for you know you'll get the same government in essential respects. In Britain, Tony Blair's New Labour explicitly adopts the legacy of Margaret Thatcher; in Canada, Chrétien's Liberals adopt and even exceed the thrust of Mulroney's Tories—a party that hasn't so much declined as, having fulfilled its historic mission by transforming all others in its image, gone to its reward in heaven. What's increasingly clear to voters is that they are not choosing the direction of their society—that has already been settled; they are voting for a cast of characters who will play the role of The Government on television and in the House of Commons for the next five years. The script is set, but you get to decide who plays the parts on TV. As politics qua culture, and as a pre-eminent media personality with a special bent for the understated timbre of TV, Pierre Trudeau was already there long ago. Maybe what people were always voting for when they voted for him was the guy they preferred to watch on TV, over the alternatives.

In one other way, Trudeau anticipated the political culture—or the politics as culture—of our era: it's with regard to the rhetoric of change. Trudeau was presented in the political arena and the media—much like Kennedy before him—as the personification of necesssary change. In the 1960s, this had to do with the inevitability of generational change. In the mid-1990s, the inevitability of change is again a central feature of discourse in the media, the academy and the political realm. But this time the inevitability has to do with technological change and in its wake change in social and economic expectations. In the 1990s, change is treated fatalistically, as something technology has made and which human beings and society resist only futilely. Some benefit: primarily those already well-endowed; others suffer. But there is little you can do, resistance is futile, as a new spirit of the age, The Phantom of the Opera—a Trudeauesque figure, come to think of it—says. As usual, popular culture mirrors these claims. Bob Dylan's "The Times They Are A-Changing," which epitomized the 1960s, gets revived as a Bank of Montreal ad in the 1990s. But the new left, as a sub-element of the 1960s experience, talked about change in a particular way: not just as something inevitable, but as something that could

and must be *made*, enacted by people choosing their future together. The kind of change invoked in our own fatalistic age has to
do with acceptance and submission, not creativity and agency.
Trudeau, in his time in politics, participated in a pallid way in the
language of agency, by speaking, especially early on—about participatory rather than parliamentary democracy—though mostly he
meant expanding the participation of MPs and of the Liberal party
in the exercise of power, not an inspired notion of the concept.
And even that language faded, just as the new left faded, after the
early promise and exuberance. Now, looking back on that time
of both Trudeau and the new left, in the shadow cast by current
grim demands for submission to technological and economic
"change," if there's anything I miss about the often shallow, always
self-infatuated phenomenon of the new left, it's the fervent and
joyous sense that human beings acting together in the name and
under the inspiration of ideals really can change their own world
and society: profoundly, within their lifetimes. I'm happy I once
was part of a time and movement that believed in that possibility,
and I regret that others, who have lived through their youthful
years since then, have yet to experience it.

Continuity and Change: Trudeau and the World

■

TOM KEATING

Tom Keating is a professor of political science at the University of Alberta, where he teaches Canadian foreign and defence policy and international politics. He has published widely in these areas, including Canada and World Order and Canada, NATO, and the Bomb *(with Larry Pratt)*.

U NLIKE HIS PREDECESSOR, Lester Pearson, Pierre Elliott
Trudeau had little experience in the area of foreign policy when he became Canada's fifteenth prime minister.
As he wrote in his *Memoirs*, he was "neither fascinated by the study
of foreign policy nor especially attracted by the practice of it." He
had travelled to exotic shores before he entered federal politics,
and, on occasion, he had written critically about foreign policy
issues such as Canada's acquisition of nuclear weapons. When he
assumed the top office on April 19, 1968, he had no experience in
hands-on management of foreign policy and little contact with foreign service officers. "I knew the world at large rather well, but I
knew the world of diplomacy scarcely at all," he reminisced. He
also lacked exposure to discussions of foreign policy during his time
in the cabinet in the mid-1960s, when foreign policy matters were
largely resolved between Pearson and his foreign minister, Paul
Martin. Expertise in foreign policy is not a prerequisite for party
leaders, but, given his record, Trudeau might have been expected
to adopt a cautious approach to international affairs. He did not.

As soon as he became prime minister, Trudeau criticized the
style and content of previous governments' external relations and
announced that his government would first review and then reform
the entire process of making and conducting foreign policy. In
his first significant foreign-policy speech delivered in May 1968,
Trudeau proposed a series of foreign-policy initiatives, including
diplomatic recognition of the People's Republic of China, reassessment of Canada's NATO commitments, and review of Canada's
assistance to Third World countries. He also launched a review of

Canadian foreign policy to find ways to serve Canada's current interests, objectives, and priorities more effectively.

The review lasted nearly two years and involved extensive consultations with parliamentarians and academics. The results of the review, which Professor Peyton Lyon labelled the Trudeau Doctrine, were published in 1970 in a set of six pamphlets. It was the first public reassessment of the country's foreign policy ever undertaken by a Canadian government. The review can be summarized in two major objectives. First, it would provide criteria against which future policy could be developed and assessed. Foreign policy would be less reactive and more proactive in planning rationally for Canada's best interests. Canada's international activities would be linked more explicitly with domestic priorities, to make foreign policy "the extension abroad of national policies." The review identified six main themes that reflected Trudeau's concern that foreign policy should serve both domestic interests and universal principles: economic growth, sovereignty and independence, peace and security, social justice, quality of life, and a harmonious natural environment. It also recognized that there were some areas much in need of attention, such as the promotion of Canada's francophone traditions in its foreign policy. As a result, Trudeau revised the country's aid policy and made efforts to establish a community of francophone states.

Second, the review informed members of the Department of External Affairs that a new leader was in charge, one with very different ideas about how policy should be made and carried out. Trudeau entered office with reservations about the department, suspicions about its tendency to control policy making, and dislike of its apparent resistance to change and innovation. The review, alongside the appointment of Ivan Head as Trudeau's principal foreign policy adviser, sent a clear message that external affairs officials would be relegated to a supporting role in the making of Canadian foreign policy. The review led to a fundamental and permanent restructuring of the foreign policy-making process in Canada.

As a first step in the reform process, Trudeau increased the work of the Prime Minister's Office and the Privy Council Office in the foreign policy-making process and delegated a significant role to

Head. Unlike previous foreign policy advisers, Head had no connection to the Department of External Affairs. Trudeau also appointed a succession of secretaries of state for external affairs who were either little known or closely connected to domestic concerns. Throughout successive Trudeau governments, the department lacked a minister who had an independent source of power and wielded effective control over policy. Instead, whenever he was inclined, Trudeau controlled foreign policy. The professional foreign service, once the most distinguishing feature of Canadian foreign policy, was weakened.

The most persistent foreign policy theme during Trudeau's sixteen years in office was the reorganization of the bureaucracy. External affairs, international trade, immigration, and development assistance were all integrated in a single structure renamed the Department of External Affairs and International Trade. Although Trudeau introduced these bureaucratic reforms to foster a more rational decision-making process, their overall effect has been to force the foreign service to work more closely with other departments in formulating policy. The emphasis has moved from politics to trade, and from ideas to selling goods. Of all Trudeau's initiatives in the foreign policy field, few have had such far-reaching effects as this institutional reform. He tried to curtail what he saw as the power of the foreign service and to upset its inherent conservatism, but he replaced the old department with an entity that is both more powerful and more conservative.

■

Trudeau's record in world affairs must be judged in the context of the international and domestic environment in which he operated. Pressing domestic concerns not only distracted his attention but limited his options. His attempt to chart a new course for Canadain international affairs also encountered many conflicting signposts. In the late 1960s the threats emanating from the Cold War conflict that had dominated international security politics for nearly two decades had diminished, and East-West relations were moving to a less hostile phase. Despite the Prague Spring of 1968 and the brutal display of Soviet power that followed, the intense pressures for bloc solidarity were easing. NATO members were considering a renewed diplomatic dialogue with their enemies in the Warsaw Pact, and the Soviets and Americans were embarking on negotiations to control the proliferation of nuclear weapons. In this environment, Trudeau had room to extend diplomatic recognition to China and to visit Moscow. By the time he returned to office for the last time in 1980, however, the world had reverted back to a more confrontational mode. American–Soviet relations had deteriorated as each side deployed a new wave of missiles against the others, the Soviet Union invaded Afghanistan, and Washington cranked up its Cold War rhetoric. As the climate chilled there was renewed pressure for alliance solidarity, including pressure to test cruise missiles in Canada. By 1983, when Trudeau embarked on his peace initiative, he could not find a receptive audience.

Canada's place in the world was also changing, partly because of what was happening in other countries. The European states had recovered from their wartime devastation and had emerged more powerful, economically and politically. In comparison, Canada's position seemed to have declined, and the country appeared to be less needed than in the past. During the 1960s a number of newly independent states had dramatically altered the makeup and agenda of institutions such as the United Nations and the Commonwealth. New demands for justice, not charity, and for radical economic and political reforms challenged the comfortable views and practices of Canada's paternalistic approach to the developing world. The United Nations was more crowded, and it became more difficult to distinguish Canada in the crowd. In these circumstances, it was essential for Canada to reassess its place in the world. When Trudeau visited Moscow in 1971 he refuted testimonials to Canada's great-power status and reminded decision makers in the Kremlin that Canada was merely the largest of the small powers. It was a common theme in his early years. Canadian academics, however, took a different view. In 1974 James Eayrs, a noted observer of Canadian foreign policy, argued that Canada had become a foremost power, in part because it possessed natural resources that had become important in the international economy. In the early 1980s political scientists John Kirton and David Dewitt described Canada as a principal power, largely because of Trudeau himself and the way he had altered Canada's foreign policy. At times, even Trudeau seemed uncertain of Canada's position in the world. While he stressed the limits of Canadian diplomacy, he also launched initiatives designed to influence the great powers in areas such as global inequality and nuclear disarmament; while he reminded Canadians of their diminutive stature, he joined the world's great powers in meetings and summits.

The 1970s were also a time when the agenda of international politics underwent significant change. The newly independent and economically disadvantaged states pushed economic issues to the top of the globe's agenda, and, in the early years of the decade, two special sessions of the United Nations were devoted to considerations of a new international economic order. Commodities, and especially oil, highlighted by the Arab oil embargo of 1973–74, became a source of power, and many Third World states saw their influence rise. By the end of the decade, North-South relations deteriorated, as negotiations broke down on economic reforms and disparities increased. Economic issues remained prominent, however, as industrialized nations fixed their gaze more narrowly on domestic needs. The plight of poorer nations was relegated to speeches delivered to humanitarian groups. The declining importance of security issues during this period brought a new set of problems to the forefront, in areas such as the environment, human rights, and economic interdependence. These issues had more direct implications for many domestic constituencies in Canada, and they reinforced demands from within the government for a closer integration of foreign and domestic policy.

Amid the conflicting political, security, and economic trends, it was difficult to find signs of progress or even stability. Foreign policy became less predictable and more difficult to manage. Any Canadian leader would have found it difficult to devise a coherent policy in the shifting contours of the international environment. What created particular difficulties for Trudeau, however, was his deliberate attempt to achieve a more coherent foreign policy and to work from an explicitly defined set of principles. Although Trudeau often criticized Canada's past policy as being too reactive, it quickly became clear that there was often little choice.

■

Trudeau had two reasons for moving control over foreign policy from the Department of External Affairs to the Prime Minister's Office: personal interest and the trend towards summitry in international relations. Summit diplomacy—direct face-to-face meetings between heads of governments—has a long and checkered history. What was once considered an infrequent and noteworthy occurrence has now become common. And Trudeau liked it. He was frequently abroad, sharing a stage with foreign leaders such as Margaret Thatcher, Fidel Castro, or Kenneth Kaunda; participating at sessions of the Commonwealth, the United Nations, or the Group of Seven; and tackling problems with Rhodesia, nuclear disarmament, or North-South relations. On every occasion, he tried to develop personal relations with foreign leaders as a means of promoting his foreign policy objectives. He encouraged Commonwealth heads of government to engage in a more extensive informal exchange of views, for example—a change that has made the Commonwealth a more effective association. In Trudeau's words: "This is perhaps the greatest strength of the Commonwealth, this opportunity on a regular basis for men of goodwill to sit down together and discuss one with another the problems which affect them and the 850 million people whom they represent."

Perhaps no summit was more important than the one to which Canada did not receive an invitation—the first meeting of what became the G7 at Rambouillet, France, in 1975. Despite his best efforts and a supportive push from the Americans, Trudeau had to wait until 1976, when the Americans hosted the event, to gain entry to this summit of summits. His subsequent performance in Puerto Rico secured a place for Canada at future meetings. This annual event became an important forum for Trudeau's attempts to promote specific foreign policy initiatives: nuclear safeguards at the

London summit of 1978, for example, North-South negotiations at Ottawa in 1981, and East-West security issues at Williamsburg in 1983 and again at London in 1984. The platform provided the necessary access to foreign leaders, but the results were usually disappointing. Whatever the merits of the club, it was not one in which members were receptive to Trudeau's world views.

On occasion, Trudeau succeeded in getting other leaders to meet, as he did at Cancun in 1981 in a final attempt to reinvigorate North-South negotiations, but the lack of results again attests to the problems Trudeau's initiatives encountered in his last years in office. First, they clashed with Margaret Thatcher's and Ronald Reagan's neoconservative philosophy, and, second, they highlighted the contradictions in Trudeau's own performance. Unlike his early years in office when Canada's record could be attributed to the previous government, by the early 1980s it was Trudeau's own performance that defined the extent of Canada's commitment to change. To argue, in spite of the record, that more needed to be done for the South, for the environment, for disarmament sounded hypocritical amid Canada' discriminatory trade practices, energy consuming megaprojects, and cruise missile testing. If a principled power like Canada was not strong enough to undertake significant change, how could Trudeau argue that others should?

Part of the mystique surrounding Trudeau's foreign policy comes from the initiatives he undertook in areas such as North-South relations and nuclear disarmament. They were highly visible and exceedingly personal, but they often lacked political and diplomatic support within his own government and in the international arena. His objective, it seemed, was to make a point or perhaps to educate. Unlike previous governments that had worked incrementally and behind the scenes to establish Canada's credibility, Trudeau apparently saw his own credibility as most important. Perhaps for this reason he personalized Canada's foreign policy in these areas and cultivated supporters abroad, while leaving undeveloped the necessary diplomatic, military, and financial resources at home to support his initiatives. The end result was often a gap between rhetoric and reality, between principle and practice. The gap was noticed more at home than abroad, but it threatened to undermine Canada's credibility overseas. Nothing exemplifies this problem more than Trudeau's foreign-policy swan song—the Peace Initiative of 1983—or relations with Europe. After Trudeau unilaterally halved Canada's military deployments in Europe and curtailed defence spending, European governments were reluctant to respond to his personal pleas for a contractual link until he showed a greater tangible interest in supporting European security concerns. The result often was a foreign policy out of touch with the country's capabilities, and capabilities out of line with the country's interests.

Sympathetic observers argue that Trudeau's foreign policy was marked by a consistent and principled world view. Thomas Axworthy, for example, wrote that Trudeau's policy in areas such as the environment, arms control, and relations with the Third World "provides [an example] of liberal idealism at work in a conservative age." Trudeau and Head repeatedly rejected realist views of international politics. In their book *The Canadian Way*, they write: "The two of us were seized of the conviction that principle and interest—idealism and realism—were not necessarily inconsistent, and certainly not contradictory . . . Power was no longer subject to traditional measurements; security was no longer solely a derivative of military might. In the circumstances, decisions based on ethical considerations were not simply tolerable, they had become necessary." Trudeau outlined these ethical considerations in an address he gave in 1975: "The role of leadership today is to encourage the embrace of a global ethic. An ethic that abhors the present imbalance in the basic human condition—an imbalance in access to health care, to a nutritious diet, to shelter, to education. An ethic that extends to all men, to all space, and through all time."

Although Trudeau repeatedly invoked such principles, they did not represent his world view in full. As the long-serving minister Mitchell Sharp writes in his memoirs: "Eloquent as those speeches were, they did more to enhance the reputation of the Prime Minister than to influence the content of Canadian foreign policy." Trudeau did not, for example, support the view that idealist principles should interfere with state sovereignty. He consistently supported the principle of non-intervention even in the face of human rights violations, and he seemed indifferent to the link between Canadian trade and violations in other states. His opposition to nationalism was also evident in his views on international politics, his response to the civil war in Nigeria, and his criticism of the West's rush "to recognize every Tom, Dick, and Harry republic that decided to proclaim its independence" in Eastern Europe after the Cold War. In observing the radical changes that have transformed East-West relations, Trudeau emphasized the importance of "stability" in the midst of competing demands for free market and democractic principles. And, while championing the needs of others, he consistently argued that foreign policy must serve Canadian interests and national objectives. Trudeau's world view, like the man and the world, was complex and multifaceted.

■

In the late 1960s, Trudeau charted a new course for Canadian foreign policy with considerable fanfare and a sizeable expenditure of political resources. His repeated references to new initiatives and a change in direction led people to think that Canada's foreign policy underwent a radical revision during his sixteen years in power. In truth, however, continuity rather than change best describes Canadian foreign policy throughout this period. In 1973 Canada supported the American peace process in Vietnam by joining yet another face-saving truce observation mission. Later that year, the government demanded not to be excluded from the UN peacekeeping operation in the Middle East after the Yom Kippur war. And in 1983, against unprecedented public opposition, Trudeau allowed the testing of cruise missiles in Canada as part of the price that good allies pay to be members of NATO. There were many critically important achievements for the Trudeau government and the country during this period: Canadian efforts to ease East-West tensions while promoting liberal values during the Conference on Security and Cooperation in Europe; to protect domestic fishing and mining interests while promoting the principles of equity and environmental protection in the Law of the Sea negotiations; and to pursue a liberalization of foreign markets while retaining some measure of protection for Canadian manufactures. But these initiatives were undertaken largely by members of the Department of External Affairs and demonstrated the continued relevance of the foreign service in multilateral negotiations.

The degree of continuity in Trudeau's foreign policy is especially evident in light of the more significant changes undertaken by his successor, Brian Mulroney. In areas as diverse as democratizing the foreign policy–making process, apartheid in South Africa, intervention in support of humanitarian objectives, openings towards Latin America and the Pacific, free trade with the United States, and establishing la Francophonie, the departures from past practice are more noticeable under Mulroney than Trudeau. This fact can partly be explained by changing external conditions. As Trudeau and Head point out in their book, they were frequently working against the tide, and especially against established interests at home and abroad. More important, however, it seems that Trudeau was more in tune with the traditions of Canadian foreign policy than was recognized or acknowledged. The Pearsonian tradition had not been so bad after all.

There is little doubt that in foreign as in domestic policy, the Trudeau legacy remains. Trudeau carried an image abroad that, in many respects, was more personal and public than that of his predecessors. He was an international figure, and his personality, along with his country, gave him a prominent place in the councils of global politics. It is also clear that his desire to question established truths and practices, as well as his invocation of principle and justice, continues to challenge Canadian policy makers. Yet, as Trudeau discovered, an effective foreign policy requires more than personality or principle, and Canada's ability to contribute to a progressive resolution of global problems owes as much to established government departments as it does to its leader. In the end, and in spite of the rhetoric of innovation and change, it was Trudeau's ability to work within the traditions of Canada's multilateral foreign policy that accounts for the successes of his government.

"Small Problems":
Trudeau and the
Americans

■

ROBERT BOTHWELL

Robert Bothwell is a prolific Canadian historian and broadcaster. *A professor at the University of Toronto, he has written extensively on Canada in the twentieth century, including* Canada and the United States *and* Pirouette: Pierre Trudeau and Canadian Foreign Policy *(with J.L. Granatstein).*

I N THE MID-1970s US secretary of state Henry Kissinger was
persuaded to devote a few hours to the question of Canadian-
American relations. The Canadian specialists in the State
Department welcomed this rare opportunity to secure top-level
recognition and affirmation for their work. But the meeting did not
progress as they had hoped. Kissinger fidgeted as his staff droned on.
Wandering eyes and tapping fingers showed that the secretary was
less than fully engrossed. Finally Kissinger motioned the diplomats
to stop. As he showed them to the door he rendered his conclusion:
"These are *small* problems. Solve them."

How small? It was a question of definition and attitude. In his
memoirs *White House Years*, Kissinger reflected that Canada's foreign policy existed in a state of contradiction. The country had
large aspirations and conducted "a global foreign policy." It had a
large economy, too, the sixth or seventh largest in the world in the
1970s, but that economy's "dependence on ours was so great as to
be a significant domestic issue within Canada."

Though he did not say so, Canada's global foreign policy was
not much of a problem to the United States or to Kissinger. Canada
was prominent, to be sure, but its influence was "marginal" and its
"military contribution" disproportionately small. Canada made up
for its limited military offerings through "the high quality of its
leadership." That leadership through Kissinger's entire time in government, 1969–77, was provided by Pierre Elliott Trudeau.

Kissinger described Trudeau as "elegant, brilliant, enigmatic, intellectual," words that might be applied to Kissinger himself. Trudeau
was something of an outsider, and so was Kissinger. Both men liked

to cut through the banalities of government, to get at the underlying principles that others ignored. They ignored, or preferred to ignore, the mundane aspects of their responsibilities—economics, for example. "Economics is the paradise of the second-rate," Kissinger is said to have quipped, words that his economics staff never forgot or forgave. Trudeau, though trained as an economist, preferred to leave economics to others. This commonality may have increased the attraction of the two men for each other. Certainly Trudeau prized the seminars on foreign affairs he could expect from Kissinger on his visits to Washington, or on Kissinger's occasional forays to Ottawa.

For the United States, there was a price for good relations with Canada. Emissaries at all levels had to repeat the clichés to guard and preserve the famous undefended border between Canada and the United States. Still, the border was something the Americans could rely on—as they had since the 1870s. Occasionally, diplomatic relations extended to the unfamiliar or the unpalatable. "I hope you haven't come to talk to me about the sex life of salmon," Kissinger groaned when one unfortunate troupe of Canadian diplomats entered his office. They had. And, from time to time, groups of Canadians objected to one aspect or another of American life and policy. On the whole, though, there was an underlying symmetry and harmony to US–Canada relations.

When Trudeau called on the recently installed American president, Gerald Ford, in December 1974, both sides seemed to be entirely satisfied with the relationship. Trudeau prudently chose to emphasize the essential similarities between the Canadian and American world-views. Such harmony was exactly what Ford wanted and needed to hear, and it was also what the Canadian public and politicians expected Trudeau to say. Good housekeeping would, it was hoped, keep the relationship that way. Good housekeeping dictated that the United States should maintain a friendly interest in Canada and extend it occasional considerations. After all, Canada resembled the United States in all things except size, and the resemblance was so close that the Canadian-American relationship could be called "special."

If the relationship was close early in Trudeau's term of office, it remained so at the end. George Shultz, who was President Ronald Reagan's secretary of state, had little to say about Trudeau, but his attitude to Canada was surprisingly similar to Kissinger's. "So few people in Washington appreciated Canada's significance to us," Shultz wrote in his memoirs, *Turmoil and Triumph*. Canada was, after all, "our largest trading partner, much larger than Japan." He recognized that "our shared objectives were of far greater importance than our differences." This realization was important, for the differences between Reagan's government and Trudeau's were not small, and they proved remarkably irritating to some of the president's entourage. Instead of retaliation, Shultz recommended cultivation, employing a gardening metaphor. Gardens had to be tended, pruned, and occasionally fertilized, not redesigned from scratch every couple of years. Things would turn out all right, Shultz told Reagan—as, on the whole, they did.

Canadian-American relations were and are a complicated affair. Different flags, different political systems, and a different language régime—these are substantial barriers, interruptions in the parade of familiarity and accommodation that characterizes life along the 49th parallel. Canadians, of course, think about the phenomenon more than Americans do. Examples, mostly unconscious, abound. Canadians use the term "North American" to signify a community of interest and experience with the United States. Americans, in contrast, use "North American" to proclaim their difference from Latin Americans, and seldom pause to think that there are other North Americans lurking at the top of the weather map.

In the absence of crisis, there is little that Canadian or American governments can do to alter a situation of subconscious satisfaction. Canada's usual concern is to avoid crises, and so it was most of the time under Trudeau. Above all, the relationship requires calm. Trudeau was prepared to be calm about the Americans. It was partly the calm of personal indifference, for Trudeau, unusually for a Canadian and especially one of his generation, was not greatly influenced by American models. The United States was not "special" to Trudeau, either positively or negatively, and some Americans found this indifference irritating. But Trudeau was quite aware of the power and size of the United States, and of the fact that economics and geography dictated as cordial a relationship as he could manage. His dealings with the United States were, accordingly, circumspect.

This caution might not seem apparent from Trudeau's early and spectacular initiatives in foreign policy. His first decision was to withdraw half of Canada's army and air force contingents on garrison duty with NATO in Europe. His second, almost simultaneous, decision was to begin negotiations for recognition of the Communist government in Beijing. Neither policy was calculated to win favour in Washington, which had for two decades held the line against recognizing Communist China. At the time, these initiatives indicated a new "made-in-Canada" brand of foreign relations, one announced in Trudeau's first meeting with Richard Nixon in March 1969. Though Nixon demurred slightly at the timing of the troop withdrawal and uttered a few caveats about China, he did not strongly object. As he hinted to Trudeau, he too hoped to bring the troops back home and, as time would show, he was open to reconciliation with China.

Had Nixon objected, would Trudeau have gone ahead with his initiatives? Possibly, but possibly not: the price of an actual quarrel with the United States government might have been higher than Trudeau, his party, or his country would have been prepared to pay. Given the fact that 80 percent of Canada's foreign investment in 1969 was American and two-thirds of its international trade was with its southern neighbour, the United States could have had considerable leverage on a wide variety of Canadian policies.

It was a leverage that the United States, at least under Nixon, did not want. Nixon and Kissinger saw that the alliance relationship was a reciprocal one and that American influence over other countries was purchased at a price. In the case of Canada, pressure over NATO and China might work, but at a price in time and effort that Nixon was unwilling to pay. Politics and economics were not necessarily "linked," Kissinger argued.

There was an apparent harmony between the American government's wish to cut its allies' dependence on it and the Canadian government's desire, buoyed by a wave of Canadian nationalism, to emphasize what Trudeau and Ivan Head, his foreign policy adviser, later called the "Canadian Way." If American allies were free to do what they wanted, within broader limits than would have been tolerated by earlier administrations, the United States was free to consult its own interests. It was a line that led directly to the "Nixon shokku."

On August 15, 1971, in a nationwide television address, Nixon announced that the days of "Uncle Sugar" were over and that "Uncle Sam" was himself again. There would be emergency tariff surtaxes and export subsidies to block foreign imports and boost American production, and no longer would the value of the US dollar be tied to gold. The world was stunned. Because the measures were immediately assumed to be directed against Japan, which Nixon had identified as the United States' largest trading partner, this announcement was dubbed a "shokku."

The news broke like a thunderclap over a vacationing Canadian government. Ottawa expressed some ritual indignation—couldn't somebody tell Nixon that *Canada*, not Japan, was the United States' largest trading partner—followed by indications of grave concern, even panic. If Canada was the Americans' largest trading partner, then Canada would suffer more than any other country. This realization brought on a crisis, or rather a pseudo-crisis, because its premise—that Canada was poised to become a martyr to American nationalism—was false.

From August until the end of 1971, Canadian and American politicians and officials snarled at one another as they debated the thrust of American trade and trading policy. The Canadians were unyielding—obdurate, in the view of the US Treasury—and the Americans were unmoved. Finally, at Head's suggestion, Kissinger crafted a meeting of the two sides at the White House in December.

The results were everything that could be desired. In public, Nixon recognized that trade was a reciprocal relationship and that Canada had a right to its own destiny—founded, of course, on significant trade with the United States. In private, he agreed to stop demanding a revaluation of the Canadian dollar in return for

American cancellation of import surtaxes. Canada was saved, yet, outwardly, its autonomy and self-sufficiency were preserved. Nixon could carve a notch for the application of what was called the Nixon Doctrine—making the allies stand on their own feet— while Trudeau could claim a victory for Canadian nationhood. It was a good script, dramatic and eloquent, lacking only a factual basis. The great Nixon shokku affected Canada hardly at all. Most Canadian exports moved to the United States duty free—and a percentage surtax on zero is zero.

Actually, Canada *had* been saved in August 1971, but not by Trudeau and Nixon. The Autopact, the Canadian-American trade agreement of 1965 that removed tariffs on most automotive products made in North America, was slated for cancellation or suspension in the original American package of economic measures. At the insistence of the State Department, the Autopact was extracted from Nixon's press release and saved. In 1971 Canada exported nearly $4 billion worth of automotive products to the United States, so this was good news—had anybody known it. But, in the interest of neighbourly relations, most Americans in the know did not tell, and the Canadians were either oblivious or refused to believe it.

What did the pseudo-crisis do, and what was its meaning? The effects of August 1971 were considerable. Ottawa, in both its political and bureaucratic limbs, was shaken. The Americans could no longer be relied on. Given the new uncertainty, Trudeau and Canadians needed to look elsewhere.

In a policy review published in the summer of 1970, *Foreign Policy for Canadians*, the Trudeau government had resisted any definition of its American policy. Critics complained that Trudeau and his colleagues had written Hamlet without the prince of Denmark, or that they had not dared publicize the extent of Canada's subservience to its American masters. The truth may have been more modest: no coherent policy could be devised that covered only the government side, or even the economic aspects, of Canadian-American relations.

With the shokku behind it, however, the government decided to try its hand. After much consideration, it published over the signature of the minister for external affairs, Mitchell Sharp, an essay entitled "Canada–U.S. Relations: Options for the Future" in the autumn 1972 issue of *International Perspectives*. The essay ranged over the whole history of Canadian-American relations, dwelling on the growth of American trade and the impact of American culture. The relationship had been beneficial, the essay argued, because imports of American goods, money, and culture had prompted Canada to become more mature and self-sufficient. At the same time, Canadian public opinion had concluded that the times required "greater Canadian independence." The time was right for action: But what?

In the only part of the long paper that is still remembered, Sharp laid out three options: first, the status quo; second, "closer integration with the United States"; or, third, "a comprehensive, long-term strategy to develop and strengthen the Canadian economy and other aspects of our national life and in the process to reduce the present Canadian vulnerability." Citing the Nixon Doctrine of self-sufficiency, Sharp concluded that the time was ripe to choose the third option. Canadian policy would be encouraged, if not directed, to grow along autonomous lines. Only this impetus, the paper promised, could resolve the ambiguity of Canadian foreign policy, the dichotomy between dependence and independence.

The third option did no such thing. Its implementation was postponed for two years while Trudeau grappled with a bruising near-defeat in the 1972 election and a minority parliament. As part of the price for a transitory parliamentary majority, Trudeau even supported a resolution condemning American bombing raids over Vietnam, a subject that, until then, he had sensibly left alone. Nixon was not pleased by this exercise of Canadian self-sufficiency, and, for a time, Canadian diplomats in the American capital were on the administration's official "shit list." But Canada was too useful to Washington, and there were too many daily issues to be dealt with, for the diplomatic apartheid to be strictly obeyed. Even Kissinger was quick to forgive and forget when, in 1973, Canada agreed to join a face-saving international commission covering American withdrawal from Vietnam.

The third option, and the assumptions on which it was founded, enjoyed a long half-life in Ottawa, well into the 1980s. When Trudeau regained a majority in parliament in July 1974, it seemed that its time had come. Yet, as a practical policy, the third option was never properly implemented. The bureaucracy and even the cabinet were divided on its wisdom, while the business community at whom it was aimed—the people who made the effective decisions about imports and exports—found it an irritating annoyance. The Americans were right next door, they spoke the same language, they had the same legal system, and they were a known commodity. Exports to the United States continued to grow, trucks bearing goods drove across the border, and the third option floated futilely above. Admittedly, it was only one commercial irritant among many. In this last flowering of Trudeau's comprehensive strategies, there were plenty of government initiatives for business to complain of, from investment review to adventures in government ownership of oil companies.

In trade policy, the 1970s witnessed a variety of government initiatives. Some officials became fascinated by elaborate schemes to develop raw material cartels, similar to the Organization of Petroleum Exporting Countries, as a way to reduce Third World dependence on the First World. The Americans took a more practical route and were disappointed not to get more Canadian support in negotiations with the Third World, either at the United Nations or in other international forums. Some Canadians toyed with the idea that Canada was both an ex-colony and a significant exporter of raw material. In the opinion of Canada's First World allies, the Canadian government was trying to walk both sides of the street in international negotiations. Was Canada a member of the First World or the Third World? American diplomats pointedly asked. The answer they received varied according to the Canadian on the receiving end. As for the Canadian government, it was far from united on the issue.

It is not hard to conclude that Canada's Third World flirtation of the 1970s was a phantom policy, unsupported by public opinion or by any strong consideration of existing Canadian interests. It is equally difficult to view the third option as much more than an intellectual conceit. Both initiatives were spawned in the same sense of disappointment and loss that followed the American economic initiatives of 1971, an experience that was easily and immediately misinterpreted in Ottawa both in its cause and its effect. The Nixon Doctrine, the umbrella under which these free-form Canadian policies sheltered, was also founded on a misinterpretation of history.

American indulgence in the face of Canadian irritation was especially needed in two cases that emerged under Nixon's successors, Gerald Ford and Jimmy Carter. First there was the Group of Seven (or Six or Five). The United States had to choose whether to exert its influence to secure Canada a seat at the World Economic Summit meetings. Until the early 1970s, the summit's European founder, French president Valéry Giscard d'Estaing, had pointedly refused to grant this privilege. But because in 1976 the summit was to be hosted by the United States, the Americans had control of the invitations. Kissinger and Gerald Ford, concluding that another North American voice at the table was preferable to a conference heavily dominated by Europeans, decided to invite Canada. In bringing Canada to the table, Ford and Kissinger refused to take seriously a number of Canadian-American disputes, such as the exclusion of Taiwan from the Montreal Olympics, even though these issues were exciting the media in both countries. Minor eruptions of this kind were "noises off" to Kissinger and his colleagues, trivial items that expressed Canada's sense of self-definition. Brent Scowcroft, Ford's national security adviser at the time, put it this way: "Well, there go the Canadians again."

In the second episode, Canadians could expect similar indulgence from the United States when their country faced, for the first time since Confederation, the serious prospect of secession. A separatist government led by René Lévesque was installed in Quebec City in November 1976. The rest of Canada was stunned. The Parti Québécois was pledged to hold a referendum on "sovereignty-association," separatism without tears. The vote would be held during the Lévesque government's electoral mandate, at a time of its choosing. If it carried the vote, the United States would have two sovereign neighbours on its northern border instead of one.

What would the Americans do? The decision lay with the incoming Democratic administration of Jimmy Carter, who had just defeated Gerald Ford and the Republicans. It was to Carter, therefore, that the US ambassador in Ottawa, Thomas Enders, directed his advice during the two-month hiatus that the American Constitution enforces between outgoing and incoming presidents. Enders became a much sought-after figure in Ottawa in the days after the separatist victory in Quebec. Trudeau, it appeared, was anxious about the attitude the United States government would take. The United States was a powerful force in the Canadian imagination, but especially in Quebec's. Many French-speaking Quebeckers, like Lévesque, preferred Americans to English Canadians, whom they characterized as a pallid imitation of the real thing. If the Americans approved of a separatist outcome, or were ostentatiously indifferent to it, their response would count for much. Equally, American acceptance could halt English-Canadian fury at Quebec's secession in its tracks. Independence, in the separatist dogma, would start off with a declaration of dependence on the United States.

What was true for Quebec was also true for Canada, as Pierre Trudeau interpreted events. The Nixon Doctrine proclaimed American self-interest. Perhaps American self-interest now dictated the breakup of Canada. In the final analysis, it appeared that Canada was not only economically dependent on the United States, as Canadian nationalists had long claimed, but politically dependent as well, and ripe for interference.

In Ambassador Enders' opinion, the transitory pleasures of interference and domination that his country might enjoy paled beside the inconveniences and disadvantages of a fragmented Canada. He advised Carter to this effect. There were, he later recalled, three main considerations for the American government. First, Canada was a democracy, in a world where functioning democracies were a fragile and uncommon species. Second, Canadian-American economic relations were vast and beneficial to the United States. Disruption was unlikely to improve economic exchange. Finally,

Canada was a North American federation, a form of government familiar and comforting to Americans. Americans knew and understood the contending forces in federations—centralism versus regionalism. What Americans would say or do when confronted with the fragments of Canada could be a volatile issue in American domestic politics—something the United States did not especially need. And so, once again, Canada's weakness, this time its structural political weakness, became an asset in dealing with the United States.

The United States, a State Department analysis concluded, did not need and should not want a rearrangement of Canada that significantly weakened the central government. If the Canadian federation devolved into a loose association of self-interested provinces, they would be bound to seek their own several ties with the United States—a complication both externally and internally for American policy. "The effect," in the State Department's opinion in August 1977, "would be that the U.S. would be faced with either new responsibilities and/or opportunities, or a number of small and weak, although probably friendly, countries to the North."

American interests called for friendly non-interference in the issue. The United States, Canadians were told, thought that Canada worked just fine as it was. In public, the United States had no opinion on the matter of separation, an internal political affair; in private, it would do what it could to forward the Canadian cause. Separatist emissaries to the United States would not be encouraged, and the Quebec government would not be allowed opportunities to bask in official American favour.

A calamitous visit by Lévesque to New York City in January 1977 was followed by and contrasted with a much more successful progress by Trudeau to Washington in February. Lévesque failed to convince an audience of New York businessmen that Quebec was really a struggling colony attempting to throw off imperial shackles, just as the United States had done two hundred years before. But Lévesque, by promising change, threatened disturbance. Nor did Americans, secure in their sense of uniqueness, welcome the news that their own revolution had an unanticipated descendant. Trudeau, in contrast, bore the message that Canada was in good hands and that no change was indicated: It was a message that Americans wanted to hear. Even better was the news that Canadian-American relations were in splendid shape, and that Trudeau could be trusted to keep them that way. Indeed, American diplomats detected an easing of official Canadian attitudes on a number of previously contentious issues. Canadian nationalism, Trudeau had presumably decided, could wait.

The separatist moment lasted four years until, in May 1980, the matter was resolved by Lévesque's long-promised referendum. Trudeau had, by then, been in and out of office, enjoyed a refreshed majority in parliament, and was ready to make his mark on Canada for the 1980s. His restoration was designed not only to shore up but to renew Canada's national institutions, including the comprehensive strategies promised by the third option. Liberated by the referendum, the Trudeau government could move against the separatists on the constitutional front and return to its earlier, assertive formulas to promote Canadian nationalism.

The result was the strongly assertive National Energy Program of October 1980. Carter's administration reacted with pained surprise, but his defeat in November by Ronald Reagan lowered Canada's erratic energy policy on his list of priorities. The Reagan Republicans were more assertive, blending threats of retaliation with a regard for Canada that was both deeply sentimental and bluntly realistic. The sentiment was what appealed to the president, who knew Canadians from Hollywood days and believed in an amorphous "North American Accord," linking Canada, the United States and Mexico in an unspecified way. The realism was deployed among his advisers, who understood that the sheer size and complexity of America's economic relationship with Canada made it difficult to select any single feature for sanctions. Steady pressure on the Canadians secured some concessions, while a decline in market prices for oil undermined the economic foundations of the Energy program. It would fall, eventually, under its own weight.

The Reagan administration was rhetorically fierce towards Trudeau and his policies, yet essentially friendly towards Canada.

Trudeau was not fond of Reagan, and he made it plain that he despised the president's intellect. Reagan's hostility to the Soviet Union alarmed Trudeau, who was also unimpressed by the American president's illiberal domestic policies. Nevertheless, Reagan was the leader of the United States, and when required, Trudeau was prepared to slather on the kind of glutinous flattery that he and his advisers deemed appropriate. Whatever the effect on Reagan, the president's entourage found Trudeau patronizing and foolish— never more so than during the prime minister's ill-conceived peace mission in 1983–84. Soon after, Trudeau had retired, and the Reagan administration breathed a sigh of collective relief. "We put up with Trudeau for so long," one White House official exclaimed.

But "put up" they did. Canada, the Americans concluded, was important; Trudeau was not. More charitably, the currents of Canadian-American relations were too strong, too significant, to allow any personality, even Trudeau's, to interfere. Curiously, when he embarked on his last quixotic travelogue in the fall of 1983, Trudeau recognized as much. Around the world, doors opened to the prime minister of Canada. But for Pierre Trudeau, citizen of the world, the result was by no means as certain. Canada gave Trudeau what Theodore Roosevelt used to call a "bully pulpit." It was too bad for Trudeau that Reagan was now his audience, not Kissinger or Carter.

In the end, the small problems of Canadian-American relations were what gave the subject its form and its importance. The small problems resisted definition and thwarted grand schemes, whether Nixon's trade policy, Kissinger's geo-strategy, or Trudeau's mission of universal world peace. They constituted a special relationship even as they made it impossible of definition.

Social Spending, Taxes, and the Debt: Trudeau's Just Society

■

ANDREW COYNE

Andrew Coyne has been national affairs columnist for Southam News since 1996, and previously he was an editorialist and columnist for both the Financial Post *and the* Globe and Mail. *He has also written for a number of magazines, including* Saturday Night, The Next City, *and* Cité libre, *and, abroad, his articles have appeared in the* Wall Street Journal, *the* Financial Times, *and the* National Review. *Currently he is at work on a book on Canadian nationalism.*

FOR A PRIME MINISTER first elected on the promise of the Just Society, Pierre Elliott Trudeau's legacy in the field of social policy is surprisingly modest. The ninefold increase in federal spending he oversaw between 1968 and 1984 might be expected to have purchased some comparable advance in social justice. Yet the social policy achievements of the four governments he led can only be described as piecemeal.

The major pillars of the Canadian welfare state, after all, were already in place before Trudeau became prime minister: unemployment insurance (1940), family allowances (1944), Old Age Security (1952), the Canada Pension Plan (1965) and Guaranteed Income Supplement (1966) for seniors, the Canada Assistance Plan (1966), and medicare (1967). The Trudeau years were marked more by incremental adjustments to existing programs—increasing GIS payments, or loosening unemployment insurance rules—than by any major new departures in social policy. Although the 1978 refundable child tax credit was a noteworthy innovation, it fell far short of the guaranteed annual income that was the real objective of social reformers of the day. By the end of the second Trudeau government, the opportunity for a more ambitious social agenda was lost, swallowed whole by provincial obstructionism, economic instability, and, more than anything else, the federal government's own mounting fiscal crisis.

Net federal debt in fiscal 1968, just before Trudeau became prime minister, was about $18 billion, or 26 percent of gross domestic product; by his final year in office, it had ballooned to $206 billion—at 46 percent of GDP, nearly twice as large relative to the economy. In an age in which we have grown used to debt-to-GDP ratios in the 75 percent range, those numbers may have lost their power to shock. It was the Conservatives who took power in 1984 who, in the nine years that followed, ran the debt up to more than $500 billion. But the truth is that the relentless rise in the debt that has all but consumed federal politics for the past decade or more was set in motion during the Trudeau years. By the last days of his régime its momentum was unstoppable.

In the twenty years after the end of the Second World War, the government of Canada ran a deficit on its operating account—that is, it spent more on programs than it collected in revenues—precisely four times. Ottawa began the period with a very large debt, most of it incurred to finance the war effort. But by running operating surpluses in most years, postwar governments offset some or all of the cost of interest on the debt: if the government did not always manage to record an overall surplus on its books, the deficit was never large. By 1965, federal finances were in as robust shape as they had ever been. Interest payments, as a share of revenue—a crucial measure of fiscal health—stood at just 11 percent.

In the first half of the Trudeau era, roughly corresponding with the first two governments, the Liberals kept to this tradition. Though spending increased at an extraordinarily rapid pace in those years, so did revenues. The government ran small operating surpluses from 1968–69 through 1974–75, enough to ensure that the overall budget deficit, including interest charges, never exceeded 2 percent of GDP. Only in Trudeau's first full year of power, 1969–70, however, was the budget actually in balance. With the economy growing strongly, the debt-to-GDP ratio continued to fall, reaching a postwar low of 18 percent in fiscal 1975. The entire accumulated federal debt at the end of that year, at $27 billion, was less than the government's annual budget.

After that, everything changed. The years from fiscal 1976 to fiscal 1985 were, fiscally speaking, a lost decade: ten straight years in which the government ran not only an overall deficit but an operating deficit. The overall deficit throughout this later phase never fell below 3 percent of GDP; it averaged 5.6 percent. In that calamitous final fiscal year of Liberal rule, 1984–85, total spending exceeded revenues by more than 50 percent. The deficit that year, at $38.5 billion, was nearly equal to 9 percent of GDP, a record in peacetime. Interest payments alone were now enough to consume nearly one-third of every revenue dollar. With interest costs compounding at a rate of 13 percent per year, and the debt doubling every three or four years, that ratio could only grow.

No wonder the Liberals' successors had such trouble bringing the debt to heel. Summing across the nine years of Conservative government, the federal government actually spent about $14 billion less on programs than it collected in revenues. Every dollar of the $300 billion added to the debt during the Tory years was interest on the debt the Liberals had left behind.

■

What explains this performance? Was the system already implicitly overloaded by the social innovations of the Pearson era, whose unaffordability was only revealed once the rapid economic growth of the 1950s and 1960s had begun to fade? Or was it the Trudeau governments' own reckless spending that left federal finances so exposed to the risk of a downturn? Or, as some have argued, is the explanation to be found in some other cause, in the ruinously high interest rates that arrived towards the end of the 1970s or in the continuing erosion of the federal revenue base throughout the decade?

Let's take the last question first. How much of the Liberals' legacy of debt should be accounted to increases in expenditures, and how much to a decline in federal revenues? Was it a case of too much spending, or too little taxes?

To answer these questions, we first need a dependable yardstick against which to measure movements in spending and revenues over the years. It is interesting, even amazing, to note that program spending, over the entire seventeen-year period, rose at an average rate of 13.3 percent per year. But that figure alone is not meaningful. Without knowing how fast prices increased in the same period, we cannot even say whether these figures represent real (adjusting for the purchasing power of the dollar) increases or decreases, let alone whether the rate of growth of either was appropriate. Mere dollar figures, in short, are not sufficient; significance is measured in relative, not absolute terms. But relative to what?

One popular measure expresses both spending and revenues as a share of GDP. From 15 percent of GDP in fiscal 1968, program spending rose like a shot to nearly 20 percent in fiscal 1976. But from there it declined for several years, to 17 percent of GDP by 1980–81—precisely the period in which Liberal profligacy is supposed to have reached its peak. Revenues, meanwhile, followed much the same pattern, rising from 16 percent of GDP in 1968 to more than 19 percent in 1975, before falling away to barely 15 percent of GDP by fiscal 1980. On this reading, then, it seems plausible to put the blame on revenues for the buildup in debt of the late 1970s. Had the federal government merely maintained its revenue take at 1975 levels, it would not have run such large deficits— indeed, it would probably have been in surplus, at least until the 1981 recession hit.

There are problems with this approach, however. The GDP yardstick implies that fiscal policy is a simple function of the resources the government has at its disposal. That assumption is fine when it comes to taxes. When we want to know how heavy the tax burden is, we put it in terms of how much of our income the government has taken, not how much revenue it has raised. Only when revenues rise or fall as a share of GDP do we say there has been a discrete shift in tax policy.

But it is quite misleading to measure spending in the same way. By this logic, spending may be said to have been "cut," no matter how fast it has grown—just so long as the economy grew a little bit faster. A government would be said to have made no change in policy if it merely raised spending in line with GDP, year after year. But this description is plainly false. The link between revenues and economic growth may be an automatic one, but no such rule applies to spending. The only reason spending would rise at such a pace is if the government decided to raise it: that is, by a series of deliberate policy changes.

As a measure of public spending, then, share-of-GDP comes with a bias to big government. The implication is that spending should always rise, not because it needs to, but because it can. A better yardstick would measure spending relative to the purposes for which it is intended. If, for example, the purchasing power of the dollar declines, or if the population that consumes government services grows, then a constant level of spending in dollar terms would mean that the government could provide fewer goods and services to each person. The steady-state policy would rather maintain a constant level of real per capita spending: Any additional spending beyond what was required to keep pace with increases in prices and population would be considered a discretionary increase, while anything less than that would be a cut.

Recasting federal spending and revenues in real per capita terms provides a clearer picture of what happened in the Trudeau years. The first two Trudeau governments again mark the period of maximum acceleration in spending. The total of $18 billion that the federal government spent on all programs in fiscal 1968, inflated into 1996 dollars, works out to about $2300 per person. By 1976, just eight years later, real per capita spending had rocketed to nearly $4000, an average annual increase of 7 percent—on top of inflation, on top of population growth. Contrary to what the GDP yardstick might have suggested, however, spending never really declined from that plateau. There was only one year of serious restraint, 1979–80, when real per capita spending fell by 5 percent—but even that decline left spending higher than in any year before 1976. From that subalpine base, spending was ready to begin the assault on Mount Recession. At its all-time peak, in 1985, the federal government was spending more than twice as many real dollars on each citizen, some $4750, as it was in 1968.

As for the revenues, here, too, there was a marked decline after 1975—but 1975 was an exceptional year, when federal revenues were inflated to record levels by the oil boom. There was no prospect of maintaining revenues at such a level, but neither was there any need. A falling tax share in a growing economy can still mean higher revenues overall. Even at their 1980 low point, real per capita federal revenues were higher than they were in any year before 1975, the last year the operating budget balanced. These revenues would have been more than adequate to pay for program spending at pre-1975 levels. In short, there was no revenue shortage. Program spending had already grown nearly 50 percent in real per capita terms from 1968 to 1974. Had it stabilized at what was then an all-time record of around $3400 per person (in constant 1996 dollars)—about where it is today, as it happens—revenues would have exceeded spending in every single year since then.

That the government was unable to exercise even this mild discipline makes the contribution of later events to the debt more or less moot. Without the string of operating deficits that drove the debt skyward in the late 1970s, the high interest rates that arrived at the end of the decade would not have had such explosive impact. Even if we assume that rates would have been no different in the presence of such restraint than in its absence, a constant real per capita spending policy would have been enough to ensure that the overall deficit never exceeded $4 billion in any year. Add another 10 percent to spending to account for the recession, and the deficit would still be less than $8 billion at its peak. The total debt accumulated by 1985 under this scenario would have been less than $50 billion—a quarter of its actual level. The recent history of Canada would have been very different.

From this review of the data it is possible to draw a few preliminary conclusions. The initial social spending buildup, to about 1972 or even 1974, was probably sustainable at historic levels of taxation—provided there was no letup in economic growth. But it left the early Trudeau governments precious little margin for error. The 1974–75 recession pushed spending to new heights that even the most robust revenue stream could not have supported. In subsequent years there was some effort to rein in spending, but not nearly enough; certainly not enough to accommodate the simultaneous relative decline in revenues. The resulting run of operating deficits could not have been more ill-timed, coinciding with the onset of double-digit inflation and even higher interest rates. By the time the second recession hit, the ship of state was already listing badly. It took only one year of flat revenues to tear a hole right through it.

■

Why did spending increase so rapidly? A noteworthy early development, as then auditor general Maxwell Henderson complained some years later, was the abolition of the officer of the Comptroller of the Treasury. Until the late 1960s every expenditure of public funds in all departments of government had to pass through a pre-audit by the comptroller. In its place, it was decided to allow the departments to pre-audit themselves. The result of this experiment, according to Henderson, was nothing less than "disastrous," and it opened the way to the vast expansion in administrative costs that followed.

If the welfare state was largely the work of its predecessors, the Trudeau government gave us the pervasive state. The Trudeau years were marked by a massive expansion in the number and scope of activities within the government's purview. Gordon Osbaldeston, former clerk of the Privy Council, counts a total of 114 agencies, boards, and commissions that the Trudeau government created in its time in office. It established seven whole new departments and twice as many ministries of state. The federal cabinet, which numbered twenty members in 1950, grew to thirty-nine by the time of the last Trudeau ministry. The federal civil service expanded from just over 200, 000 employees in 1968 to 244,000 in 1985. Wages and benefits, which had once tracked neatly with private sector norms, escalated markedly after the mid-1960s. By the early 1970s, total compensation for the average federal employee exceeded that of his private sector counterpart by more than 20 percent.

As much as the government's own spending might have increased, however, it could not compare with the growth in transfers to the provinces, notably for health care, post-secondary education, and social assistance. The Pearson government had established these programs on a shared-cost 50–50 basis with the provinces. But while the federal government footed half of the costs, it was the provinces that decided how much to spend. In effect, Ottawa had surrendered control of a large section of its budget to another level of government, for which the delights of spending 50 cent dollars proved irresistible. It seems clear that no one in federal circles had any idea of what the government was letting itself in for: in 1966 the Pearson cabinet reckoned the combined federal-provincial cost of medicare at about $80 million. The cost today is closer to $60 *billion*.

From 1967 through 1975, figures from the national accounts show federal transfers to provincial and local governments increasing by 10.8 percent per year, after inflation—more than two-and-a-half times the rate of growth in ordinary departmental spending. Alarmed, Ottawa began negotiations with the provinces to limit its contributions, resulting in the 1977 Established Programs Financing Arrangement that governed transfers for health and higher education (it was left to the Conservatives, some years later, to impose similar limits on social assistance, the infamous "cap on CAP"). Henceforth, the federal government would make a fixed per capita contribution to these programs, indexed to the rate of growth in the economy. This agreement restored some predictability to federal finances and slowed real growth in federal-provincial transfers over the next decade to less than one-third its previous rate.

But there was a cost. Not only were the transfers converted to block grants, removing the conditions that had previously been attached, but Ottawa was also prevailed upon to cede more tax "room" to the provinces as part of the deal. Though some limits were placed on the cash component of EPF in later years, the transferred tax points increased in value along with economic growth: a Department of Finance study put the total cost to the federal treasury between 1978 and 1985 at nearly $38 billion, or more than 8 percent of federal revenues. And there were more goodies. The terms of the equalization program were expanded over the years, broadening the definition of a "have-not" province and embracing many more provincial revenue sources in calculations of revenues to be equalized. The provinces were also compensated for revenues lost as a result of tax reforms introduced in 1971. By 1984–85, the value of all federal grants, transfers, equalization payments, and tax points ceded to the provinces totalled $26 billion, equal to one-quarter of all federal spending in that year.

This was, to be sure, in a long tradition of federal concessions to the provinces. Indeed, one of the more striking trends of the Trudeau years, contrary to the myth of centralization and conflict, was the almost continual backpedalling in the face of provincial demands for more money, more power, or, best of all, more of both. The practice of transferring tax room had begun in 1957, with the relaxation of the wartime tax "rental" agreements under which Ottawa had taken over the income-tax field from the provinces. The Pearson government had ceded further tax room to provinces (read: Quebec) that wished to "opt out" of shared-cost social programs. But it was in the early 1970s that a pivotal change was made. Where previously the provinces had been "abated" a share of federal income taxes—a practice that, at least in theory, set a ceiling on the total tax bite—provincial taxes were now simply added on top, as a sort of surcharge on the federal tax. With no limit remaining on the combined tax load, the way was prepared for the rapid expansion of provincial taxes that followed. In 1967 the provinces controlled 40 percent of total government revenues; by 1984 their share had risen to more than 52 percent.

■

Transfers to persons increased almost as fast as transfers to governments—7 percent per year, after inflation, over the entire seventeen-year period. One event in particular stands out here: the 1971 reforms to unemployment insurance, brainchild of employment and immigration minister Bryce Mackasey. No single measure is more redolent of the era: Benefits were increased from 40 percent of earnings to two-thirds; and as little as eight weeks of work was required to be eligible for benefits, which could then be paid out for as much as fifty-one weeks. The program, until then self-financing, was topped up with a huge subsidy out of general revenue to pay for extended benefits in regions of high unemployment. The Mackasey reforms are credited with adding as much as two percentage points to the base rate of non-cyclical unemployment, and, in turn, they substantially raised the cost of the program. From less than $700 million in 1970, UI benefits soared to nearly $1.9 billion in 1972; to $3.8 billion in 1977; to more than $10 billion in 1985. Governments have been slowly pruning the UI program of the Mackasey excesses ever since, but the system of regionally extended benefits remains to this day.

There was more where that came from. The age of eligibility for old age security was progressively reduced from age seventy to age sixty-five. Pensions and family allowances were indexed, then raised further beyond inflation. Even as the deficit mounted to previously unthinkable levels in the late 1970s and early 1980s, the guaranteed income supplement for seniors was increased not once but three times. Yet in the one area of social policy where Trudeau's advisers most hoped to make gains, social assistance, they were stymied, unable to proceed without provincial cooperation. The 1973 social policy review, known as the orange paper, had recommended the creation of a guaranteed annual income for all Canadians, a perennial Liberal goal, to be financed jointly between the federal government and the provinces. The provinces at first seemed interested, but, with the economy turning sour and unemployment on the rise, they baulked, fearing—prophetically—that Ottawa could not be counted on to maintain its share of funding for the program.

No area of program spending grew more rapidly, or with fewer evident attempts to control it, than subsidies to business and other agencies and groups, including Crown corporations. From 1967 to 1975, subsidies and capital assistance combined grew by nearly 17 percent per year, in constant dollar terms; over the entire Trudeau era, they increased fivefold. Much of this money was funnelled through the burgeoning regional development programs, administered through the new Department of Regional Economic Expansion. All sorts of spending programs were created in the name of job creation and community development; Opportunities for Youth and the Local Initiatives Program were two of the more ambitious.

There were grants for native groups, women's groups, and cultural groups. And virtually any interest could find shelter under the secretary of state's broad umbrella, in the name of advancing its participation in Canadian life.

Then there were the Crown corporations, whose claim on the public purse grew continually, until, by 1985, the government was spending more than $6 billion to subsidize its own creations. The Canada Development Corporation, set up in 1971 as a holding company for the government's investments in "strategic" industries, wound up absorbing much of what passed for an aerospace industry in Canada, including such sinkholes as de Havilland (cost to the taxpayer, $400 million) and Canadair ($1.5 billion, most of it in development costs for the Challenger jet). The post office, which became Canada Post Corporation in 1981, cost the taxpayer nearly $1 billion a year in subsidies at its peak. Canadian National Railways was a constant drain on public funds, as was Via Rail, the publicly owned passenger rail service formed in 1978. Housing subsidies, administered through the Canada Mortgage and Housing Corporation and other agencies, proved an especially lucrative source of funds for the construction industry. From next to nothing in 1968, federal expenditures on housing grew to more than $2 billion by 1985.

In later years, Petro-Canada, which opened for business in 1976 as the government's "window" on the oil industry, proved an increasingly costly fiasco. All told, journalist Peter Foster, in *Self-Serve: How Petro-Canada Pumped Canadians Dry*, estimates the cost of PetroCan's adventures to the taxpayer, including the acquisitions of Atlantic Richfield, Pacific Petroleum, and Petrofina, at about $14 billion. Nothing so addled government senses in the mid-to-late 1970s as oil, and the gusher of royalties that was expected to flow from the relentless rise in international oil prices. In the early days there were oil import subsidies, meant to spare Canadian business the full impact of the oil price explosion; later there were oil exploration grants, notably the Petroleum Incentive Payments introduced under the 1980 National Energy Program, intended to make Canada self-sufficient in oil. "Canadianization" of the oil patch became a top government priority in the early 1980s—just in time for oil prices to crash. Dome Petroleum's debt-fuelled buying spree and subsequent bailout left the taxpayer on the hook for hundreds of millions of dollars.

The merits of such corporate welfare may be doubted, but at least they had some public policy rationale, however contentious. Not so for what grew to be far and away the largest single federal budget item, and the fastest growing: interest on the public debt. From $1.3 billion in 1967–68, public debt charges grew to an incredible $22.5 billion in 1984–85. Interest costs now accounted for more than one-fifth of all spending. That left less and less room for spending on social programs. Ottawa was now spending more on interest than it was on health, education, social assistance, and unemployment insurance combined. Small wonder that the Trudeau team's more ambitious social policy plans were set aside.

No doubt the astronomic interest rates of the late 1970s and early 1980s contributed mightily to the rise in public debt charges, but they cannot be considered as wholly independent events. Interest rates rose as creditors strove to protect their returns from the effects of rising inflation. Double-digit inflation was in turn driven by excess money creation on the part of the Bank of Canada. And how did the bank come to pour so much money into the economy? Through the purchase of large amounts of Canada bonds, to help the government finance its enormous deficits. The direction of causality is clear: federal deficits were more the cause of higher interest rates than the reverse.

■

The oddity is that Trudeau came to power preaching fiscal restraint. The promise of a Just Society did not come with much in the way of concrete commitments, or none that would upset the Liberals' 1968 campaign promise to balance the budget. Trudeau himself seemed to consider his main task in the early years to be one of lowering public expectations of the welfare state, after the uncontrolled expansion of the Pearson years. "We are not promising things for everybody and we are not seeing great visions," he insisted. The throne speech that first year lectured Canadians on the reality that "government spending . . . cannot increase faster than productivity if we wish to restrain the increase in levels of taxation."

But the means chosen for rationalizing government operations, a series of elaborate planning exercises yielding ever more complex management structures, seemed only to expand the supply of government services. Similarly, the strategy for impressing on the public the limits of the state, providing interest groups with public funds in hopes of co-opting them into the process, instead simply stimulated the demand. After the near-defeat at the polls in 1972, widely blamed on the philosopher king's aloof and professorial style of governing, the Liberals abandoned any pretence at rationalizing public expenditures. Whether this was the price of the NDP support for his minority government, or a reflection of the divisions and uncertainty brought on by the first oil crisis, the result was that neither Trudeau nor his ministers seemed concerned after 1972 with the state of the government's finances.

As in other respects, Trudeau the prime minister diverged markedly from Trudeau the thinker. By the time he went to Ottawa, Trudeau had put aside the socialist convictions of his youth. He was, it is true, something of a policy magpie, as susceptible to persuasion by a neoclassical economist like Albert Breton as by the broad interventions prescribed by J.K. Galbraith. But he was never an enthusiastic proponent of higher debt for its own sake. Nor was he entirely uninterested in economics, as legend has it. The more likely explanation is that balancing the books did not strike him as a priority. Through the 1970s, the country's debts were at historically low levels, relative to GDP. There were many other pressing issues to address: The country was fracturing as never before under the combined strains of separatism and economic dislocation, and politics, as he learned after that disastrous first term, required a certain realism. Public spending, like patronage, had its uses. The cost could be counted later.

To be sure, each year's budget was marked by the usual rhetoric of restraint. "We must do all we can to restrain the growth of governmental expenditures," Finance Minister John Turner told the House of Commons in November 1974, as he introduced a budget that would increase spending 20 percent. "We are now seeing the solid results of our commitment to get government expenditure growth below the growth rate of GDP," his successor, Donald Macdonald, announced in March 1977. But spending was still rising: 10 percent in that year alone. It had acquired a momentum of its own, as all of those new departments and agencies sought to justify their existence. And it even prompted Trudeau, in another of his about-faces, to make his most celebrated venture into the field of public finance: the sudden, and unilateral, decision in August 1978 to cut $2.5 billion out of spending—allegedly after being scolded for his government's profligacy by German chancellor Helmut Schmidt at an economic summit. Too little, perhaps, but certainly too late.

■

Whatever restraint was exercised on the spending side was more than offset in later years by the steady erosion of the tax base: yet another retreat, given efforts at tax reform under Trudeau's first finance minister, Edgar Benson. A much-quoted article by two Statistics Canada researchers explained the increase in deficits after 1975 as arising "more from a shortfall of revenues than higher spending."

The most significant early measure was the 1973 indexation of the personal income tax system, where both personal exemptions and tax brackets were adjusted each year to keep pace with increases in the consumer price index. By and large, this was good public policy: Failure to index the system had exposed taxpayers to "bracket creep" as inflation mounted in the late 1960s and early 1970s. In effect, indexation allowed the government to raise taxes without seeking parliament's authority. Yet if indexation was a praiseworthy move, it was no less costly: a Finance Department study put the revenue loss in 1979 alone at $6 billion, or about one-third of personal income tax revenues in that year.

Other tax measures introduced around the same time included the three personal income tax cuts enacted from 1973 through 1975, increases in personal and employment expense deductions, the $1000 interest income deduction, and the investment tax credit. Then there was the $1000 deduction for pension income, the radical expansion of the Registered Retirement Savings Plan program in 1972, and the Registered Home Ownership Savings Plan. Most important of all was the 1978 Child Tax Credit, providing parents with a basic payment of $200 per child per year. If not quite a guaranteed annual income, it had much in it that resembled its close relative, the negative income tax: the benefit was delivered through the tax system, a first in Canada, and varied with family income. It was much in keeping with the bureaucratic preference for the "building blocks" approach to income security over a full-blown guaranteed annual income. Just as the Guaranteed Income Supplement added an income-tested boost to the universal Old Age Security program, the child tax credit now did the same for family allowances. (In recent years, these two-headed programs have been rationalized into, respectively, the Seniors' Benefit and the Child Tax Benefit).

On the corporate side, successive finance ministers introduced ever more generous and complex tax preferences as the 1970s wore on in a desperate and largely fruitless bid to prop up economic growth. Manufacturers, in particular, benefited from a series of measures, including accelerated depreciation, a reduction in the basic tax rate, and inventory writeoffs. In addition, the federal sales tax, which applied only to manufacturers, was reduced from 12 percent to 9 percent in 1978. Resource producers, though saddled with hefty export taxes and royalties under the National Energy Program, also benefited from their own investment tax credits, writeoffs, and exemptions. The high-tech sector was the intended beneficiary of the Scientific Research Tax Credit, though by the time the program was suspended, its exorbitant costs—$2.8 billion in foregone revenues, as of 1984—left no doubt that it had been widely abused.

All told, discretionary tax measures, personal and corporate, are estimated to have reduced federal revenues by as much as $14 billion in 1979—or about $2 billion more than the federal deficit in that year. In 1981 the famous "MacEachen budget" attempted to close many of these tax preferences, to the dismay of the business community. Allan MacEachen proposed some 150 new tax measures, with a view to boosting federal revenues by $3.4 billion over two years. Perhaps the messenger lacked credibility one year after the NEP tax grab, but the budget was a public-relations disaster and was largely withdrawn. With that the government more or less gave up the fight against the deficit. It is not too much to say that, by the early 1980s, federal finances were simply out of control. Marc Lalonde, the last of Trudeau's finance ministers, abandoned even the rhetoric of restraint. The deficit, he said in 1984, "has provided considerable support to the welfare of individual Canadians and the promotion of economic activity," though he allowed that "deficits must be reduced as investment recovers and the economy expands." Easier said than done.

Trudeau himself remains remarkably unmoved by the carnage he left behind. In his *Memoirs*, he does not defend his governments' fiscal record, but merely notes that in the context of the performance of "the economy in general," he can look back on his legacy "without shame."

■

What do we conclude from all this? It would certainly be untrue to say that social spending, on its own, was responsible for the massive debts the federal government incurred during the Trudeau years. Though the social envelope, broadly defined (transfers for health, education, old age security, family allowances, and unemployment insurance, plus federal housing and labour market programs), expanded in that time from 44 percent of program spending to 51 percent, even that rate of increase would not have strained federal revenues unduly. What was not possible was to finance this amount of social spending in addition to the almost-as-rapid growth in the rest of the federal budget, including internal departmental spending and subsidies to business and other groups. Had these expenditures been held constant in real per capita terms throughout this period—

that is, at 1968 levels, plus inflation and population growth—total program spending in 1984–85 would have been about $20 billion less than it was: enough to keep the budget in balance on an operating basis. There would have been no less social spending, and no more revenues, than was actually the case.

It is perhaps too easy to say that transfers to the provinces should not have been allowed to grow so quickly: They were, after all, subject to multi-year federal-provincial agreements, and they could not easily or quickly be altered. Similarly, increases in transfers to persons might be put down, at least in part, to demographic or economic trends. But the remainder of program spending was entirely and unambiguously within the federal government's power to control. Any increases here were purely discretionary. If the government's own spending had been more closely restrained, then program spending as a whole would not have been excessive. And, as we have seen, if spending itself had been kept on a sustainable path, neither the relative decline in revenues nor even the rise in interest rates would have had much impact.

Whatever might have been is of no consequence to history, and it could not have spared social programs from the remorseless arithmetic of compound interest. Whether or not social spending was part of the debt problem, it became of necessity part of the solution. If the deficit had to be reduced (and it did) and if spending cuts were required (and they were), it was hardly realistic to mark over one-half of the budget as off-limits. Perhaps spending in other areas, outside the social envelope, should not have been allowed to grow so quickly, but having done so, it was difficult to undo. By 1984–85 the deficit had grown to exceed spending on all other federal programs, excluding transfers: The entire government apparatus could have been shut down, everyone laid off, and still the debt would have continued to grow. To make real progress against the deficit, social programs would have to come under the knife.

This is one of the many ironies of the Trudeau years. The federalist who believed in a strong central government left it cruelly weakened at the end. The nationalist who wished to preserve Canada's independence left it utterly dependent on foreign capital.

The social democrat who wanted to expand the welfare state instead left social programs to be consumed by the debt.

Canada is certainly a more just society than it was when Trudeau made his pledge: there is less poverty; more students go on to higher education; and medical insurance is universal. But, thirty years and a half trillion dollars in debt later, the promise is unfulfilled.

Maverick
without a Cause:
Trudeau and Taxes

■

LINDA McQUAIG

Linda McQuaig has written widely on politics, economics, and the financial dealings of Canada's establishment. Her investigative reporting in the Globe and Mail *drew public attention to scandals and injustices in the Canadian tax system during the Trudeau years, and her subsequent book,* Behind Closed Doors, *examined how the business community was able to enrich itself by winning tax concessions from the Trudeau and Mulroney governments. She has also investigated the story behind the deficit in* Shooting the Hippo, *and her most recent book,* The Cult of Impotence, *refutes the notion that governments are powerless in the global economy to deliver full employment and well-funded social programs.*

O N A COOL OTTAWA EVENING in November 1981 the
finance minister rose in the House of Commons to deliver his budget speech, strangely unsuspecting the
political storm that lay ahead. His naiveté was surprising; if anyone
understood politics, it was Allan MacEachen. After serving twenty-
four years in parliament, including an effective stint as government
house leader, MacEachen's antennae for political trouble and his
knack for steering the Liberals into safe waters had become legendary. This ability had clearly helped him win the respect and trust
of Pierre Elliott Trudeau—something not many anglophone politicians ever succeeded in doing. Trudeau had signalled that respect
by appointing the shy Cape Bretonner to the powerful Finance
portfolio, as well as elevating him to deputy prime minister. Indeed,
Trudeau seemed to be grooming MacEachen to be his successor.
But the hopes that MacEachen had harboured along those lines
came to an end that evening when he presented what quickly became the most fiercely attacked budget of the past two decades.

MacEachen's budget was a bold assault on the tax privileges of
the well-to-do, who wasted little time rallying their forces against
it. In the days and weeks that followed, he was continually besieged
by powerful members of the business and financial communities and
their allies in the press, particularly the *Globe and Mail* editorial board.
The daily parliamentary Question Period turned into a barrage of

*I would like to thank Neil Brooks, Charlotte Montgomery, and Thomas
Walkom for their insights on this subject.*

criticism against the budget. And MacEachen, who had saved the political hides of many of his Liberal colleagues, found himself for the most part facing the barrage alone, with surprisingly little support from his cabinet colleagues. "It was remarkable how they ran for cover," MacEachen later recalled. "It was not a marked example of political courage."

The events surrounding that November 1981 budget shed some light on aspects of Trudeau, as a person and as a politician. Despite the intensity and relentlessness of the attacks, MacEachen maintains that Trudeau never pressured him to back down from the controversial budget measures or to leave the finance portfolio. After ten months under siege, MacEachen himself requested to be moved, and Trudeau eased him into the more comfortable and prestigious post of external affairs minister, where he retained his position as deputy prime minister. When MacEachen retired three years later, Trudeau appointed him to the Senate. Although Trudeau continued to bestow privileges and honours on his trusted colleague, he failed to come to MacEachen's aid when his finance minister most needed it—when he was being pummelled day after day over the 1981 budget. As MacEachen learned, there were limits to Trudeau's loyalty.

Perhaps what is most interesting about the whole fiasco—and what it tells us in retrospect about Trudeau—is that such a radical budget ever saw the light of day. For that matter, it is revealing that Trudeau ever entrusted the highly sensitive finance portfolio to MacEachen, a left-leaning reformer who championed social legislation and never abandoned the radical Catholicism he had been immersed in as a youth in poverty-stricken Cape Breton. The 1981 budget, which became a huge source of antagonism between business and the Trudeau government, was the logical extension of MacEachen's lifelong commitment to greater social equity.

What Trudeau's appointment of MacEachen reveals more than anything was Trudeau's independence from—even slight indifference to—the enormously powerful business and financial élite. In the administrations that have followed, we have seen no such independence. Indeed, we have witnessed an almost total adherence to Bay Street orthodoxy on economic and financial matters. The

Trudeau régime was the last Canadian government that, when it came to economics and finance, was at least unpredictable.

While tax policy in the Trudeau years may seem like an obscure area to explore, in fact, it offers an interesting window for an assessment of Trudeau, his economic ideas, and his relationship with powerful corporate interests. There are, of course, many areas of concern to the business élite, but few approach tax policy in importance. The desire of corporations to reduce their tax burden or shift it onto other segments of society is intense. So governments find themselves under constant pressure to shape tax policy in ways that will benefit some of the most powerful interests in the country.

■

What is striking about tax policy in the Trudeau years is how widely divergent it was—a bizarre mixture of slavish kowtowing to Bay Street's demands and bold and innovative reforms that would be unthinkable as government policy proposals today. Essentially, it reflected Trudeau's lack of strict adherence to a clear economic philosophy as well as his ambivalent attitude towards the nation's economic élite. As a crafty politician, Trudeau knew that powerful members of the establishment could not be ignored, but he also had little real interest in catering to them. The result was an era in which the élite was generally able to get its way when it protested with sufficient force, but its hegemony was far less seamless and certain than it often seems to be in the 1990s.

Perhaps what most distinguished Trudeau from his successors on economic issues was his unwillingness to focus his political energies on delivering the agenda of the élite. Brian Mulroney's career in business and politics was built around delivering what was wanted by his powerful employers and financial backers, both inside and outside the country. Jean Chrétien, ostensibly more populist while in opposition and on the campaign trail, has done an about-face in office, redirecting his attention towards satisfying the élite's demands for deep spending cuts and deficit reduction, and cosying up to business with his Team Canada missions.

It is hard to imagine Trudeau compromising his style or his interests to cater to the corporate élite. When their interests coincided—such as their mutual desire to derail Québécois aspirations for independence—Trudeau and the élite got on well, and he generally produced the results the élite desired. But in areas such as tax policy, which were of little interest to him but of enormous concern to members of the élite, Trudeau's performance was unreliable and, from their point of view, reckless.

Trudeau's distance from the business community should not be mistaken for any deep commitment to social justice or the common people. Trudeau came from a privileged background, and he went on to receive a grounding in free market economics at Harvard. He flirted with socialist ideas in the 1950s, partly due to the influence of left-leaning intellectuals like McGill law professor Frank Scott (who was also national president of the Co-operative Commonwealth Federation) and philosophy professor Charles Taylor. In his writings for *Cité libre* later in that decade, Trudeau argued that capitalism "exploits the worker" and that the "proletarian condition" of workers prevented Quebec from being "a society of equals." But by the early 1960s, he had begun to distance himself from such anti-capitalist ideas. Increasingly concerned with resisting Quebec separatism, he had become disdainful of the left-leaning intellectuals in the separatist movement. His economic ideas, returning to their Harvard roots and freshly influenced by Quebec free-market economist Albert Breton, became more focused on how to increase the size of the economic pie than on how to divide it.

By the time Trudeau became prime minister in 1968, his earlier economic radicalism had largely disappeared, and his interests were clearly directed towards constitutional and national unity issues. To the extent that he turned his attention to economics, it was now a more mainstream kind of market economics. But Trudeau was not particularly dogmatic about his economic views, nor did he regard a strict adherence to free market ideology as an essential quality in someone who was to be entrusted with supervising the economy. Some of the key individuals Trudeau appointed to high-level economic posts were, like MacEachen, outside the Bay Street mould and foreign to its way of thinking.

It is important to note that the mood of the times was very different than it is today. The orthodoxy of market economics—sometimes referred to as neoliberalism—was not nearly so entrenched or pervasive in the United States, Britain, or Canada as it was to become later in the 1980s and throughout the 1990s. There was a more open and balanced public debate on all economic issues, and the notion that there was no alternative to strict market orthodoxy had not yet taken root. This greater openness to economic debate was partly reflected in the Department of Finance. Although it has since become a bastion of free-market ideology, the department that was in place when Trudeau became prime minister subscribed to the notion that government had a key role to play in the management of the economy. Under deputy minister Robert Bryce, the department epitomized the strong, independent civil service that had developed during and after the Second World War. Bryce had studied under John Maynard Keynes in England in the 1930s and was committed to a strong role for government in regulating the marketplace. The department treated the financial community as just one of the interest groups—albeit an important and powerful one—it had to deal with in shaping the nation's economic policy.

So Trudeau's independence from Bay Street reflected both the greater openness of the times and the kind of advice he received from the finance department of the day. But it also reflected something about Trudeau himself—his independent-mindedness, his intellectual intensity, and his aloofness. Trudeau never really understood business leaders. He was not one of them, he didn't think like them, and he didn't relate to their old-boy camaraderie. He didn't even understand their antipathy towards him or the trouble they could create for him. They just weren't the kind of people he knew how to deal with. He was far more comfortable with people like MacEachen. Even if MacEachen's political goals were different from Trudeau's, the two men were both intensely intellectual and extremely private.

As prime minister, Trudeau was not involved in the intricate details of tax laws, but his choice of individuals to oversee the broad thrust of tax policy reflects his own thinking and the importance (or lack of importance) he attached to satisfying Bay Street interests. Trudeau's ambivalence on economic matters and his somewhat distant relationship with the financial community is reflected in his wide-ranging selection of finance ministers and deputy finance ministers. His finance ministers included such opposites as corporate lawyer John Turner, who had close relations with the business community, and MacEachen, who had virtually no connection to Bay Street and little interest in the values and goals of business leaders. Similarly, deputy finance ministers in the Trudeau years included Mickey Cohen, a corporate tax lawyer who was keen to make the tax system more to Bay Street's liking, and Ian Stewart, a distinguished economist from within the civil service who had a strong taste for economic theory and social justice.

It is not surprising that tax policy in the Trudeau years was somewhat incoherent. The whole issue of taxation was not one that had occupied Trudeau's attention, yet, as soon as he became prime minister, he was confronted with a huge problem on the tax front which he inherited from previous administrations. The Diefenbaker government had appointed the Royal Commission on Taxation in 1962 as a way of placating the financial community, which was constantly complaining of being overtaxed. The commission, headed by Bay Street accountant Kenneth Carter, had surprised everyone by producing a report that focused on the need to reform the tax system by removing special privileges, including the exemption of capital gains from taxation. The result would have been sharply higher taxes on the rich—exactly the opposite of what the business community had had in mind. Prominent members of the business and financial establishment loudly attacked the Carter report. The Liberal government of Lester Pearson, which was in power when the report was released in 1967, tried to dodge the issue and passed it on to the Trudeau government unresolved.

The finance department had hired conservative accountant Jim Brown to help it find some common ground between the solutions advocated in the report and those desired by the business community. Brown's distinctly Bay Street influence was countered, however, by that of Bryce. The result was a mixture: the department produced a white paper on tax reform in 1969 which, while generally not going as far as the Carter report, recommended reforms along the same line. In one of its proposals, the white paper actually went farther than anything Carter had recommended. This radical proposal—which had been the brainchild of Bryce and had been opposed by Brown—called for what amounted to a wealth tax, an obligatory evaluation of unrealized capital gains every five years for the purposes of taxation.

A furious financial community unleashed a torrent of abuse on the white paper proposals. This reaction put enormous pressure on Trudeau's first finance minister, Edgar Benson, an accountant who had previously taught commerce at Queen's University and been supportive of the thrust of the Carter report. But the established voices of business and finance found their most effective venue for protest at the Senate Banking Committee. The committee's thirty-three members, who held a total of 211 corporate directorships among them, were like a subcommittee of the Canadian establishment, and they welcomed harsh words against the white paper proposals—indeed, they encouraged presenters to be even harsher in their criticism. For months, leading Canadian business figures voiced their protests before the committee, arguing that the reforms would destroy much of the Canadian way of life, including even the sport of hockey. In the end, the government introduced legislation that retreated from the white paper proposals, which were themselves a retreat from the bold Carter plan.

Nevertheless, the new tax legislation did eliminate many loopholes and was regarded in business circles as being tough. The combination of the Benson white paper and the tax reform legislation created deep concerns among key establishment figures about the thinking in the upper levels of the Trudeau government. These concerns prompted a small group of powerful CEOs, including Noranda president Alfred Powis and Imperial Oil president W.O. Twaits, to write a letter to Trudeau in 1972 outlining some issues, including taxation and competition policy, on which they felt strongly. Trudeau responded by inviting the group to Ottawa to meet with him. When the meeting went well, the group was invited back for several more encounters. This response inspired Powis and Twaits to develop the group into a formal organization of top CEOs—the Business Council on National Issues. The creation of this sophisticated new lobbying machine for big business had been largely prompted by concerns within the corporate community that Trudeau couldn't be trusted on key economic matters such as taxation.

After the difficult experience with tax reform in the early 1970s, Trudeau adopted a more conciliatory approach towards business with his appointment of John Turner as finance minister. Under Turner (and later under Donald Macdonald and Jean Chrétien), the finance department became much more responsive to the demands of business. Turner's budgets introduced many generous new corporate tax writeoffs and indexed the entire tax system to the cost of living, so that individuals would not automatically be bumped into a higher tax bracket as their incomes rose with inflation. With Mickey Cohen now the assistant deputy minister for tax policy, the Trudeau government became highly accommodating to the demands of business on the tax front. Cohen's approach was to create "breathing space" so that high-income taxpayers weren't tempted to try to evade the rules of a tight tax system. The result was a tremendous loosening up of the tax laws. Corporations and the well-to-do were able to win back many of the tax concessions that they had lost in the 1971 legislation, as well as many new breaks.

Ironically, it was these huge tax reductions in the the Turner budgets of the mid-1970s that laid the foundation for the federal deficit problems of later years. It is worth taking a minute to elaborate on this point, since it goes against conventional wisdom and has implications for a key aspect of the Trudeau legacy. According to the common view, hefty increases in spending on social programs by the Trudeau government led to the burgeoning deficits of the later Trudeau years. In fact, there was little increase in the size and scope of social programs after the early 1970s. As Irwin Gillespie, an economist at Carleton University, notes in *Unnecessary*

Debts: "The growth in government spending was never more than a minor contributor to increasing deficits . . . The primary cause of the increase in deficit financing since the mid-1970s was the decline in total tax revenues, relative to the size of the economy." Gillespie points in particular to the corporate tax reductions of budgets in the mid to late 1970s. He quotes Turner to show that the finance minister clearly understood that his corporate tax cuts would deprive the country of revenue: "This radical revision of the corporate tax system as it affects manufacturing and processors will require us to forego revenue."

This erosion of the tax base was later to have major consequences for the deficit. As Osgoode Hall law professor Neil Brooks has shown, if the Trudeau government had simply maintained the level of taxation it had in 1974, the deficit would have been only about half the size it became by the early 1980s. Brooks has also made the provocative point that, if Ottawa had imposed the same level of taxation that the European countries had imposed during the 1980s, Canada wouldn't have had a deficit problem at all in those years. Rather, we would have been generating large surpluses.

Thus, the deficit problems of the 1980s are correctly identified in popular lore as the heritage of the Trudeau government, but they are often incorrectly attributed to its spending rather than to its tax policies. (The other key factor was the Bank of Canada's high interest rates, which greatly increased the government's borrowing costs in the early 1980s and drove up unemployment, thereby further reducing the tax base.) Certainly, Trudeau's tax giveaways are one of the main deficit culprits. If he infuriated the business community with his bold tax-the-rich schemes at one point, he lavished tax favours on them at another.

By the early 1980s, the rich were about to take another hit from the Trudeau government with MacEachen's 1981 budget. The intensity of the business community's response on the tax front in the early 1970s should have impressed on Trudeau the dangers of tampering with the tax privileges of the well-to-do. But, preoccupied with constitutional issues, he apparently was not paying close attention. In appointing MacEachen as finance minister and Stewart as his deputy, Trudeau was clearly not catering to the business élite. Undoubtedly, he felt he was handing the key management functions of the economy to a highly adept team. Both MacEachen and Stewart were extremely clever men with graduate training in economics from major US universities. Their economic ideas, however, turned out to be radically different from those favoured by Bay Street.

MacEachen's controversial 1981 budget—built on the principles of simplicity and fairness that were the hallmarks of the Carter report—had a strong intellectual basis and the potential to be greatly admired. In some ways, it set out to correct the growing deficit problem that Turner had knowingly created by allowing tax breaks to drain revenue from government coffers. A document published by the finance department in April 1980 had shown that tax breaks introduced in Liberal budgets throughout the 1970s reduced corporate, personal, and sales tax revenue by more than $14 billion a year by the end of that decade. It was easy to see how the country was sinking dangerously into debt.

But the unfairness of the tax system was the prime factor motivating MacEachen and Stewart. The benefits of tax breaks were heavily skewed towards high-income Canadians, making a mockery of the supposed progressivity of the tax system. Highlighting this unfairness promised to make the budget saleable to the wider Canadian public. To this end, Stewart had the department draw up a provocative document that spelled out the amount of tax break benefits that were going to those in higher income brackets. It showed, for instance, how low-income Canadians saved an average of $771 a year in tax breaks, while those in the top income group were saving an average of $46,000 a year. The document noted that if all tax breaks were eliminated, there would be sufficient revenue to cut tax rates virtually in half. The document was released along with the budget, and its startling contents were expected to make the budget a hit with most Canadians. But the public never got the message: the media ignored it.

MacEachen's failure to go out and sell the budget to the broader public meant that he had nothing to counteract the enormous outpouring of anger from the influential and outspoken Canadians who were losing their tax breaks. With Trudeau leaving Mac-Eachen to deal with the aggrieved parties on his own, MacEachen felt he had little choice but to retreat, which he did. Ironically, the principle that the removal of tax breaks could result in lower overall rates was introduced, but only for the rich. The budget had reduced the top marginal rate from 65 to 50 percent, in order to provide the rich with partial compensation for the loss of their tax privileges. After those privileges were restored, the rich once again had their old tax breaks, but also now enjoyed a lower marginal tax rate.

Given this sort of result, it is perhaps odd to look back on the handling of tax policy in the Trudeau years as anything other than a disaster, which in many ways it was. By creating so many loopholes in the tax system, the Trudeau government contributed to its inequities, as well as to the growth of the deficit in the late 1970s and early 1980s.

Still, what distinguishes the tax policy of the Trudeau years was its relative independence. Trudeau was surprisingly unsolicitous of the view of business leaders on contentious tax issues. And the finance department operated with some distance from the financial community and from free-market orthodoxy. Values and ideas other than those found on Bay Street sometimes influenced policy.

This *could have* made a significant difference. If Trudeau had coupled this independent spirit with some political conviction to implement the bold reforms put forward by his administration, we might well have ended up with a fairer distribution of resources and healthier public finances. Sadly, however, this wasn't the case. The daring initiatives that occasionally came out of the Trudeau government in the area of tax policy were almost always followed by a massive retreat. In Trudeau, we had a prime minister with a refreshing degree of independence from Bay Street, but little inclination to use that independence to champion the economic interests of ordinary Canadians.

Trudeau and the Canadian Charter of Rights and Freedoms: A Question of Constitutional Maturation

■

LORRAINE EISENSTAT
WEINRIB

Lorraine E. Weinrib, a law professor at the University of Toronto, has appeared for Ontario in a number of Charter cases, including the major case on the notwithstanding clause in the Supreme Court. She has had a number of conversations with Pierre Trudeau on the political developments that led to the adoption of the Charter in its final form as well as its interpretation in light of those developments. She is currently writing a book on the institutional and conceptual coherence of the Charter and its role as a model for rights-protection in other countries.

I have always wished to ensure myself that the changes would be for the best and not for the worst . . . [C]onstitutions are made for men and not men for constitutions. However, one tends to forget that constitutions must also be made *by* men and not by force of brutal circumstance or blind disorder. In this arena, more than any other, one must know where a policy leads.

The state, whether provincial, federal, or perhaps later supra-national, must seek the general welfare of all its citizens regardless of sex, colour, race, religious beliefs, or ethnic origin.

– Trudeau, *Federalism and the French Canadians*, 1968

T HE ADOPTION of the Canadian Charter of Rights and Freedoms is Pierre Elliott Trudeau's greatest political achievement and his most important political legacy. Overcoming obstacles that had baffled his predecessors, Trudeau secured a constitutional change that offered the tantalizing possibility of a new type of national self-understanding. Rather than an evocation of shared blood and history, which could only invite discord in a land of aboriginal peoples, colonial conquest, and increasingly diverse immigration, the Charter bound a pluralistic and far-flung population into a nation of free and equal rights-bearing citizens.

I would like to thank Jonathan Ptak for valuable research assistance.

Given Trudeau's crystallized ideas before he entered national politics in 1965, his constitutional achievement is not surprising. He had been preoccupied with the relationship between the individual and the state all his adult life. He did not, however, enter politics to reform the Constitution. He believed there was no constitutional impediment to moving forward on the pressing political issues of the day, including the Quebec agenda. Unlike many of his contemporaries, he reasoned that it was premature to make changes to Canada's fundamental constitutional arrangements just as Quebec was embarking on a long-delayed process of modernization. "Before sitting down to rewrite the constitution," he wrote in *Maclean's* in 1964, "one must have some idea of what kind of society it is intended to govern." Otherwise, one could expect endless negotiation to meet ever-changing demands. In this prediction, Trudeau the politician proved Trudeau the theorist correct.

A constitutional bill of rights was the one exception to Trudeau's distaste for constitutional change. He thought that the sustained debate on the subject during the previous decades, the inadequacy of rights protection under the existing Constitution, and the adoption of statutory bills of rights in the provinces provided a sufficient basis on which to proceed. Moreover, the provision of constitutional protection for language and educational rights, as well as for other basic liberties, would undercut growing French-Canadian nationalism in Quebec by releasing French Canadians from their notional Quebec "ghetto." A bill of rights would fulfil one goal of the original Canadian Constitution—to allow all its citizens to "consider the whole of Canada their country and field of endeavour." Although securing a constitutional bill of rights was not Trudeau's reason for entering politics, it was a congenial prospect once constitutional change became unavoidable.

■

Trudeau's political ideas about rights took shape in academic study filtered through experience. Quebec premier Maurice Duplessis presided over an authoritarian, corrupt, and nationalist régime that held the province back from general postwar development. The government sacrificed the rule of law to political ends, denied freedom of speech to critics and non-conformists, denied freedom of association to those battling for economic rights against big business, and denied religious freedom to Jehovah's Witnesses. The Roman Catholic Church wielded extensive authority, maintaining the social order and controlling education. When he left Quebec to study and travel, Trudeau set out to reflect upon and experience other cultures, ways of thinking, and modes of governance. His political views meant he would get no academic employment in Quebec as long as Duplessis was in power. This misfortune, combined with his family wealth, gave Trudeau time to write and work as an activist lawyer in the fields of human rights and labour law. By the time he moved into public life, after a short period as a law professor, he had clearly articulated his political thought and honed his considerable analytic and polemical skills.

Duplessis' Quebec provided the perfect environment for creating an obsession with liberal democracy. Trudeau came to support the values of individual freedom and self-fulfilment and to champion a comprehensive world-view free of state-imposed nationalist, religious, or ideological preferences. His emphasis on individual freedom merged with an attention to cultural identity, an opposition to nationalism, and a defence of federalism—all elements of his later constitutional politics.

Trudeau considered nationalism the enemy of individual freedom and material well-being. Coming of age in the postwar world, he knew the role that nationalism had recently played in wide-ranging wars, collective hatreds, and unsurpassed atrocities. Even without these excesses, nationalism tended to xenophobia and closed-minded solidarity, thereby preventing any beneficial cross-fertilization among cultures and languages.

Trudeau's championing of individual liberty, however, did not lead him to the position that political theorists would later denigrate as "atomism," where the individual is considered independent of society and culture. Although he opposed state-engendered nationalism, he valued cultural identity, and he regarded the protection of language as a means of assuring its continuity. He thought that the state should protect cultural values, so long as it did so "as a natural consequence of the equality of all citizens, not as a special privilege of the largest group." This distinctiveness would countermand the tendency of modern technology and systems of communication to create homogeneous consumers. To Trudeau, a secure and confident cultural identity was as necessary as individual freedom to the flourishing of the individual, the group, and society at large.

Trudeau admired the federal state as an antidote to nationalism. By dividing authority among one central and several regional governments, democratic federalism required compromise among countervailing visions, powers, and priorities. A larger and ethnically more heterogenous political unit would avoid the tendency to chauvinism and intolerance in the unitary nation-state. Citizens would have choices and potential mobility. Moreover, by accommodating the pluralist, multicultural societies of the postwar world, federalism would facilitate the developing patterns of interstate cooperation. Trudeau's vision was not so much anti-nationalist as multinationalist.

He regarded the federal structure, with its allocation of economic powers to the central government, and social and cultural matters to the provincial governments, as appropriate for Canada's intractable half-continent. He particularly admired the practice of equalizing the spending power of provinces—to standardize economic opportunity and well-being across the country. The protection of institutional bilingualism at the federal level and in Quebec acknowledged the full and equal citizenship of those speaking the minority language. The minority language education rights, which he understood were embodied in the protection of dissenting religious schools, assured the intergenerational transmission of both language and culture.

Trudeau was well aware of the growing discontent with the federal system in Quebec, but he thought the critics were laying their complaints at the wrong door. The system afforded Quebec the freedom and the opportunity to develop itself. Sovereign status, in a world of emerging trade alliances, would not offer more. The logic of the nationalist position seemed absurd, first, because its claims to self-determination denied the parallel claims of minorities within the province and, second, because the geographic definition of the nation-state ignored French Canadians outside the province.

Trudeau found fault with three features of the Canadian federal system as it had evolved. Its tendency to consider Quebec as the home for French Canadians produced a ghetto mentality in that province, a general sense of Anglo-Canadian superiority, and an erosion of the French-Canadian presence in other parts of the country. Moreover, the underrepresentation of Quebec in the central administration and the dominance of English meant that French Canadians could not be "at home" in their central government. Finally, the tendency to homogenize everyone into a melting pot of Anglo-Canadian nationalism had the effects of relegating French Canadians to their province and stimulating Quebec nationalism as a counter-force.

The maturation of the Canadian constitutional system might be advanced, Trudeau argued, through adoption of a bill of rights. Such a bill would bolster democracy, individual liberty, and equality. It would also secure minority language rights so that all Canadians, and French Canadians in particular, could engage at both the provincial and the national level throughout the country and have confidence that their children would be educated anywhere in Canada in their own language and cultural heritage. A bill of rights would provide a stable basis, in terms of democratic function as well as individual liberty and identity, to think about other changes.

A constitutional bill of rights would also, he thought, have benign institutional effects. The existing constitutional system burdened the Supreme Court with political responsibilities because it was judging legislation without being restricted by the norms of public law that a constitutional bill of rights would provide. These norms, far from throttling provincial autonomy, would, he argued in "Comparative Federalism" in 1963, allow the provinces to "exercise their autonomy with all the more freedom, since this freedom would come within certain civilizing and democratic standards." The idea that freedom for political institutions consists not in a lack of constraint but in a conformity to normative standards echoes Trudeau's personal experience under Duplessis and fore-shadows his later debates with the opponents of the Charter about judicial and legislative roles.

■

In his early political career, Trudeau demonstrated his ability to carry controversial projects by clearly communicating the importance of the liberal values at stake. It is said that Paul Martin Sr. advised rookie members of parliament to avoid the issues of homosexuality, birth control, abortion and divorce. If he gave that advice to Pierre Trudeau, it must have raised the new recruit's penchant for contrariness—for his agenda for law reform included every one of these forbidden categories. As minister of justice, he introduced legislation permitting therapeutic abortions, legalizing adult consensual homosexual acts, legalizing the dissemination of birth control materials and contraceptive information, and introducing judicial divorce based on a range of fault and no-fault grounds. These statutory reforms effected advances in the protection of individual rights that were realized in other countries not by statute but by court rulings under a constitutional bill of rights.

These initiatives expressed some of Trudeau's deepest political commitments. The changes reflected his understanding that the legal system should have regard for crime, not for sin; they widened the separation between church and state; and they reflected his antipathy for state-imposed ideologies and moralities and their attendant behaviours. He encapsulated his approach in his well-remembered reiteration of a sentence from a newspaper editorial: "The state has no place in the bedrooms of the nation."

Later, in his first term as prime minister, he built on the work of the Royal Commission on Bilingualism and Biculturalism to enact the Official Languages Act. Here, to the extent possible under federal legislative jurisdiction, parliament secured by statute the official status of both English and French as well as their use in the executive, legislative, and judicial branches of the federal government. This act was a triumph for the man who, in a brief stint in the federal civil service twenty years earlier, had been incredulous at the fact that he, a French Canadian, could not write a memorandum in French to his superior, also a French Canadian, and marvelled at the absence of a French sign designating the prime minister's office.

The Front de libération du Québec crisis of October 1970 forced Trudeau to make hard decisions about the limits of individual freedom within civil society. Faced with concerted, criminal acts in the name of Quebec independence, he exercised statutory powers to send the army into Quebec to maintain order. He also proclaimed the War Measures Act, which restricted the ordinary procedural protections of the criminal process. His actions responded to urgent requests by the premier of Quebec and the mayor of Montreal, who considered the situation beyond their control. Although his action enjoyed support across the country, Trudeau drew heavy criticism from civil libertarians as well as those who believed he had seized the opportunity to destroy Quebec nationalism, not merely the political terrorism carried out in its name. Trudeau rejected this criticism. He argued that all liberty presupposes the stability of the political order. Perhaps reflecting on his study of the Weimar Republic, he stipulated that the state must ensure that no exercise of freedom negates the freedom of others. While all accounts recall his taunt "Just watch me!" in response to a reporter's query about his intentions, he also said in that exchange: "Society must take every means at its disposal to defend itself against the emergence of a parallel power which defies the elected power in this country." This is not to say that Trudeau believed that the powers he had exercised raised no proper concerns. Two years earlier, as minister of justice, he had proposed various ways to integrate necessary emergency powers into a regime of rights-protection, and in 1978 he insisted in the House that his Charter of Rights take precedence over all legislation, including the War Measures Act. Although this episode remains controversial, Trudeau's response did quell violence in the nationalist movement in Quebec.

Trudeau's early political actions suggest that the Canadian political system was sufficiently resilient to meet both its aspirations and its crises without undertaking an ambitious agenda of constitutional reform. We do not know what law reform priorities Trudeau might have pursued had his predecessor, Lester Pearson, not put the Constitution onto the national agenda as the way to deal with surging Quebec nationalism. As the recognized expert on federalism in the federal cabinet, Trudeau was the person to whom the government, and later the country, turned.

■

From 1967 on, a constitutional declaration of rights was the cornerstone of Trudeau's constitutional policy. Inevitably, such a declaration would involve the most intractable issue within Canadian constitutionalism: patriation of the British North America Act, 1867. Canada's written Constitution was, in part, a statute amendable only by the body that had first enacted it, the parliament of the United Kingdom. Canada functioned as a fully independent country in every respect but this one. Constitutional amendment required what Frank Scott, the esteemed constitutional law professor at McGill Law School and Trudeau's acknowledged mentor, called "our rendezvous with the B.N.A. *Act*." Canada would have to go back to Westminster one last time to have it enact a domestic amending formula.

No one doubted the desirability of vesting Canada with full legal independence from Britain, but what was the new amending formula to be? The quest for unanimous provincial agreement on this issue had stymied Trudeau's predecessors. A holdout province could make demands, beyond the terms of the formula itself, as the price of its consent—as Quebec had done on several occasions despite having already secured the highest prize, a veto over future constitutional change. The desire of other governments to effect patriation was hostage to one province's ever-enlarging appetite for increased powers.

Trudeau expended considerable effort as prime minister seeking unanimous agreement on a new amending formula. At his moment of triumph in 1981, he finally secured the agreement of all provinces except Quebec on the basic plan he had announced in 1967 as minister of justice: patriation with a constitutional declaration of rights. In the interval, he had tested every conceivable substantive and procedural variation on this theme in the hope of securing unanimity. On the substantive side, his government widened the agenda to include a range of other significant changes sought by the provinces, including reform of the Senate and the Supreme Court and changes to the division of powers between the federal and provincial governments. That dynamic failed because there was no basis on which to call closure to the list of provincial demands or to sustain a meaningful federal state, given the combined effect of the changes proposed. So Trudeau offered patriation alone and subsequent discussion of further reform. His early hope for a wide-ranging Charter of Rights and Freedoms succumbed to the realization that the negotiation process would produce consensus, if at all, only on a relatively ineffective Charter. In terms of process, the range of possibilities also spanned the spectrum: patriation with unanimous provincial consent, with some provincial support, and without provincial consent. In a futile effort, before losing power in 1979, Trudeau even moved off his constitutional agenda, suggesting a statutory bill of rights at the federal level, with provision for the provinces to opt in later.

Until his final term as prime minister, Trudeau's rendezvous with the B.N.A. Act remained beyond his grasp. It is likely that any other politician would have put the project aside, as previous prime ministers had done in the 1940s and 1950s. But there were three factors that militated against this course of action. First, Trudeau seemed to have an endless store of personal resources for this battle. The Constitution was his personal project, originating in his academic understanding of individual liberty as the goal of social organization and his related belief in federalism as the appropriate system for pluralist societies. This was not abstract theorizing for Trudeau: it was daily affirmed by his presence, as a member of Canada's French-speaking minority, in the central government, surrounded by other French-Canadian politicians and bureaucrats.

Second, events precluded abandonment of the project. Trudeau felt he could gauge the reasonableness of the provincial premiers' demands. As long as the process made some sense, he continued to engage. His commitment ebbed when it became apparent to him that the process was futile because federal concessions only increased provincial demands. In exasperation at the process in the late 1970s, he stated, "I have given away the store." "Who," he demanded, "will speak for Canada?" Not his provincial interlocutors and not the federal Conservative Party. Their vision of Canada, in his view, amounted to nothing more than a confederation of shopping centres; their ideal prime minister would be a head waiter satisfying the provinces' increasing appetites for more power. Nevertheless, Quebec's evolving nationalist agenda kept the Constitution on the front burner.

Third, the prospect of a constitutional declaration of rights enjoyed sustained and growing support across the country. Even the provincial premiers could not object to its substance, for by the time the Charter became the central issue in the constitutional wars, all the provinces had their own statutory bills of rights. The fact that Trudeau's project captured the imagination of Canadians proved the decisive factor in its ultimate adoption.

The defeat of the Liberals in May 1979 seemed to mark the end of Trudeau's hoped-for resolution. The minority government of Joe Clark took a more flexible approach to both federalism and the Charter. It accorded pre-eminence not to individual freedom, but to majority rule based on moral, spiritual, and family values. These efforts met with no success. Perhaps the short-lived Clark government simply ran out of time.

The separatist government of René Lévesque had delayed its promised referendum on Quebec sovereignty in the expectation that Trudeau would lose the 1979 election to a Conservative government without representation in Quebec. As fate would have it, however, the Conservative minority government fell unexpectedly, and in 1980 Lévesque found himself facing a re-elected and re-energized Trudeau, bolstered by a mandate of seventy-four out of the seventy-five Quebec seats in parliament. Trudeau had intervened effectively in the dying days of the referendum campaign, invoking his particular form of Canadian patriotism and offering Quebeckers "constitutional reform" in return for their No vote. This promise was so vague that many Quebeckers cried foul when Trudeau subsequently stood poised to deliver nothing more than his classic vision of patriation and a Charter, rather than a new place for Quebec within the federation. But Trudeau maintained that his referendum speeches, and indeed his life's work, had raised no broader expectations.

The Charter that he offered the country in a nationally televised speech in October 1980 included a full range of guarantees: fundamental freedoms, democratic rights, mobility rights, legal rights, equality rights, and language rights. The guarantee clause made rights claims "subject only to such reasonable limits as are generally accepted in a free and democratic society with a parliamentary system of government," a formula designed, despite the cabinet's intention to offer a "first-class" or "Cadillac" Charter, to mollify those provinces anxious to preserve the legislative upper hand. The package also offered a future referendum for the people to choose between two alternative approaches to a new amending formula: the Victoria Charter formula of 1971, a region-based formula that effectively gave vetoes to both Quebec and Ontario, with an added referendum mechanism to introduce public consultation if the federal-provincial dynamic created deadlock; and a provincial proposal. The referendum proposal was an attempt to emancipate the process—not the substance—of constitutional change from the dead hand of the first ministers. Despite the popularity of the Charter, as revealed by polling and nurtured by an intensive federal advertising campaign, Trudeau envisaged no public involvement by Canadians in formulating the terms of their future rights.

The government's intention was to ride the wave of the Charter's popularity to a quickly enacted amendment by the British parliament. The Charter was to apply to the provinces, even without their agreement. Trudeau declared the end of bargaining "freedom against fish, fundamental rights against oil, the independence of our country against long-distance rates." His opponents ultimately succeeded in slowing him down, but not stopping him. In the fascinating way that process intertwines with substance, the effect was to improve the Charter immeasurably—by Trudeau's standards.

Three of the opposing provinces—Manitoba, Quebec, and Newfoundland—asked the courts whether Trudeau's "unilateral" initiative could result in a British amendment having legal force in Canada and whether Trudeau was departing from past constitutional convention. No one in the constitutional trenches expected the provinces to win in the courts, but the judges might cast some light on an issue sizzling unproductively in the federal-provincial frying pan.

The federal Conservatives proposed a nationally televised, joint committee of the Senate and the House of Commons to review the terms of the government proposal. This move was not without risk. Someone surely anticipated, despite public disenchantment with Trudeau's unilateral approach, that the Charter's popularity across the country would ultimately help the Liberals. Previous efforts to tap public opinion on the Charter had revealed a public increasingly passionate and informed on the terms of the debate. The joint committee provided the opportunity for unprecedented public engagement in the Charter project. Experts in rights-protection came forward with blistering criticism of the draft Charter. Day after day, public interest groups presented detailed analyses of the Charter's shortcomings. Ninety of the committee's 267 televised hours had focused on the Charter. There was every indication that the country was watching, and the result was a much improved Charter text—as a legal instrument but also as a document bearing the legitimacy of public participation and attention.

Among experts, professionals, and members of the general public, few rejected the values expressed in a constitutional guarantee of rights. Controversy flourished on the best delivery system: Should questions of liberty, equality, and fairness continue to be resolved by elected and accountable politicians in the give and take of ordinary politics, or should the Constitution vest their determination in the courts? Those who supported the Charter believed that these values were of such prime importance that the Constitution should withdraw them from the political arena and secure their guarantee by judicial review—through the application by judges of legal analysis divorced from political considerations and cost-benefit analysis. The critics of the Charter saw this role as an anti-democratic rule by élite, unrepresentative, life-appointed judges. Conservative critics feared that the courts would be too liberal; liberal critics predicted the opposite result. The premiers were split on this question. Polls suggested that the public was divided as well: Support for the Charter was enthusiastic, but Canadians, with an eye to past practice, doubted whether judges could adequately do the job.

This institutional question became the focal point of the Joint Committee's deliberations. The Charter text under examination protected the guarantees only tentatively, permitting governments to impose "generally acceptable" encroachments. Experts and the representatives of a wide range of interest groups were extremely critical. What past denial of rights had not enjoyed "general acceptance?" Representatives of the very people for whom rights protection offered most—women, the disabled, the aged, religious and ethnic minorities, aboriginals—said they would forgo this Charter because it would waste what might be the only chance for constitutional change. They denounced the federal cabinet's "Cadillac" Charter as a "Mack Truck" version—because one could have driven a huge vehicle through it.

Justice Minister Chrétien welcomed the criticism because it meant he could return to the Liberal government's original design. Limitations on Charter rights would have to be "prescribed by law," "demonstrably justifiable," and consistent with a "free and democratic society." These impenetrable words strengthened the Charter immeasurably by invoking the language of postwar rights-protecting systems, both national constitutions and the international human rights-protecting instruments. They meant that governments would have to work very hard to encroach on a Charter guarantee. Charter rights were to be the norm; limits on rights were to be rare, requiring full justification.

The rights guarantees improved as well. The equality rights, particularly those relating to sex and disability, gained ground. The

minority language education rights expanded. Changes strengthened the hand of trial courts to exclude evidence derived in breach
of Charter guarantees where the administration of justice would be
called into disrepute. Judges were charged to read the Charter consistently with the "preservation and enhancement of the multicultural heritage of Canadians." Beyond the parameter of the Charter
text, the committee's work led to the constitutional recognition of
aboriginal and treaty rights for the first time.

With the revised Charter text back in the House of Commons,
but blocked by an opposition filibuster, Trudeau agreed to await
the Supreme Court of Canada's decision on the appeal of the
provincial reference cases. In September 1981 the Supreme Court
settled the legal question as expected. A Charter enacted over the
objections of the provinces would have legal force in Canada. But,
because there was no precedent, the majority recognized a non-
binding constitutional practice requiring at least "substantial"
provincial consent for an amendment having such restricting effect
on provincial powers. This extraordinary judgment perhaps reflected the Court's discomfort with the prospect of enforcing a
Charter against eight legislatures whose governments objected to
it. The Court might be understood as reformulating the dominant
refrain in the Joint Committee, though on the grounds of the process of constitutional reform rather than its substance: A Charter
enacted as Trudeau proposed might lack political legitimacy and
thus be worse than no Charter at all.

The Court's endorsement on the legal issue might have sent
Trudeau's proposal on its way to the Parliament of the United
Kingdom had he had full confidence that the British government
would act expeditiously on a request for amendment lacking
much provincial support. Despite his public bravado—" Let them
hold their noses"—he must have harboured doubts. Margaret
Thatcher's government was cool to the Charter—why should the
United Kingdom do this for Canada? A committee of the British
House of Commons discovered a residual colonial responsibility to
protect Canada's federal structure. The provinces, particularly Quebec and Alberta, having apparently despaired of appealing to their

constituents at home, dropped a small fortune in wining and dining UK backbenchers to their point of view. In addition, Trudeau knew that the judicial recognition of a conventional requirement of "substantial" provincial support in Canada would suggest the existence of a reciprocal rule of practice binding on the UK Parliament as well.

Trudeau now faced resistance from most of the provinces, the highest court in the land, the federal Conservatives, and the British government. He had to cede. He called "one last" first ministers' conference for early November 1981. Most observers anticipated continued deadlock between an obsessed prime minister and eight intransigent provincial premiers, but the end was in sight. In retrospect, one realizes that a number of factors had strengthened Trudeau's hand. The Charter's new legitimacy, endorsed by the work of the Joint Committee, precluded the old game of reducing the rights, enlarging the basis of their limitation, or adding opt-out clauses. In place of the presumed unanimity rule, which had made it cost free for a number of fence-sitting premiers to band together with Trudeau's strongest opponents, the Supreme Court had supplied, but not defined, a requirement of "substantial" consent. Ottawa likely lacked any means of sweetening the deal for Quebec, since the cause of separation precluded any demonstration that "federalism worked." But in seeking "substantial" support, Trudeau had only to win over several of the least-committed members of the "Gang of Eight."

In addition, the premiers had no reason to doubt that Trudeau would proceed unilaterally. He faced at best some constitutional embarrassment in getting what he wanted. Alternatively, a refusal by the UK Parliament to act on his request would have precipitated an unprecedented constitutional crisis, which Trudeau might use to build support for his initiative as an affirmation of full independence of Canada from its former imperial parliament.

Trudeau made the expected move in an unexpected way. He broke the solidarity of the Gang of Eight by isolating his strongest opponent, Quebec's René Lévesque. As a new champion of public participation in constitutional change, Trudeau suggested a referendum on the Charter in two years. The idea appealed to the separatist premier, who could not challenge the legitimacy of consulting the people and who seemed to relish the idea of a rematch in which he would battle Trudeau to defeat on his Charter. We don't know if Trudeau anticipated this response. It is more likely that he thought a referendum might offset the lack of provincial executive approval in the eyes of the British. In any event, Lévesque's reaction effectively shattered the rule of unanimity subscribed to by the gang. The other premiers had no referendum score to settle with Trudeau, and they could see no advantage in a campaign against a popular "people's package" of constitutional reforms.

The pieces of a deal quickly fell into place. With the exception of Quebec, the holdout premiers accepted the Charter, with the addition of a "notwithstanding provision," variations of which had been their mainstay throughout the drafting process. This provision enabled the federal and provincial governments to subordinate some Charter rights through legislation expressly indicating this effect. The suspension would have a five-year sunset clause, so that elections would offer the opportunity to debate the suspension of the Charter guarantees. The premiers also secured adoption of their preferred amending formula. The process had exhausted itself—or so it appeared. In the final horse-trading, some of the protection for equality rights for women and guarantees to the aboriginal peoples had fallen by the wayside. The grassroots forces unleashed by the Joint Committee arose in protest. Surprised at the organizational skills and intensity of the lobbying efforts, the premiers agreed to reinstate these guarantees. Efforts to bring Lévesque into the agreement with further offers failed—although the Quebec populace, and its representatives in parliament, supported the Charter.

Quebec lost heavily in this round of constitutional renewal. The court references it had initiated with two other provinces resulted in the declared end of its strongest card—the presumed unanimity requirement for patriation. The new amending formula lacked the Quebec veto on constitutional change that Trudeau had willingly offered for more than a decade. Lévesque had reluctantly supported this formula for the sake of creating some shared policy for the opposing provinces, taking what seemed at the time the small risk that it would find itself in a deal binding Quebec. The gamble failed. Turning to the courts to secure legal protection against its own political strategy, Quebec learned from the Supreme Court what it feared—that Lévesque's ploy had solidified into constitutional law. Quebec also lost some of its legislative authority over language policy owing to the guarantee of minority language rights and the exclusion of these rights from reach of the "notwithstanding clause." Considering that it had kick-started the constitutional reform process for its own gain, these results marked no measure of success.

It is commonplace now in Quebec politics to direct scorn at the round of deliberations that culminated in the 1981 amendments. The assertion is that Quebec was left out in the final deal, deserted by its fellow provinces and betrayed by Ottawa. This account is a strangely simplistic description of the complicated dealings that lasted more than a decade—one that assumes that the separatist government was seeking anything except the collapse of the constitutional negotiations. The astonishing risk that Lévesque took with the amending formula indicates that his intention was to scuttle Trudeau's project rather than to secure Quebec's place within it. In any case, his nationalist aspiration for Quebec sovereignty was inconsistent with Trudeau's rejection of nationalism in favour of individual liberty, federalism, and the full integration of Quebeckers in a national, multicultural state.

■

Despite his singular achievement in securing a constitutional Charter for Canada, Trudeau has complained that political exigencies forced him to settle for a flawed instrument, a Charter that failed to put fundamental rights and freedoms beyond the reach of the legislative process. He has been particularly critical of the notwithstanding clause—embodied in the final compromise—which permits legislatures to subordinate fundamental, legal, and equality rights, if they do so expressly in the body of a statute, for a maximum, renewable five-year period.

Trudeau's objection to the notwithstanding clause warrants examination. Was the Charter draft he championed in the final negotiations, with its remarkably wide clause that permitted a limitation
on rights, more clearly aligned to his political philosophy than the
Charter that was finally formulated in the courts, with its principled,
narrow limitation clause and legislative notwithstanding clause?
Where Trudeau the politician felt the sting of political compromise,
might Trudeau the political theorist have recognized an innovative
complex of institutional roles having the potential to realize some of
his deepest political commitments?

To its critics, the notwithstanding clause gives politicians an
easy escape route from the Charter's strictures. Those who supported the Charter laid a similar charge against the wide limitation
clause in the penultimate formulation, arguing that it would, in effect, have granted judges carte blanche to do what elected representatives were free to do without the Charter—subordinate rights
to "reasonable" and "generally acceptable" political preference.
Although they secured the narrower and more principled limitation clause, many believed that the victory was rendered valueless
by the adoption of the notwithstanding clause.

The combination of the narrow limitation clause with the
notwithstanding clause, however counter-intuitive it seems, may
serve rights protection effectively. These two provisions enlist
the institutional strengths of both courts of law and representative,
accountable legislatures in forwarding the Charter's guarantees.
Neither has an easy way out.

In combining these two institutional provisions, the final text of
the Charter created an innovation in the institutional arrangements
for rights protection. It charges the courts with the task of principled articulation of the content of the rights, the fact of infringement in individual cases, and consideration of the justificatory force
of the government's proffered limitation argument. (Yet, ironically,
the trend in the case law in the Supreme Court of Canada has been
away from the narrow and principled limitation of values encapsulated in the final text.) The notwithstanding clause supports this narrow judicial function. It does not simply permit the system to revert

to majoritarian legislative sovereignty, but provides a narrow power restricted so as to intensify the legislators' broader representative responsibilities and accountability.

Designating a law as contrary to Charter rights sets in motion political repercussions beyond what its policy content would generate within ordinary majoritarian politics. Such a law can unleash a wide range of protest, to the extent that there is a strong commitment to rights protection in the immediate constituency, across Canada, and in the world at large. Premier Bouchard has recognized this possibility and has declined to use the clause to extend the sign law, contrary to Charter rights, or to reinstate the provisions of the Quebec referendum law, when they were invalidated for the same reason. As explanation, he has cited the strictures of the Quebec Charter, the Canadian Charter, and obligations under international law. He realizes that reliance on the notwithstanding clause would undermine the long-term sovereigntist project, which requires a good international reputation on rights and minorities. Finally, the pan-Canadian firestorm generated in Alberta in the spring of 1998, when the government announced that it would use the notwithstanding clause to remove equality rights from those people who had been sterilized under the province's former eugenics law, demonstrates that suspension power under the notwithstanding clause is temporary; and that a law so sheltered from Charter challenge can become an ongoing political irritant, particularly at election time.

In this institutional structure we see realized Trudeau's commitment to liberal democracy, postwar constitutionalism, and the pluralist and multicultural society bound together by rights-based constitutionalism. Consistent with his approach to institutional responsibility, courts would operate under the discipline of public law principles. And consistent with his life's work as a parliamentarian, legislative representatives would continue to hold responsibility for protecting and forwarding the values of the Constitution.

One cannot help but think that Trudeau, dissociated from his own involvement, would appreciate this complex interplay of constitutional values within and beyond Canada, the propriety of an institutional role, and continuing public engagement. One could even identify the general disdain for legislative invocation of the notwithstanding clause as the post–Charter manifestation of the public support of the Charter that provided the legitimating foundation for his sustained commitment to its adoption.

■

Trudeau's commitment to the charter was sufficiently strong for him to denouce the proposed constitutional amendments contained in the Meech Lake and Charlottetown accords, which were conceived by Brian Mulroney to bring Quebec back within the constitutional fold. The full story of Trudeau's relationship to the Charter must therefore include the extraordinary battle he waged, as a private citizen, for its full retention.

Trudeau faulted the Meech Lake accord, in part, because it included a directive to the courts to interpret the Constitution, including the Charter, consistent with the "recognition of Quebec within Canada [as] a distinct society." In addition, the text affirmed the role of the legislature and government of Quebec to both "preserve and promote" its "distinct identity." Trudeau analysed the effect of these proposals on the Charter in these words: "the accord has empowered one provincial government to subordinate the rights of every individual Canadian living within its borders to the rights of a chosen community, presumably, the French-speaking majority." To illustrate his point, he noted that Premier Robert Bourassa, who had sought this amendment, had expressed a similar assessment of its effect when he had used the notwithstanding clause to reinstate his French-only sign law, after the Supreme Court had invalidated the statute for breaching Quebeckers' Charter guarantees to freedom of expression. National public opinion had protested that action. Bourassa, in contrast, exulted in having subordinated individual rights to collective rights. He also predicted that the promised distinct society clause would in effect expand the National Assembly's powers to encroach on Charter rights, without exacting the political price, at home and abroad, of using the notwithstanding clause. Moreover, the proposed distinct society clause would contract within Quebec the guarantee of those rights which in 1982 had been put beyond the reach of the notwithstanding clause—democratic, mobility, and linguistic rights. The distinct society clause would thus undermine the most basic principle that had animated Trudeau's desire for a Charter—indeed, the most basic principle of a rights-protecting regime—that all citizens are equal rights-holders.

Trudeau was even more critical of the Charlottetown accord. Its distinct society clause was one of a number designed to subordinate Charter guarantees—such as gender, ethnic, and racial equality—to Quebec's mandate in respect to its "unique culture" and French-speaking majority. Trudeau characterized the purpose of these clauses succinctly: to provide governments with protection from the constraints imposed by the Charter's guarantees of equal, individual rights. While Trudeau had worked to limit government in favour of the individual on the basis of cultural and ethnic equality, Mulroney's constitutional agenda meant reducing those limitations in the name of cultural and linguistic solidarity.

In the debate on both the Meech and Charlottetown initiatives, Canadians re-experienced Trudeau's ability to mobilize public support for his vision of the relationship between the individual and the state. As prime minister, he was able to win the public over to his idea for entrenched rights and freedoms despite opposition from all quarters; later, as a private citizen, he acted to protect the Charter from attempts to dislodge its primacy and, in particular, to undermine its promise of equal citizenship.

Since 1982, the Charter has become part of the basic fabric of our lives, shaping the legislative policy process and providing citizens and public interest groups with the possibility of asserting their rights in courts of law. No major issue passes through our lives without some reflection on its Charter implications: the permissibility of euthanasia; the rights of homosexuals to state support for their relationships and for health and employment benefits; the treatment of the disabled; restrictions on biker gangs; deportation of alleged murderers to the United States, where they might face the death penalty; or the Ontario government's transformation of local government. Trudeau's idea of Canada as a community of rightsholders is taking root.

Trudeau's desire for public engagement in constitutional questions has also taken root. The Meech Lake accord went down, in part, because of the perception that the first ministers had reverted to the pre-1981 process, making the final deal entirely through executive accommodation without much concern for legislative process or public participation. For that reason, the federal government approached the Charlottetown accord in a different way, widening its substantive appeal by including aboriginal self-government and making the agreement subject to a national referendum. A remarkable indication of the changed nature of our constitutional politics was the success of the grassroots movement to force the Mulroney government to release the draft constitutional text before the referendum, so that citizens might cast their votes informed by the effect the amendments might have, not just the political aspirations of the negotiating parties. Some governments have now indicated that they will seek public agreement in a referendum before seeking approval for future constitutional proposals in their legislatures. The Constitution has been opened up to the claims of a wider constituency.

■

Those who would minimize the extraordinary role that Trudeau played in Canada's acquisition of a constitutional bill of rights in 1982 might suggest that Canada had merely fallen in step with the general postwar proliferation of such documents, especially in former British colonies. It is true that Britain provided others of its colonies, such as India, with bills of rights when they secured independence. But this pattern emerged too late for Canada. The securing of a constitutional declaration of rights in Canada was a domestic project.

Canada also departed from the pattern of those countries that acquired their bills of rights in the context of extensive, often unprecedented, political upheaval. For the United States and France, the precipitating event had been revolutionary rejection of monarchy. Equality entitlements had entered the US Bill of Rights after the Civil War. Defeat in the Second World War led to the imposition of democracy and bills of rights on Japan and Germany. Peaceful transforming circumstances have been no less dramatic—for example, the end of the Cold War for Eastern Europe and the end of apartheid in South Africa. Canada's story pales by any measure of comparison. How then to explain Canada's experience?

The historical record reveals that, among his Canadian predecessors and successors alike, Trudeau alone saw his objective through to completion. Demands for constitutional change were building, initially in Quebec and later in the western provinces; but Trudeau did not simply react. He realized the full extent of Quebec's challenge to Canadian unity and the need to bring the Constitution into line with Canada's, and the world's, evolution. He formulated a constitutional future that he believed would accommodate French Canada within Canada. He often set the terms of debate and dictated the political options. In the final period, he brought Canada to the brink of constitutional crisis for the sake of constitutional reform.

In an interview published in *Cité libre* in 1997, Trudeau affirmed his commitments to individual over national sovereignty and the need for the Charter to embody not only the traditional liberal rights and freedoms he considered generic but also the language rights necessary to constitute linguistic justice in the particular circumstances of Canadian federalism. These are the ideas the young law professor brought with him to Ottawa over thirty years ago. The consistency of Trudeau's vision over time did not produce his ideal Charter. But his commitment to a Charter embodying his principles produced an intensive debate, yielding a distinctive articulation of rights guarantees as well as a new institutional arrangement in which rights are framed by a judicially applied limitation clause and a legislative notwithstanding clause. These features of the Charter strongly influenced the emerging constitutional systems in Israel and South Africa, as those divided countries looked to Canada's recent constitutional history to understand what is generic and what is specific in the constitutional protection of rights. Canada's Charter has become a model to many countries that are moving from legislative sovereignty to rights protection. What appeared to be chaotic to those who lived through the Charter's evolution now appears to others as creative steps in the development of operative constitutional systems.

Trudeau has said that the politician is a teacher. His political career provided a twenty-year national seminar on the nature of citizenship in the modern, liberal, multicultural state. He gave Canada the clearest and most coherent articulation of how its history could support its destiny—a vision informed by constitutional theory and presented as a model for the emerging multicultural and economically integrated world. In this vision, the common bond of equal rights binds together a pluralistic and far-flung, even a divided, population. Whether one agrees with Trudeau or not, one cannot deny the clarity, consistency, and logic of his united Canada.

Constitutions are organic instruments. Canadians' ideas about rights, nationalism, and federalism will continue to evolve. If Trudeau's legacy is valued, individual liberty and equality, group support, and public engagement in constitutional development will continue to be integral components of that process.

Trudeau:

Hedgehog or Fox?

■

BOB RAE

Bob Rae is partner at the Canadian international law firm of Goodman Phillips & Vineberg. His Canadian clients have included companies, trade unions, charitable and non-governmental organizations, and governments themselves. Rae served as premier of Ontario from 1990 to 1995, and was elected eight times to federal and provincial parliaments before his retirement from politics in 1996. He led the New Democratic Party of Ontario from 1982 to 1996, and served as leader of the official opposition before becoming premier. He was also the federal NDP finance critic from 1978–1982. He is the author of From Protest to Power *and* The Three Questions: Prosperity and the Public Good, *due out in the fall of 1998.*

I SAIAH BERLIN recalls the old fable, "the fox knows many things, but the hedgehog knows one big thing," and reminds us that: "there exists a great schism between those, on one side, who relate everything to a single centered vision . . . and, on the other side, those who pursuc many ends, often unrelated and even contradictory" (The Proper Study of Mankind, 1997). If we apply this moral to Pierre Elliott Trudeau, we see that his greatest strength has also been his greatest weakness. His political life centred on "one big thing"—the demolition of Quebec nationalism. This fixity became his greatest strength, for, like many others, his talents and invective were always put to best use when he was in his "J'accuse" mode. But it was also his greatest weakness, for he became the prisoner of his own rhetoric, an ideologue despite himself, and curiously rigid as he attacked anyone who chose to disagree.

Like many in my generation, I have not been consistent in my own assessment of Trudeau. As an undergraduate in the 1960s I was an early supporter. My enthusiasm soon faded, however, and, after his election in 1968, I wrote that he was sounding more and more like "William Lyon Mackenzie King in a mini-skirt." I was a strong critic of his approach to the economy in my time as finance spokesman of the New Democratic Party, and an equally fervent ally on patriation of the Constitution. We parted company over thr Meech and Charlottetown aaccords, but agreed on free trade and the North American Free Trade Agreement. At a personal level, we have never exchanged more than a few words in private and the usual range of partisan barbs in public.

It is somewhat ironic that a man who led the governing party of Canada for more than sixteen years, and whose span as prime minister was only slightly shorter, would portray himself in his last book as paddling constantly "against the current." From another perspective, his life seems downstream with a full wind behind him all the way. His perspective speaks to the importance of his formative years in opposition and the power of his self-image as the lonely world citizen fighting the forces of reaction all around him.

One of the mythologies popularized by the English-language media in the late 1960s was that Trudeau sprang fully grown as a "new politician," with no baggage from the bad old days. In the cult of the new and the young so prevalent at the time, English Canadians embraced Trudeau as the man without a past, someone of apparently pure intellect who, by his presence alone, aroused emotional mania. That the professor would become a brilliant stump politician, even a demagogue, was a discovery reserved for later years.

In fact, Trudeau was an "opposition leader" for the first fifteen years of his career. A teacher, journalist, and commentator, what he said and wrote between 1950 and 1965 was a reflection of his political engagement against Maurice Duplessis and the Quebec nationalist establishment of his day. He developed a style that never left him. Lucid, unequivocal, brilliant, acerbic, he revelled in the tricks and excesses of rhetorical debate. It is impossible to read his work of those days without admiring his skill and the verve of his argument. Yet the perpetual undergraduate quality of a man infatuated with his own cleverness grates as well. More than anything else, he wanted to win the argument.

Trudeau's first argument, that the Duplessis political order was corrupt and archaic, was right then, as it is now. His support for the essential elements of a democratic civil society was eloquent and unequivocal. He showed courage and dedication in his support for trade unions in a deeply conservative and repressive political context. His treatment of nationalism in all its manifestations is much more problematic and would lead to even bigger difficulties in the years ahead.

Trudeau was a member of a broad coalition of forces caught up in the struggle against the Duplessis government and its allies. A government that appeared so reactionary and corrupt produced an opposition that covered a wide spectrum of views. Many of the members of the Quiet Revolution were, as we now know, as firmly nationalistic as any of Duplessis' friends. Indeed, soon after the formation of the government of Jean Lesage in 1960, Trudeau was already proving to be a strong critic of what he saw as the perpetuation of Quebec's nationalist myth. He broke with René Lévesque initially on the subject of hydroelectric nationalization, about which he remained a strong sceptic.

Trudeau's political voice found an strong and clear expression in these opposition years. His description of Quebec's history and political culture in the opening chapters of *The Asbestos Strike*, its tirades on the "treason of the intellectuals," its broadsides against corruption and what he saw as a weak and vacillating parliamentary opposition, remain classics of liberal democratic writing in modern Canada. Clever, scathing, and funny, they reflect the enthusiasm of the battle and the joy of argument itself. There is no question that, to be at his best, Trudeau needed an enemy, and he was never stronger or clearer or more effective than when eviscerating an opponent. It was this spirit that always gave life to his political personality. When he lacked an enemy or a clear sense of purpose or direction, which was clearly the case between 1968 and 1972, and again during the "phony war" with the separatists in the late 1970s, Trudeau reverted to a language that was at once technocratic, remote, and aloof. It spoke to the conservative side of his personality, and the often cautious nature of his actions.

Trudeau's need for something to oppose also meant that, on occasion, he seemed to be synthesizing his enemies, making them sound more evil than they could possibly be. Trudeau is not the first politician to create a series of straw arguments and fabricated opponents to make himself look good. It is yet another irony of his life that the man of reason, of cool intellect, as he liked to think of himself, was in fact a politician who was never afraid to play on emotion and who, in key political arguments, reverted to demagoguery of the simplest kind.

Like all great men, Trudeau is hard to characterize. In attempting to bring him down to size and to dismiss him as "nothing but a conservative" or "nothing but a socialist" or "nothing but a sellout," his fiercest opponents on the left or the right, or from Quebec's nationalist community often missed the point. It was Trudeau himself who liked to quote the famous aphorism that "the style is the man himself." That is entirely true. No assessment of Trudeau that tries to pigeonhole him, or to explain his resonance, his extraordinary political success, and his longevity in a simple phrase, is worth very much if it is based on some ideological standard. Trudeau is without question the most successful political figure in Canada since the Second World War, and his influence continues to affect the efforts of his successors.

Trudeau's first brush with the federal Liberal Party was hardly a friendly one. He launched a vitriolic attack on Lester Pearson for his Scarborough speech of 1963, the speech where Pearson finally recognized the futility of John Diefenbaker's Bomarc policy and the risk to the Canada–US relationship posed by the contradictions of the Conservatives' attitudes to defence. There was neither generosity nor balance in Trudeau's assault on Pearson. It had the kind of undergraduate quality that always marked his diatribes at their worst: personal, unfair, never allowing for a moment the possibility that someone of integrity might take a different view. It says a great deal for Pearson's own generosity that he quickly overlooked this outburst in appointing Trudeau as his parliamentary secretary in 1965 and, two years later, as attorney general and minister of justice. Trudeau's ministerial career was marked by the landmark legislation that allowed for a liberal reform of the Criminal Code. It suited Trudeau's temperament and policy directions perfectly. The reforms on abortion and homosexuality, while controversial at the time and offensive to certain conservative sensibilities, permitted Trudeau to express some fundamental thoughts on privacy and the distinction between private moral judgment and criminal activity. They were humane and necessary.

Trudeau's role as constitutional adviser to Pearson pointed to a shift in Liberal policy that was to be consolidated after Trudeau himself became prime minister in 1968. Pearson's vision of cooperative federalism clearly allowed for some recognition of the emerging and progressive nationalism marked by the Quiet Revolution in Quebec. With the appointment of the Royal Commission on Bilingualism and Biculturalism, and the compromises reached over the Canada Assistance Plan and the Canada Pension Plan, Canada's duality and partial asymmetry were quietly being accepted and recognized. Lesage's defeat and replacement by a more determined nationalist in Daniel Johnson, together with Pearson's personal outrage at General Charles de Gaulle's "Vive le Québec libre" speech in the summer of 1967, gave rise to support for the very different approach advocated by Trudeau. A language of rights, a strengthened francophone presence within the federal government, and a determination to ensure an unequivocal role for Ottawa, along with a loathing of anything that smacked of "special status" for Quebec, would become the hallmarks of Trudeau's approach to federal/provincial relations. Lines that Pearson had preferred to leave somewhat unclear, in the name of diplomatic solutions, were suddenly drawn in the sand. The language of partnership that appeared to be emerging between Premiers John Robarts of Ontario and Daniel Johnson of Quebec was replaced by an unambiguous assertion of a determinedly symmetrical federalism, in which the powers of all the provinces would be recognized only to the extent that a "strict construction" of the Constitution would allow.

Many previous prime ministers had wanted to patriate the Constitution, but none was so ideologically committed as Trudeau to patriation accompanied by a Charter of Rights as an assertion of constitutional maturity and citizenship. Trudeau's first efforts in constitutional reform culminated, after long negotiating sessions with the premiers, in the Victoria Charter in 1971. When Quebec premier Robert Bourassa reneged on the agreement, Trudeau never quite trusted him again. This perception, together with Bourassa's indecision in the aftermath of the kidnapping and murder of Pierre

Laporte in October 1970, fuelled the breach between Trudeau and subsequent Quebec Liberal governments.

There is no question that it was during the October Crisis in 1970 that Canadians saw for the first time Trudeau's new dimension as a defender of authority. He was not afraid to be ruthless in the circumstances and had little time for those in opposition who expressed doubts, reservations, and even hostility to the first use of emergency powers in modern Canada in peacetime. It became a defining moment in understanding the extent to which Trudeau was prepared to use the powers of the state to deal with criminal activity that was quickly elevated to "apprehended insurrection." Many could never forgive Trudeau for what they saw as an abuse of power. But, at the same time, he clearly lost all patience with those critics who, in his view, were not prepared to deal with the realities of modern political terrorism. The disillusionment was deep, and it was mutual.

While many in the progressive movement were less than impressed with the technocratic Trudeau after 1968, the War Measures Act produced a split of a qualitatively different kind—more severe, more harsh, more personal. It was at that moment that Trudeau made his spectacularly cool assessment of Claude Ryan, publisher of the respected Quebec newspaper *Le Devoir*, which had dared to criticize him: "absolute powerlessness corrupts absolutely." Many New Democrats regard the party's lonely battle against the War Measures Act as its most unpopular but most necessary fight. Clearly, Trudeau had aroused public opinion to a point of near unanimity in his favour, but it was also the moment that showed his demagogic side. The debate over the apprehended insurrection will never be closed, but one point is clear: once Bourassa asked the Trudeau government to act, it moved without hesitation. Critics were relegated to the ranks of hand-wringing "nervous Nellies."

It is ironic that, in the 1980 referendum, Trudeau's love of doing battle and winning led him to fight René Lévesque on his own ground. Now, eighteen years after that first referendum, the federal government is finally considering the possibilities of secession, which should surely have been expressed unambiguously when the first referendum was debated. No doubt Trudeau was overwhelmingly confident that he could win the issue while fighting on the intellectual terrain defined by his opponents. Yet there is no question that the task of future governments was made more difficult by his acceptance of the premises of the first referendum. This is a curious inconsistency in what is otherwise a root-and-branch questioning of the premises of Quebec nationalism.

Yet another irony is the fact that the man many describe as an unbending ideologue was forced by the Supreme Court ruling of 1981 to introduce the "notwithstanding clause" to the Charter of Rights and Freedoms. On many subsequent occasions, Trudeau expressed profound regret that this compromise was necessary, and he attacked the Supreme Court majority in a speech at the University of Toronto in 1991.

No doubt it was his lingering resentment at the compromise forced upon him that explains Trudeau's venom over the Meech Lake and Charlottetown accords. It was not simply that he found fault with the substance of the Supreme Court judgment of 1981 and the particular clauses in the accords. Rather, it was his sense that his opponents were either charlatans or dunces, or both. No argument was too low or too personal. Brian Mulroney was a "sly fox" and a weakling; Quebec supporters of Meech were "snivellers"; the premiers were all "cowards." There was no end to the number of straw men he was prepared to drag across the theatre of ridicule. He spoke for a constituency truly bewildering in its breadth: charter centralizers who saw any reference to provincial rights as an assault on the welfare state; "one Canada" supporters who, like Diefenbaker before them, preferred the unambiguous assertion of unity to a world of mixed identities and dual loyalties; and nativists who saw Trudeau as the best hammer with which to bash French Canada. This coalition of American style constitutionalists, unreconstructed Fabians, and incipient western reformers proved to be an unbeatable combination. A know-nothing populism had as its main spokesman the most articulate symbol of "reason over passion."

What Trudeau was never prepared to admit was that it was the concession on the notwithstanding clause that gave more powers to Quebec than anything proposed in either the Meech or Charlettown accords. Further, it was his own fiscal policies over sixteen years which did more to decentralize and limit the power of the central government than anything proposed in either document. Subsequent Liberal governments will end up conceding and admitting to the basic premises contained in Meech and Charlettown, with the appropriate refinements that time and further discussion will produce. The street fighter could win against his opponents, who were all "losers" and "nobodies" in any event. But he will not win the battle because, in all his rhetoric, he failed to recognize that further constitutional reform is required, that the purpose of patriation was not to freeze the Constitution for all time but to make it our own to allow for future change. In that sense, Trudeau's lack of generosity to his successors reflects a churlishness that hardly does him proud. But he would not be himself were he not churlish as well as brilliant, emotional as well as rational, conservative as well as radical. "Do I contradict myself?" he asked. "Very well, then, I contradict myself."

Is an accommodation with Quebec nationalism possible within the Canadian federation, or is it a delusion to think that some middle ground exists between Trudeau's awful symmetry and separation? Trudeau's political life was based on the simple notion that French Canadians should seek their full expression of citizenship in Canada itself, not in Quebec. Patriation, the Charter, minority language rights, official bilingualism, opposition to Meech and Charlottetown were all manifestations of this "one big thing."

Yet the previous great prime ministers—John A. Macdonald, Wilfrid Laurier, Mackenzie King, Louis St. Laurent, and Lester Pearson—would have seen Meech and Charlottetown as worthy successors to their efforts at accommodation and compromise. It's all very well to mock the accords, as Trudeau did, as a "dog's breakfast." So was the British North America Act itself. Constitutions do not emerge perfectly formed from the brains of the philosopher kings, as Trudeau himself discovered in 1980 and 1981. They are always messy processes that are easier to knock down or tear apart than they are to construct. Macdonald knew that Quebec nationalism was not about to disappear, which is why he, together with the key leadership of Upper Canada, ditched Lord Durham's impossible effort to create "one Canada." His key successors reached the same conclusion, knowing that Canada's duality is not its only characteristic, but it is certainly one of them. They learned from Macdonald's famous dictum: "Treat them as a nation and they will act as people generally do—generously. Call them a faction and they become factions." Trudeau never did learn this truth.

Trudeau's hostility to Duplessis, along with the strength of his own liberal ideology, puts him in the camp of those who see all manifestations of nationalism as a retrograde craving that progress, culture, and enlightenment will make redundant. To use another phrase often quoted by Isaiah Berlin, Trudeau never absorbed the wisdom of Kant's maxim: "From the crooked timber of humanity nothing straight is ever made."

In its excesses, Quebec nationalism can be as offensive as any; but it cannot be understood only by its excesses. The need to belong to a family and a community, to treasure a language and a native tongue, to value a land because it is home and nurtures common values and traditions: These are not signs of civil or weakness or a crass perversion of human ideals. Durham's vision of a culturally inferior French population disappearing in the wake of a technologically advanced English "civilization" proved to be quite wrong, precisely because of the depth of nationalist feeling in Quebec and the fact that 1867 reserved significant powers for the provinces.

This is not to say that Trudeau was wrong in his assault on the premises of René Lévesque and Lucien Bouchard. Rather, in his taste for winning the argument pure and simple, Trudeau failed to seek the middle ground. At its best, political life is not a debating society; it is about finding a better balance.

Looking back now we can see more clearly than ever how much the world, and Canada, has changed since the start of Trudeau's tenure. Canada is less a national economy than a group of regional economies increasingly faced with global integration. We have gone from the late industrial to the information age; from a time of steady growth and low debts to an era of low growth, high debts, and greater disparities between rich and poor. Some of these changes Trudeau resisted; some he contributed to. It would be a stretch to say that he really understood them: few modern liberal democratic leaders have shown such fitful attention to the economy. Knowing only one big thing has its price: we got our patriated Constitution in 1981, but it came at some cost. The "Canadian crisis" identified by the Royal Commission on Bilingualism and Biculturalism in 1965 was not resolved, but continued in another form.

Constitutional scholar Frank Scott attacked Mackenzie King because he "blunted us . . . never doing by halves what could be done by quarters." Trudeau did not blunt us. He amused us, inspired us, enraged us, enlightened us, disappointed us, and, ultimately, eluded us.

Changing Positions: Reflections on Pierre Trudeau and the October Crisis

■

J. L. GRANATSTEIN

J. L. Granatstein is one of Canada's best-known academics, writers, and broadcast commentators. He taught history at York University from 1966 to 1995, and in 1998 became CEO and director of the Canadian War Museum. His many publications have focused on Canadian national history, Canada-US relations, the public service, universities, and the teaching of history. Although he never voted for Pierre Elliott Trudeau, he has supported Trudeau's constitutional views.

THERE HAD NEVER BEFORE been a crowd at York University like it. Gathered around the flagpole in the centre of the still-growing campus that October noon in 1970 were at least five thousand students and faculty, pressed close together and surrounding the small stage. This was the university's "Rally for Canada," a response to the crisis in Quebec that had led the federal government to impose the War Measures Act and arrest almost five hundred suspected "terrorists" and their supporters.

The night before, one of my departmental colleagues, a young historian who had just arrived at York from Harvard University and who understood nothing whatsoever about what was happening, had called to ask me to speak at the rally. "But I don't support the government and its actions," I said. "That doesn't matter," came his very American reply, "come and speak for Canada."

So I did. There were other speakers, including historians Ramsay Cook and John Saywell, but in my memory I was the only one to oppose the government's actions forthrightly. I cannot remember my exact words, but I suggested that the imposition of the War Measures Act was a direct attack on the civil liberties of all Canadians, that it was using a mallet to kill a flea, and that, under its terms, not only the Front de libération du Québec terrorists but activists, hippies, Vietnam draft dodgers, and troublemakers could be arrested anywhere in Canada. That morning, the newspapers had reported that the mayor of Vancouver had greeted the imposition of the act with pleasure as a way to clean up his city.

I have never before or since been afraid of a crowd, never feared being torn limb from limb, but that day I was frightened. The shouts from the students that interrupted my speech were frequent and hostile; the visceral hatred of the FLQ kidnappers and murderers, and, as I interpreted it, of all Québécois, was palpable. I was very pleased to get off that platform and into my office before I was attacked and beaten.

The same vengeful mood pervaded my classroom the next day. One hundred students were enrolled in my third-year course on post–Confederation Canada, and I asked how many supported the government's policy. Every hand but one went up, a result that mirrored the national opinion polls. A Canadian Institute of Public Opinion poll taken on October 17 found that 88 percent of Canadians thought the government actions either not tough enough or about right; in Quebec, 86 percent felt that way. Understandably, none of the students was for terrorism, and everyone believed that Pierre Trudeau had acted with appropriate force to deal with the crisis created by the kidnapping of British trade commissioner James Cross and the kidnapping and murder of Pierre Laporte, Quebec's labour minister. Several female students referred to a comment by Jean Marchand, the minister of regional economic expansion who was also Trudeau's friend, that a woman had been found in Hull with "FLQ" scratched on her stomach. In other words, no one was safe. Marchand also painted the FLQ as having up to three thousand activists with weapons such as rifles and machine guns and two tons of explosives, and, for good measure, he labelled the Montreal civic action party, the Front d'action politique, or FRAP, which was fighting a city election against Mayor Jean Drapeau, as quasi-terrorists. Like the minister and the Quebec and federal governments, my students were frightened, concerned, and certain that Trudeau was the leader to put Quebec finally and firmly in its place.

It wasn't only students who felt that way. I recall very clearly a meeting of the board of the *Canadian Forum*, the left-centrist monthly of small circulation and, we fondly believed, much influence that had been publishing since 1920. Abe Rotstein of the University of Toronto was the editor, and we always met at his home. The question in the immediate aftermath of the FLQ crisis was what position the *Forum* editorial would take. The majority, of which I was part, was firmly for denouncing Trudeau's position, but a significant minority supported the government's actions. Ken McNaught, the University of Toronto historian and biographer of J.S. Woodsworth, was the main proponent of this view, and the discussion was fierce. In the end, the *Forum* attacked the government, and McNaught resigned from the editorial board. Years later, shortly before his death in 1997, he reminded me that at one point in the discussion I had threatened to punch him in the nose. Happily, I didn't.

Two years after the October Crisis, at a time when public opinion had begun to move massively against the Trudeau government and when many had begun to forget their strong anti-Quebec/pro-government responses at the time, the University of Toronto Press published *Forum: Canadian Life and Letters 1920–70: Selections from The Canadian Forum*. There was a grand party at Rotstein's house, and the book was hailed. At one point during the evening, Frank Scott, the constitutional expert, civil libertarian, poet, old socialist, and frequent *Forum* writer in the 1930s and 1940s, was asked to say a few words. In his celebratory remarks he referred to the *Forum*'s editorial about the imposition of the War Measures Act with a tone of mild criticism, and there were some kindly hisses—if hisses can ever be characterized that way, those ones were. I still remember the amazement with which I was soon hearing from people who hadn't attended the party that Scott had been shouted down because he still supported the imposition of the War Measures Act. Many professed pleasure that the socialist-turned-reactionary Scott had been so treated. As that small incident suggested, the strong feelings about Trudeau's actions still persisted, though the swing in opinion was well under way.

Now, a quarter-century later, scarcely anyone appears to remember that the Canadian public, including the Quebec public, was solidly behind Trudeau and the War Measures Act in October 1970. A recent conversation with a young francophone journalist, to whom I told my story about the York rally, drew only puzzlement from her. You mean, she asked, that the students opposed you because you supported Trudeau? That it was the other way round she could scarcely believe.

■

Today, the students and faculty who gathered at the flagpole at York University that day in 1970 would, if asked about their position on the FLQ crisis, likely claim to have opposed the War Measures Act. "Trudeau overreacted," they would say. "Yes, the FLQ had to be dealt with, but the arrests, the troops in the street, that was just too much. Worse still," they might continue, "Trudeau's actions fostered the growth of the Parti Québécois." Canadians, in retrospect, always seem to be more in favour of civil liberties than they ever have been in times of crisis.

Why have we changed our collective mind about October 1970? Certainly it is not because there is any new support for terrorist actions, or any greater acceptance in English Canada of Quebec separatism. The never-ending constitutional struggles, the referenda, and the continuing blackmail game played so successfully by Quebec City and Quebec MPs in Ottawa guarantee that the vast majority of anglophone Canadians remain as hostile to the idea of Quebec independence, Quebec as a nation, or Quebeckers as a *peuple* as they did in October 1970. In Quebec, the belief that Trudeau was a bully serving the Anglos and inflicting yet another humiliation on Quebec in the crisis has taken firm root, an attitude reinforced by the way Trudeau fought the 1980 referendum and then patriated the Constitution over the opposition of the *nationalistes*. In Quebec's flexible, fallible public memory, no one supported Trudeau in October 1970—the opinion polls must have been wrong!

What has changed, in other words, is the perception of Trudeau. The trampoline-bouncing candidate of 1968 turned into the grim-visaged and remorseless opponent of terrorism in October 1970, and Canadians accepted and admired him for his defence of the state. "Just watch me!" he said on television on October 13, 1970, and all but the "weak-kneed bleeding hearts" watched what he did with approval.

But when Trudeau's arrogance began to grate on the public ("Why should I sell your wheat?" "Where's Biafra?"), and when, inevitably, he proved unable to resolve all Canada's problems, the mood changed. The hero of 1968 and 1970 was beginning to be scorned by the time of the election of 1972, which produced a narrow minority government dependent on the NDP for its continued existence. Liberal free-spending produced a majority in 1974, but in 1979 the bland, unknown Joe Clark defeated Trudeau's discredited Liberals. The age of Trudeau seemed over, and the assessments at the time of the man's record suggested limited achievements and a still-growing distaste for the strong-arm methods of 1970. René Lévesque and the Parti Québécois had won power in Quebec in 1976, and the first referendum on separation was drawing near.

But Trudeau came back when Clark threw away his opportunity at government, won the election of 1980 with a majority, and proceeded to defeat Lévesque handily in the referendum that year. For a time, Trudeau the hero was back, but only briefly, and the tepid government of the next four years was weakly led. The peace initiative of the last months seemed only a tired, futile gesture, and the famous "walk in the snow" that produced Trudeau's decision to retire from office was inevitable. John Turner briefly succeeded him, but, saddled with the legacy of fifteen years of Trudeau, Turner proved easy meat for Brian Mulroney's Tories.

Curiously, even Mulroney's failures at constitutional reform, failures that galvanized the separatists who had been gravely weakened by the 1980 referendum defeat, did not alter the firm perception that Trudeau had overreacted in October 1970. Perhaps it was the 1982 addition to the Constitution of the Charter of Rights and Freedoms that gave Canadians a new sense of their liberties. Perhaps it was the repeal of the War Measures Act itself, or, possibly, the failure of Trudeau's government ever to explain the basis for its actions in the crisis. Whatever the reasons, the public mind now seems fixed: Trudeau used a mallet to crush a flea, almost exactly as I had said in October 1970 at York University.

So why am I not happy that I was proven right? Because, like the Canadian public, I too have changed my position. Over the last dozen years I have come to believe that Trudeau acted properly during the FLQ crisis. The FLQ had been exploding bombs since 1963, attacking CBC property, armouries, and mailboxes and toppling the monument to General Wolfe in Quebec City. People were killed by the frustrated, angry *felquistes*, but ordinary police methods seemed able to control matters. In October 1970 they did not seem sufficient. Terrorism can never be tolerated. Advocating Quebec (or British Columbia) separatism is a legitimate political activity in a Canadian democracy, but kidnapping and murder are not.

The government of Canada could not allow its duly elected politicians or foreign diplomats to be at the mercy of anti-democratic political thugs. Virtually every measure to create and maintain public order in such circumstances was justified. Should the federal government have stood idly by and done nothing? Should the FLQ hoodlums—who were not freedom fighters, intellectuals, or heroes of any kind—have been allowed licence to kill? Nothing Trudeau and the government did, however extreme the rhetoric at times, crossed the line into unjustifiable areas. I am prepared to grant that the unwarranted arrest of 497 nationalists and democratic separatists, almost all on lists prepared by the Quebec Sûreté and the Montreal Police, not the RCMP or the federal authorities, was an overreaction of a shocking sort. The Aislin cartoon of Jean Marchand holding a Montreal telephone book and saying he had a list of suspects seemed all too accurate at the time, though in later television interviews Marchand explained that the federal government had, in fact, intervened to reduce the number. The last of those arrested was released on January 1, 1971.

Yet even the detentions had their justification. The situation in Montreal in particular, where recent police and taxi-driver strikes had degenerated into violence, and in Quebec in general, was on the verge of slipping out of control, tending towards the "apprehended insurrection" that the imposition of the War Measures Act had aimed to squash. Students, unionists, and separatist radicals—cheered on by what historian Desmond Morton called "the affluent dilettantes of revolutionary violence"—were creating a psychological atmosphere of crisis and fear in which a political *putsch*, massive civic unrest, or the collapse of the just-elected Quebec Liberal government of Robert Bourassa began to seem very real possibilities. The killing of protesting anti-war students by National Guard troops at Kent State University in Ohio had occurred a few months before, and ministers, generals, and police must have been haunted by the fear that something similar could occur at Université de Montréal.

The most visible sign of the growing sense of destabilization and crisis came on October 15, when *Le Devoir* published a document signed by a group of leading Quebec business, academic, trade union, and political figures which called, in inflammatory language, on the Quebec government to negotiate "an exchange between hostages and political prisoners." The group and the document it produced were the inspirations of René Lévesque, the Parti Québécois leader who, while strongly condemning terrorism, had his own game to play in destabilizing Quebec and attacking Ottawa. The hostages were Pierre Laporte and James Cross; the "political prisoners" were the FLQ activists, hoodlums who had been jailed for their part in bombings in the 1960s. After this incredible statement, Trudeau and his advisers clearly concluded that only the firmest action could bring a dangerous and rapidly collapsing situation under control. In retrospect, the arrests of militants, the troops on the street, and the sense that the federal government, if not Mayor Drapeau or Premier Bourassa, was taking firm action were necessary. The imposition of the War Measures Act, the awareness that the state would use its full powers, was precisely the boost that the forces of order and public confidence required. It worked, and the government's firmness won it the same overwhelming support in Quebec as in Canada.

Yes, the FLQ murdered Pierre Laporte as its counter to the imposition of the War Measures Act. But the terrorists might well have done the same thing at any time that the Quebec labour minister's death served their purposes. Yes, the Parti Québécois won the election of 1976 (campaigning not for independence, but against the Bourassa government's corruption and incompetence), and there is little doubt that the backlash against the War Measures Act contributed to its stunning success. But since October 1970 there have been no acts of terrorism, no bombings, and no kidnappings. Trudeau may have hoped and even expected that the October Crisis would destroy separatism once and for all; if so, he was wrong. But there can be no question that Trudeau's bold actions had moved the idea of separatism completely out of the conspiracy-charged FLQ cells and into the bright light of public debate. That, at least, was a major accomplishment, and the issue ever after would be fought out in a civilized fashion in public forums. If Canada loses and separatism wins, it will not be because of the way Trudeau dealt with the events of October 1970.

Frank Scott, the great man that I jocularly hissed that night in 1972, was right and I was unquestionably wrong during the FLQ crisis. The proclamation of the War Measures Act was "drastic," he wrote in a letter in January 1971, but "there was no other means at hand . . . While there was no likelihood of any 'insurrection' here, there was an imminent collapse of civil government. Unfortunately we live in a fragile civilization which can be brought to the brink of disaster by a few ruthless and determined men." Scott had watched the NDP, led by his old colleague David Lewis, along with a few Tories and civil libertarians, oppose the Trudeau government's actions, and he could understand why they did so. "But they hadn't been living in Quebec under seven years of bombing and they hadn't been living in Quebec in a volatile atmosphere," he said; "they hadn't seen seven thousand or six thousand students approving the FLQ manifesto." Nor had they seen Quebec's attorney general taking refuge on the top floor of the Queen Elizabeth Hotel in a suite guarded by the police. The rule of law was threatened. The leaders of the government of Quebec may have been scared silly, Scott said, but "they were the legitimate government of Quebec and I was going to defend their right to govern against any terrorist."

Trudeau, I believe, took this same view in October 1970, and it shaped his government's actions. As he wrote in his memoirs, "it is the duty of any democracy to protect itself against the forces of dissolution as soon as they raise their heads . . . never giving in to chaos or terror." Essentially, the Canadian state chose to defend itself against the campaign of terror launched by a handful of ideological pygmies, as it had to do, and Trudeau used the only means predecessor governments had left at his disposal. No one was killed by the state and, though some temporarily lost their liberty, democracy was preserved. Trudeau himself (as Margaret Trudeau wrote in her first volume of memoirs) was shaken by the way old civil libertarian friends turned against him and, she noted, he wept when Pierre Laporte was murdered.

Canada itself, also shaken to its roots, continued to exist, and a badly shaken Quebec remained a part of the nation. Trudeau was right; yet, in a curious way, the fact that Canadians could turn so quickly against the leader who had brought them through the October Crisis was the best sign of their democracy's strength.

Trudeau's Canada:
The Vision and
the Visionary

■

ANDREW COHEN

Andrew Cohen is a foreign correspondent for the Globe and Mail, *based in Washington, D.C. A native of Montreal, he studied political science at McGill University and earned graduate degrees in journalism and international affairs at Carleton University.*

He has worked for the Financial Post, *the* Ottawa Citizen, *and* United Press International, *where he covered the last government of Pierre Trudeau. In 1990, he wrote* A Deal Undone: The Making and Breaking of the Meech Lake Accord, *a bestselling study of Canada's constitutional politics.*

As a member of the Editorial Board of the Globe, *he won National Newspaper Awards in 1995 and 1996.*

O N JANUARY 24, 1998, the *Globe and Mail* published a withering denunciation of Pierre Elliott Trudeau under the name of its editor-in-chief, William Thorsell. A few days before, the former prime minister had visited Toronto to celebrate the launch of an English-language edition of *Cité libre*, the audacious journal he had co-founded in 1950. Thorsell, it seemed, would not be taking out a subscription.

Trudeau was "a bust in English-speaking Canada" and "the greatest disappointment since John Diefenbaker." His return in 1980 was an "accident of history"; almost everything he did subsequently was "decisive, dramatic and disastrous." His investment and energy policies were repealed; his peace mission was disarmed. Only on the Constitution did Trudeau leave "a permanent mark" —and it was not altogether positive.

To Thorsell, Trudeau had wounded Canada grievously when he patriated the Constitution without the consent of the government of Quebec and later resisted two exhaustive negotiations to redress it. Lucien Bouchard was "Pierre Trudeau's child and the Bloc Québécois his most enduring legacy outside the Charter of Rights." So repugnant was his record that even his Liberal Party had made "a desperate effort to escape him." How to explain, then, the enduring adulation for a leader who had left the country in ruins and showed "barely concealed contempt" for his public? Thorsell offered this elegant interpretation: "The shrinking band of Mr. Trudeau's acolytes played on in downtown Toronto this week, the thriller and the thrilled entwined in their old neurotic dance, insisting that the mania in Trudeaumania live up to its billing. Never in Canada's history has psychology dominated policy like this."

There it was, the legacy of Pierre Elliott Trudeau. A bust, a disappointment, an accident. The tribune of contempt. The father of secession. The man in search of his mania.

Oh, Trudeau. He taunts us still.

■

Thorsell isn't alone in rethinking Trudeau these days. In the ivory tower, his record is under relentless attack. Political scientists Guy Laforest (*Trudeau and the End of a Canadian Dream*) and Kenneth McRoberts (*Misconceiving Canada: The Struggle for National Unity*) accuse the country's fifteeth prime minister of destroying the duality that had defined Canada. Their dissatisfaction is shared by many of the twenty-five historians who rated Canada's prime ministers for *Maclean's* magazine in March 1997. Desmond Morton, for example, branded him "the disappointment of the century . . . who left Canada dramatically more divided and drastically poorer than he found it." Altogether, they placed Trudeau in the third rank— neither great nor near great, above Lester Pearson but below Louis St. Laurent—and suggested that he was there more by virtue of endurance than achievement.

More telling, Trudeau's stature is said to be so low in his native Quebec that he had to sit out the referendum in 1995. "His name and legacy may well have become a political liability for federalists in Quebec," say Richard Nadeau, one of a team of political scientists tracking public opinion over recent decades. "For many Quebeckers . . . his name mainly represents a certain way of dealing with constitutional issues, a way they no longer find appealing."

It was that "way", of course, which brought Trudeau to parliament in 1965 and to the prime ministry in 1968. His ambition wasn't to tame inflation or thaw the Cold War (though he tried to do both). It wasn't to lower taxes or reduce the size of government. Rather, politics for Trudeau was about Quebec. His *raison d'être* was to find the ways and means of making Canada broad enough to accommodate the aspirations of its French-speaking minority. He wanted to keep Canada whole.

A generation later, critics count his failures. They say his economics yielded deficits and bloated government; his liberalism failed to redistribute income or reduce poverty; his internationalism was capricious. To a large degree, they are right. Yet, at the end of the day it is unlikely that Trudeau will be judged on his economic, social, or foreign policies. Important as they are, they pale beside the national question, the central issue of his time. Trudeau will be remembered for the Constitution, not the deficit, just as Ronald Reagan is remembered for the Cold War, not the deficit. Fair or not, history has a way of asking the big questions. It doesn't raise statues to leaders for balancing the budget. Visionaries know that; certainly Trudeau did. In the next century, the measure of his legacy will be his vision of Canada.

Both the vision and the visionary have cast a long, lingering shadow. In the thirty years since he came to office in 1968, there has scarcely been a passage in the relationship between English Canada and French Canada in which he was not influential, if not decisive. From his opening skirmish as justice minister with Daniel Johnson in 1968 to his last volley as private citizen with Lucien Bouchard in 1996, Trudeau has been at the centre of our national conversation.

As biographers Christina McCall and Stephen Clarkson put it, the Constitution was "his magnificent obsession." He entered politics with a deep-seated view of the country and spent his career giving life to it. When he left office he said that the Constitution was the only issue that could bring him back, and three times it did. This matter of the Constitution was a different calculus for Trudeau. For all his avowed devotion to reason over passion, his sense here was visceral as much as cerebral. As prime minister he could reverse himself on wage and price controls or cruise missile testing, but never on his kind of Canada. Whether it was the role of francophones, the balance between individual rights and provincial rights, or the value of popular sovereignty, Trudeau's thinking never "evolved" like that of other politicians. As he led an unequivocal

life, seeking excellence in all that he did, he followed an unequivocal ideal, which left little room for compromise in its fundamentals.

For a generation, Trudeau was Canada's constitutional com-
pass. His commitment to a charter of rights, a strong central government, equality of the provinces, and the protection of minority
language was the orthodoxy. More than any other figure of his
time, his constancy and eloquence gave him a claim of ownership.
At the height of his powers, he set the tone and tempo of the
debate. He was to politics what Bobby Orr was to hockey—the
player who could dominate the play and, on a good day, determine
the outcome of the game itself.

Trudeau represented true north. His beliefs were forged in a
lifetime of thought and practice and they became the standard of
comparison for all others. Two nations, special status, a community
of communities, sovereignty-association and distinct society were
doctrines judged in relation to his own. Those that deviated a few
degrees—say, a modest devolution of power to the regions—were
negotiable. Those that deviated substantially—say, the creation of
two nations—were untenable. And those that would detach Quebec from Canada—whether by outright independence or asym-
metrical federalism—were contemptible.

Trudeau gave no quarter in his defence of Canada. Between
1968 and 1996, in seven tests of will, he declared, enacted, and defended his vision. By any standard, it was an extraordinary act of
citizenship. He was at once patriot, philosopher, warrior, polemecist, even tragedian. His adversaries were nationalists, terrorists,
separatists and provincialists, Quebeckers or Albertans, Conservatives or Liberals, populists or demagogues—it scarcely mattered.
Trudeau engaged everyone, and every time he won.

■

The first time Trudeau gave full voice to his idea of Canada was as
minister of justice in 1968. Since he had arrived in Parliament three
years earlier, and particularly since the Liberal Party had reviewed
its position in caucus in September, 1967, Trudeau had been press-

ing for rejection of any form of special status for Quebec. As Donald Peacock remembers in *Journey to Power*, Trudeau told his colleagues there was a choice: "either one nation with two languages, or, ultimately, two separate nations." His colleagues worried about the challenge, fearing it would divide Canada. "Trudeau feared Canada would break up by default if the challenge were *not* made," Peacock wrote. Against the odds, supported by Jean Marchand and Gérard Pelletier, Trudeau won over caucus and cabinet.

On February 5, 1968, Lester Pearson opened a federal-provincial conference in Ottawa. He said that Canada was at "a fork in the road," warning that its survival was at stake. Across the table, Trudeau faced Daniel Johnson of Quebec. In papers presented to the conference, Trudeau had set out his view: "Canada's identity is its diversity *and* its unity; we lose ourselves if we lose our two linguistic communities, our diverse cultural heritages, or our several regional identities. We lose them all if we lose the Canada in which they have been able to exist and develop."

The next day, on national television, Johnson attacked Trudeau. He claimed Trudeau was pushing a powerful centrism out of political ambition, trying "to prove to the rest of Canada they won't be pushed around by Quebec." He said the willingness of other provinces to accept the Commission on Bilingualism and Biculturalism was little more than "an aspirin." Only special powers to Quebec would preserve its distinctiveness, providing equality.

Trudeau, much to Pearson's alarm, returned barb for barb. When the premier called the minister "the member from Mount Royal," Trudeau called the premier "the deputy from Bagot." He accused Johnson of trying to undermine Quebec's members of parliament. If Quebec had more power in the province than Ottawa, why have a federal government? He mocked Johnson's request for more powers from the English-speaking provinces: "If we could have our cake and eat it, and the candles and the icing," he said, "I would be happy."

Beyond the theatrics, new lines of argument were emerging. Trudeau trumpeted "the Canadian Charter of Human Rights" and mused about a political community in which both French and

English Canadians could move freely, live and work in Canada. Trudeau knew that the greatest threat to special status for Quebec was the idea that Quebeckers could be at home everywhere in Canada, not just in *la belle province*.

Historian Jean-Louis Roy called Trudeau's exchange with Johnson "one of the most spectacular duels in Canadian politics." Biographer Richard Gwyn said "he slugged it out, in Single Combat . . . winning on all cards, in the conference chamber and on the television screens." The celebrated confrontation did something more than make Trudeau prime minister. It showed why this iconoclast had come to Ottawa and how he would challenge convention there. It showed that in Ottawa, as in Quebec, he was prepared to offer a pan-Canadian vision against those who would retreat into Quebec. In challenging Johnson, he drew his line in the snow.

Thus, at Pearson's fork in the road, Canada faced a choice between special status or a broader community. Trudeau declared his Canada, and his Canada prevailed.

■

The next passage in relations between Quebec and Canada came in the October Crisis of 1970. When the Front de libération du Québec kidnapped James Cross, the British trade commissioner and Pierre Laporte, Quebec's labour minister, Canada sailed into uncharted waters. "Canada enters the Revolutionary Age," said *Time* magazine.

Trudeau immediately saw the danger. He knew the demands of the FLQ were inherently undemocratic, a threat to the popular will. No self-respecting leader could release "political prisoners" who were in jail for their crimes, not their beliefs. To free them would legitimize blackmail and invite more.

As clearly as Trudeau recognized the threat, he feared that others did not. What was decisive for him was a declaration signed on October 15 by leading Quebeckers, including René Lévesque, Jacques Parizeau, and Claude Ryan. It encouraged the provincial government to negotiate "an exchange between hostages and political prisoners." To Trudeau, to use "political prisoners" was to adopt the language of the terrorists. Trudeau worried about a deterioration of public will. The justice minister of Quebec had proposed releasing political prisoners, the police were exhausted, and there was talk of student demonstrations, inviting violence. The prospect of politicians, scholars, and unionists negotiating with terrorists suggested, in Trudeau's words, "an extremely disordered state."

At the request of Premier Robert Bourassa, Trudeau had already sent federal troops to Quebec. Now, in imposing the War Measures Act, he chose a blunter instrument. He never denied that there were abuses and as a civil libertarian, he felt them keenly. His government later repealed the act and introduced an entrenched bill of rights.

The purpose of the War Measures Act wasn't to crush separatism but to restore order. Secessionists argued that the government imposed the act unilaterally, but it did not. Perhaps Trudeau could have refused Bourassa's appeal, but what would have been the response if Ottawa had done nothing and chaos had followed?

The October Crisis marked the end of terrorism in Quebec. For seven years, the FLQ had been maiming and killing Quebeckers. René Lévesque could sneer that "Trudeau's stupidity will not have prevented more kidnappings," but he was wrong. "In my judgement Pierre Trudeau kept Quebec in Canada when no one else in Canada could have done it," Former senator Eugene Forsey wrote of the crisis. "In my judgement also, he saved us from Baader-Meinhof gangs and Red Brigades."

Trudeau's response wasn't subtle. If the choice, as he saw it, was between democracy and the mob, he would chose democracy. Trudeau defended his Canada, and his Canada prevailed.

■

The next challenge to national unity came in the referendum in Quebec in 1980. By that winter, when the question was being debated in the National Assembly, almost 60 percent of Quebeckers supported sovereignty-association. With Joe Clark as prime minister and Claude Ryan as leader of the Quebec Liberals, the Parti Québécois was mounting a forceful campaign, and it was winning.

No one can say that Trudeau single-handedly reversed opinion and won the referendum. The polls showed a steady erosion of sovereigntist support over the last six weeks of the campaign, but they also showed that the early soundings may have overstated support for separatism. Still, if ever a leader made a difference in his time, the time was that spring and the leader was Trudeau.

The prospects for the No side improved markedly when he returned to power on February 18, 1980 with seventy-four of seventy-five seats from Quebec and a clutch of Quebeckers in senior portfolios. The secessionists would now have to face a federalist from Quebec. His success was the strongest antidote to their argument that Quebeckers could look only to Quebec City to protect their interests.

The referendum of 1980 was Trudeau's greatest test. Having been defeated for re-election in 1979, when he insisted on making the Constitution the focus of his losing campaign, he felt new life. Now, girding for battle, he marshalled his resources and rationed his appearances. In his first speech on April 15, he declared that sovereignty-association was impossible because the nine other provinces were uninterested in association. As for sovereignty, he couldn't negotiate it because he had just been re-elected with a mandate to exercise sovereignty over all Canada. In speeches in Quebec on May 2 and May 9, Trudeau mocked Lévesque's vision and offered his own, challenging Quebeckers to find their identity in a larger entity, not to cower behind the walls of the ghetto.

But it was his speech on May 16, at the Paul Sauvé Arena in Montreal, that was pivotal. Responding to taunts from Lévesque over his middle name, Trudeau invoked "Elliott" to illustrate the intolerance of his adversaries. He promised constitutional change, and he made the referendum not just a No to sovereignty-association but a commitment to constitutional reform. Defeating sovereignty-association could have killed any negotiation; now Trudeau promised to open a new one.

Once the referendum was lost, the threat was blunted. If Trudeau was not solely responsible for the victory, he was certainly responsible for changing the country. As Joe Clark put it: "The kind of Canada that Mr. Lévesque wants to separate from no longer exists."

It was a choice between a little Quebec and a broad Canada, between division and unity. Here, too, Trudeau preserved his Canada, and his Canada prevailed.

■

Having won the referendum, Trudeau unveiled his plans to bring home the British North America Act, entrench a Charter of Rights, and establish an amending formula. Everything was negotiable, he said—rights, roles, and responsibilities—and he meant those of the provinces, too.

The debate over the next eighteen months would give shape to Trudeau's Canada and test his will. It would take place in parliament, the courts, and intergovernmental conferences, generating a cacaphony of threats, cries, and laments. By its end, from its blast furnace, would come the steel of Trudeau's Canada.

Since 1955, Trudeau had proposed placing a bill of rights in the Constitution. A charter would realize his dream of a society of two peoples, largely but not exclusively French and English, securing their futures in the broad pan-Canadian state. The vehicle would be the patriation of the BNA Act of 1867. Having presided over several unsuccessful rounds of federal-provincial talks since 1968, including the acceptance and rejection of the Victoria Charter in 1971, Trudeau knew the risks. He also knew that he had promised Quebeckers "renewed federalism."

His predecessors had tried for more than half a century to free the Constitution from British trusteeship. Opposing him were the premiers, each with his own interests, including an avowed separatist who would reject anything that strengthened Confederation. Collectively, the challenge they posed to Trudeau's Canada was not Johnson's special status or Lévesque's sovereignty-association. This time it was provincialism.

From the moment the premiers met Trudeau at 24 Sussex Drive in October 1980, they were intransigent. They would do what the premiers had always done in these negotiations—trade rights for fish. It wasn't patriation or the Charter that mattered to them, it was the division of powers. It was what they could extract from Ottawa. Without concessions, there would be no consent.

No wonder the meeting began badly. The premiers presented a list of demands that no prime minister, particularly this one, could accept. Forestry, communications, culture, the fishery and other areas of federal jurisdiction were all demanded by the provinces as the price of their agreement. When the flinty Brian Peckford declared that his vision of Canada was closer to Lévesque's than to the prime minister's, Trudeau recoiled.

Facing opposition from the premiers, the Conservatives and the government of Great Britain, Trudeau persevered. He would woo the New Democrats in parliament, divide the provinces (by co-opting Ontario and New Brunswick), and go straight to Westminster in London. If necessary, he would call an election, even a referendum. The Constitution would be home by July 1, 1981.

Ultimately, Trudeau compromised—even though he said years later that he never wanted to. He referred the matter to the Supreme Court, and when the justices failed to deliver the endorsement he wanted, he reconvened the first ministers. In splitting Lévesque from the premiers of the Gang of Eight, he reached agreement with them on the Charter. He accepted the notwithstanding clause, which he disliked for the opportunity it gave the provinces to opt out; he accepted a modest transfer of power; and he accepted an amending formula without a veto for Quebec. He did what he had to do.

If patriation was the symbol of nationhood, the Charter of Rights was its ark and covenant. Trudeau had succeeded where every prime minister had failed since the first attempt by Mackenzie King. No one else in Canada could have done it, for no one else had the single-mindedness and the bloody-mindedness. Only a leader with a clarity of purpose and a sense of destiny could have carried it off.

A weaker prime minister might have offered more powers to the premiers, bowed to Westminster, diluted the Charter, placated the secessionists. Trudeau stood firm, showing the confidence of a Venetian doge entrusted with the people's faith. He never shambled or shuffled. Feet apart, thumbs in belt, cheek bones high, Trudeau was a figure of resolve. For him, it was a choice between his political community or their community of communities. Trudeau shaped his Canada, and his Canada prevailed.

■

Trudeau left office in 1984. Although he took a vow of silence, he broke it three times over the next dozen years. Twice he tried to stop his successors from rewriting the Constitution; the third time he intervened to defend his record after he was attacked by secessionists in the referendum of 1995. In retirement, Trudeau was watchful. Like Cincinnatus, the general who left the plough to take up the sword for Rome, Trudeau returned to defend his Canada.

The first of his interventions as a private citizen came during the Meech Lake Accord in 1987. Trudeau had thought that separatism was dying when he left office three years earlier. His Constitution, he boasted in an infelicitous choice of words, would last "a thousand years." The Parti Québécois was disintegrating and his successor, Brian Mulroney, presented himself as a federalist of his ilk. Although the framers of the Accord declared it a moderate proposal—in relative terms, it was—and although Trudeau himself had offered some of its elements to the provinces at different times, he called it a repudiation of his Canada. The greatest affront was recognizing Quebec as a "distinct society." For Trudeau, this was special status, *redux*.

Trudeau had hoped that someone would question the accord, but no one did. "So I took it upon myself to remind Canadians that there is another view of Canada than the one proposed in the Meech Lake Accord," he writes in his *Memoirs*. In an article published on May 27, 1987, he savaged the accord and its authors in searing polemic, informed by logic, inflamed by hyberbole. Over the next three years, until the accord died in 1990, he restated his argument in interviews with the media, in testimony before two parliamentary committees, and in a best-selling collection of essays on his government.

Here was Trudeau as polemecist and pamphleteer. The words were poison darts; the arguments were extreme; the mood black. The accord was an end to bilingualism and a sellout to the provinces. Owing nothing to anyone, Trudeau railed at the vandals desecrating his Canada. Many hoped he would fall silent, muttering that former prime ministers should retire and shut up. Not this former prime minister.

His intervention unsettled the premiers, angered the prime minister, comforted the dissidents and sowed doubt among Canadians. He couldn't stop the accord, which was signed in June, though two premiers, in tacit response to the reservations he had raised, insisted on imposing conditions on the power of the distinct society. Trudeau acted as he always had in times of crisis: He weighed his options, chose his timing, and exercised his conjurer's powers.

When the accord collapsed, he could claim some credit. Pollsters said that his intervention moved public opinion from support to opposition. Certainly, as the strongman from Quebec, the winner of the referendum, and the father of the Charter, he had credibility on Quebec, if not in Quebec, where his stature was eroding. He made opposition to Meech Lake respectable.

To Pierre Trudeau, the Meech Lake Accord represented the ruin of Canada, and the repudiation of his vision. Here he restored his Canada, and his Canada prevailed.

■

In 1992, Trudeau entered the debate again, this time in response to the Charlottetown Accord. As the referendum campaign opened that autumn, there was scarcely a dissenting voice in the land. Beyond the unanimity among the first ministers and the leaders of the opposition, business and the media also supported the agreement.

Then Trudeau reappeared, like Banquo's Ghost, first with articles in *l'Actualité* and *Maclean's*, then in a speech at a Chinese restaurant in Montreal, which became known, somewhat grandly, as the "Maison Egg Roll" address. In proposing the distinct society (more qualified this time), the hierarchy of citizenship, a transfer of power to the provinces, and the assurance of more constitutional negotiations, the agreement was a junk bond and a promissory note. "They have created this mess, and it deserves a big NO!" he thundered.

The arguments were familar, inviting his critics to argue that he could never move beyond them. He took this as praise, thinking his consistency enlightened rather than foolish. In 1980 he could say that Quebeckers always knew what his promise of "renewed federalism" meant; in 1992 they knew what his rejection meant, even as he momentarily left retirement to reaffirm it. There was no mystery to his position.

Pollsters say that support for Charlottetown in English Canada dropped twenty points after his remarks. Although Trudeau found himself on the same side as Preston Manning and the Reform Party, his voice conferred credibility on the ragtag band of opponents. The referendum lost. Trudeau, ever the patrician populist, cheered the blow to the conventional wisdom of the elites. Once again, he had gone over the heads of the politicians. As he wrote in his *Memoirs*: "The Canadian people did exactly what I had hoped they would do: they established that the locus of the sovereignty of Canada is the people . . . What they did really amounted to a revolt of the people against the political class."

Trudeau had intervened again, perhaps decisively, to thwart the emergence of a Canada built on the distinct society, devolution, and aboriginal self-government. In a choice between his federalism and their provincialism, he had protected his Canada, and, once again, his Canada prevailed.

■

The last time Trudeau's Canada was in question was the Quebec referendum in 1995. Trudeau wanted to enter the debate, as he always had, but Ottawa asked him to stay away. He obliged. On the day thousands of Canadians marched in Place du Canada in Montreal, Trudeau watched forlornly from his office high above Boulevard René Lévesque. Then he went for lunch.

That Trudeau was silent did not mean he was absent. More than once Lucien Bouchard invoked the "humiliation" of patriation in 1982, as if it were an ancient stain on the family honour. Reveling in the affront, he held up newspapers from November 5, 1981, the morning after "the Night of the Long Knives," repeating the charge that Ottawa and the other provinces had met secretly and agreed to patriate the Constitution without consulting Quebec. You see, said Bouchard pointing to a photograph of the prime minister, Trudeau is laughing! He's laughing at us! He's mocking us! Trudeau held his tongue, but not for long.

In an open letter to Bouchard on February 3, 1996, Trudeau challenged his version of history. "I accuse Lucien Bouchard of having misled the population of Quebec during last October's referendum campaign," he wrote. "By distorting the political history of his province and of his country, by spreading discord among its citizens with his demagogic rhetoric and by preaching contempt for those Canadians who did not share his views, Lucien Bouchard went beyond the limits of honest and democratic debate."

Point by point, the old logician refuted the "stupid allegations" that Bouchard had made in the campaign—that negotiations between Quebec and Canada had always failed; that Quebec's negotiators were always sound; that the Night of the Long Knives was a betrayal. He denied Bouchard's interpretation of events in 1981 and said that the Premier lied in claiming that the Constitution reduced Quebec's power in language and education. Ironically, he even said that Bouchard had wrongly accused English Canada of killing the Meech Lake Accord; Quebec, by and large, had been responsible. Then came his stinging denunciation: "By calling upon fallacies and untruths to advance the cause of hateful demagoguery, Lucien Bouchard misled the electors . . . By his actions, he tarnished Quebec's good reputation as a democratic society and he does not deserve the trust of the people of this province." Here was a declaration of honour, a man speaking to history. It was characteristically Trudeau.

Bouchard replied. Although he didn't answer most of Trudeau's accusations, he revisited the hoary myth of Quebec's mistreatment within Canada, evoking the October Crisis to question Trudeau's credentials as a democrat.

Trudeau responded in a letter of February 17, in which he attacked Bouchard's "historical relativism." When Bouchard said he was happy to be placed among democrats such as Lévesque and Jean Lesage who had felt Trudeau's scorn, Trudeau sniffed: "Mr. Bouchard, you misread me—I never accused you of being a democrat."

In what now seems like a valedictory, Trudeau revisited the vision of Canada he had always embraced. Quebeckers, he said, should not look for their "identity" and "distinctiveness" in the Constitution but "in their confidence in themselves and the full exercise of their rights as citizens equal to all other citizens of Canada." While he did not doubt that they could create an independent country, he implored them to choose a more enlightened destiny. "I have always believed that they have the stature to face a more difficult and nobler challenge—that of participating in the construction of the Canadian nation founded on democratic pluralism, institutional bilingualism and the sense of sharing." He said the very notion of sovereignty was obsolete at the end of the century. He continued: "To weaken it [Canada] by dividing it would be a historic blunder of infinite proportion. We must not rend the fabric of this still-young country, we must give it the chance to grow and to prosper."

Trudeau was writing his epitaph. Age was advancing. In Montreal, where he had retreated to his art deco mansion in 1984, it was whispered that he had Alzheimer's or Parkinson's Disease. Of the three wise men, Jean Marchand was dead and, within a year, Gérard Pelletier would be too, a loss which would devastate Trudeau. After the referendum, Trudeau seemed dispirited and spent. "I have no new ideas," he sighed.

■

As Trudeau withdraws, his vision of Canada seems in eclipse, if not in ruins. In Quebec, a demagogic premier prepares to seek re-election, threatening another referendum. In Ottawa, the Liberals govern by dint of central Canada, led by a discredited Quebecker who sometimes speaks a language of nationalism to Quebec that Trudeau distrusts. The official opposition, rooted in the West, espouses a view of Quebec as a province like the others, a view seemingly close to his own until under scrutiny its coded prejudices emerge. In the academy, scholars pronounce the end of Canada and offer panaceas antithetical to his own.

Is it all over, then? Did Pierre Trudeau fight all those battles only to lose the war? Was it all in vain? Is the vision of the pan-Canadian identity obsolete in the twilight of the century? The answer can only be no.

The fundamental truth is that today's Canada is still Trudeau's Canada. Just as he won every battle to defend his vision as prime minister, he defeated every attempt to destroy it as a private citizen. His legacy is all around us: the Charter of Rights, official bilingualism, multiculturalism, the amending formula, equality of the provinces, the prominence of francophones in national life.

The Constitution Act of 1982 remains the law. The House of Commons, the Senate, and the Supreme Court remain unchanged, despite efforts to make them more "representative." The Charter of Rights remains in place, creating a generation of "Charter Canadians" who see it as the foundation of their citizenship. The distribution of powers between governments remains largely unaltered, despite unrelenting demands from the provinces. True, there has been a shift of powers to the provinces, largely through declining federal spending and intergovernmental administrative agreements, some of them negotiated by Trudeau's government. True, as well, that federalism is far from perfect—the economic union is still elusive and multiculturalism frustrates a national identity and the Senate is an anachronism.

But the elements of Trudeau's Canada endure. It isn't accidental, for example, that the governor general, the chief justice of the Supreme Court, the head of the armed forces, the Clerk of the

Privy Council and Canada's ambassador to Washington are franco-phones. In a sense, they are Trudeau's children.

For almost thirty years, Trudeau has shown Sisyphean persistence. In 1968 he reversed the drift to two Canadas and defined his own pan-Canadianism. In 1970 he challenged terrorism, ensuring that it would no longer distort the debate. In 1980 he scorned sovereignty-association and promised a new federalism. In 1982 he rejected any trading of rights for powers and cast his Canada in law. In 1987, 1992, and 1996, he fought efforts to undo his work. As Trudeau went from Northern Magus to Cincinnatus, as Canada turned from the philosopher king to Larry King, Trudeau always remained true to himself.

Deux nations, égalité où indépendance, special status. Flexible federalism, profitable federalism, executive federalism. Sovereignty-association and the distinct society. Johnson, Lévesque, Parizeau. Ideas and advocates came and went. Trudeau stayed.

It is fashionable in some quarters to say that Trudeau is passé, and that his final repudiation will come when Quebec declares its independence. (Kenneth McRoberts, for example, says that "the referendum was the ultimate proof that the Trudeau national unity strategy had failed.") If Quebec goes, critics will blame Trudeau's opposition to greater powers for Quebec. After all, they conclude, it was he who reversed Canada's long-standing accommodation of Quebec, polarized the debate, revived separatism, and thwarted efforts to reconcile the two Canadas on any terms but his own.

This criticism gives false comfort to those who could never accept the victory of his vision over theirs. But what if Trudeau had not acted at those critical moments? Would Canada be bounding happily into the sunlit uplands of the new millenium?

Consider, for a moment, the Canada that might have emerged if it had taken Pearson's other fork in the road. In 1968 a government led by Liberal Robert Winters—or Conservative Robert Stanfield—embraces deux nations, softpedals bilingualism and offers Quebec special status. Quebec becomes more French, Canada becomes more English. Would that accommodation have stopped the rise of René Lévesque and his Parti Québécois, a movement born the year *before* Trudeau came to power, repudiating Pearson's flexible federalism and the "duality" of Confederation?

In 1970 the government negotiates with the FLQ. Would that have suffocated terrorism? In 1980, Joe Clark sits out the referendum (or campaigns, with equal ineffectiveness.) Would sovereignty-association have lost decisively? In 1982 the government abandons patriation, or accepts it in exchange for massive decentralization. Would that have ended the debate? Would Quebec have signed, and if it had, would those hard-line separatists have been content to pack up and go home?

In 1987 Meech Lake passes. Perhaps it might have pre-empted Charlottetown and kept Bouchard in Ottawa. But would it have kept the Parti Québécois from returning to power in 1994 in a province that hadn't elected a government to a third term in forty years? Would it have ended the debate with two constitutional conferences a year, as required by Meech Lake, *ad infinitum*? Recall Bourassa's promise to present a new list of demands in a second constitutional round. Consult Bouchard's pyschologist. Read the history of federal-provincial relations. To think the Meech Lake Accord would have ended the discussion is staggering naïveté.

In this light, Canada would be no better off, and probably far worse. Canada would be a country in name only, its centre weak, its will drained, a sad association of duchies united only by envy and resentment. The BNA Act would reside in Britain. The Charter would remain an idea. The premiers would still be talking. The separatists would still be wailing. Indeed, but for Trudeau's efforts to shape a broader Canada—a Canada that Quebeckers, whatever their ambivalence, still tell surveys they admire—the seccessionists might have succeeded by now, and Canada would not be here at all.

If Canada does fail in the next century, let the sages of history turn their gaze on Trudeau's successors, principally Brian Mulroney, who reopened the Constitution and truly created Bouchard, however confidently some ascribe paternity to Trudeau. Of course, these prisoners of the contemporary cant will blame Trudeau for a generation, denying him the statute of limitations that even war criminals enjoy.

To them, it doesn't matter that Trudeau is almost a decade and a half out of office; that he won majorities in Quebec five times; that twice Quebeckers have defeated secession; that the Charter remains popular in Quebec and in Canada; that he agreed to a notwithstanding clause which gave Quebec the right to preserve its restrictive language law. Nor does it matter that Quebec and the other provinces gained powers under his leadership in a highly decentralized federation or that Trudeau tried to restore the veto which Quebec itself had relinquished. None of these arguments is likely to dislodge the image of the illegitimate, absolutist, uncompromising idealogue, the self-hating Quebecker determined to put Quebec in its place.

■

No matter. Trudeau can rest now, confident in the honour of his struggle and the consistency of his vision. His was a noble, moral vision, appealing to the human spirit, bidding it to rise above the parochialism of little nationalisms that afflict today's world. It was vision for the ages, and Canada has become an exemplar to the world. It has lost appeal in Quebec, to be sure, though that may have more to do with the failure of salesmanship (largely because Trudeau failed to recruit a successor) than the absence of substance. Indeed, if Canada flourishes in the next century and Quebec makes its peace with Confederation, Trudeau may well emerge as the Churchillian figure of his time, a voice of reason amid the hysteria, a titan who stood alone at the bridge and ensured that the centre would hold and the people would rule and union would endure.

Today, though, the greatest argument for Trudeau's vision is the survival and the success of Canada. For all the remaking of institutions and redrawing of powers, for all the threats from separatists and the ambitions of provincialists, the unlikely country remains whole. The fractious, dysfunctional country, the Canada which remains wasted on Canadians, continues to work better in practice than in theory. Loath as we are to self-congratulation, it remains a dominion of security, prosperity and generosity.

When he left office, Pierre Elliott Trudeau was asked to name his greatest accomplishment. He shrugged and said, "I survived." He was wrong. It wasn't that Trudeau survived. It was that Trudeau's Canada survives—and will.

Who Speaks for Canada? Trudeau and the Constitutional Crisis

■

MICHAEL D. BEHIELS

Michael D. Behiels is a professor in the Department of History at University of Ottawa who specializes in Canadian and Quebec political history in the twentieth century, Canadian federalism, and constitutional renewal. He has published numerous books and magazine articles, including Prelude to Quebec's Quiet Revolution: Liberalism versus Neo-Nationalism, 1945-1960 *and* The Meech Lake Primer: Conflicting Views on the 1987 Constitutional Accord.

I N THE 1995 Quebec referendum, Canada barely avoided a
momentous political meltdown. Premier Jacques Parizeau came
within a whisker of declaring the unilateral independence of
Quebec. How had this near disaster come about? It was due, in part,
to the fact that Prime Minister Jean Chrétien and his entourage insisted that Pierre Elliott Trudeau remain silent throughout the campaign. The intellectually bankrupt No forces went on to squander a
sizeable lead in the polls once Lucien Bouchard replaced Parizeau at
the head of the Yes forces. Yet, during the 1980 referendum, the
Meech Lake accord débacle of 1987–90, and the 1992 referendum
on the Charlottetown accord, Trudeau played significant and possibly decisive roles in maintaining Canada's constitutional integrity.
Three times he had beaten back the Quebec secessionists. Indeed,
since the 1960s, he has been at the heart of our constitutional debates. Thanks to a combination of character and circumstance, he
educated a generation of Canadians about their constitutional past,
present, and future. With the support and participation of a wide
cross-section of Canadians, Trudeau undertook the challenge of
transforming the deferential Canadian political culture into one of
genuine democratic deliberation. As a result, Canadians are finally
coming to perceive themselves as a sovereign people.

Such a profound transformation of our political culture was neither understood nor appreciated by our political and chattering
classes. They struggled valiantly to stem the erosion of their ability
to control and ultimately dictate the evolution of Canada's constitutional development in a manner that would enhance their powers
and privileges. They feared and despised Trudeau's presence in the

debate. They tried unsuccessfully to curtail the participation of a whole range of women's, aboriginal, and linguistic minority groups —defined as the Charter federalists because of their links with the 1982 Charter of Rights and Freedoms—that lobbied intensively for the clarification, implementation, and expansion of those rights.

This political war over the theme "Who speaks for Canada: The people or the politicians?" began with the debate over the Meech Lake accord. It continued during two years of constitutional wrangling, culminating in the omnibus Charlottetown deal and referendum of October 1992. Exercising their constitutional sovereignty, a majority of Canadians rejected the ambiguous deal. Why did Trudeau feel compelled to play such a determining role in these struggles? Was he driven by a self-serving desire to protect the place he had carved out for himself in Canada's constitutional history? Or was Trudeau drawn out of retirement to defend the very integrity of the Canadian nation-state by championing the sovereignty of all Canadian citizens to decide, in a democratic manner, their own constitutional future? No doubt, Trudeau was eager to defend his government's constitutional accomplishments, especially the Charter. Although he reluctantly acknowledged the flaws of the Constitution Act, 1982—its notwithstanding clause, the absence of Quebec's signature, and the lack of a referendum mechanism—he was determined to defend its fundamental precepts, the sovereignty of the people symbolized by the transfer of power from governments to citizens.

For Trudeau, all constitutional amendments must promote the vision of a sovereign Canada and a sovereign people. Polls showed that a majority of Canadians, including those in Quebec, supported the passage of the Constitution Act, 1982. Most Canadians hoped that the tiresome constitutional wrangling had come to an end, and they felt that the secessionist movement in Quebec was in decline. Very few Canadians, including Trudeau, suspected that his successor had a far different constitutional vision in store for them. Eager to be elected prime minister and prompted by his friendship with Lucien Bouchard, Brian Mulroney reopened the constitutional debate in the 1984 election campaign by promising Quebec voters to do whatever was necessary to get Quebec City's "signature on our Constitution, with honour and enthusiasm." Once in office, Mulroney rolled the constitutional dice to cement his profitable alliance with the Liberal government of Quebec premier Robert Bourassa. Together, their decision to release the genie from the constitutional bottle created a disruptive train of events that threatened the fabric of the Canadian nation-state. No wonder the lion was drawn out of his lair! Over the next five years a classic battle played out between two political titans, the passionate rationalist Trudeau and the ambitious, opportunistic Mulroney.

■

Within a month of the announcement of the Meech accord, the battle was joined. In a harshly worded letter dripping with sarcasm and contempt, printed in the *Toronto Star* and *La Presse* on May 27, 1987, Trudeau described the accord as a "total bungle" and Mulroney as the destroyer of the "Dream of One Canada." For Trudeau, the 1982 amending formula had strengthened Ottawa's bargaining power because unanimity, which had stalled patriation for sixty years, was no longer required for most issues. "Alas, only one eventuality had not been foreseen," concluded the irate Trudeau, "that one day the government of Canada might fall into the hands of a wimp. It has now happened. And the Right Honourable Brian Mulroney, PC, MP, with the complicity of 10 provincial premiers, has already entered into history as the author of a constitutional document which—if it is accepted by the people and their legislators—will render the Canadian state totally impotent. That would destine it, given the dynamics of power, to be governed by eunuchs." What Trudeau failed to mention was that the 1982 formula, based on the dubious premise of the equality of provinces, also gave every premier a veto over crucial matters. Paradoxically, it was this veto that proved to be the undoing of the Mulroney government's constitutional deal.

Trudeau's scathing attack stiffened Mulroney's resolve to prove that the charge of disloyalty was wrong. When the first ministers

met on June 2 to approve the legal draft of the principles set out in
the accord, he counter-attacked. Fearing that Trudeau's interference had dissolved the fragile unanimity, Mulroney devoted his
opening remarks to questioning his predecessor's motives. The
Liberals had made such a mess of constitutional reform in 1982 by
deliberately excluding Quebec that they had absolutely no right to
criticize anyone trying to remedy the situation; moreover, he, not
Trudeau, was prime minister. The tactic paid off. The premiers
realized that to renege on their signatures would merely confirm
Trudeau's unflattering characterization of them as self-serving political opportunists hell-bent on destroying national unity by "selling out" to Quebec nationalists. Nevertheless, Trudeau's forceful
intervention, including two days of television interviews, forced
the first ministers to make a significant alteration to the fundamental characteristics clause of the accord. The terms "French Canada"
and "English Canada" were altered to "French-speaking Canadians" and "English-speaking Canadians." This move away from a
collective, two-nations definition of Canada only partly appeased
Trudeau. He preferred that Canada be described succinctly as a
bilingual nation-state with official language minority rights.

What was a former prime minister to do but join the fray?
Trudeau pursued two strategies. He attempted through rational
argument to convince the first ministers to fix the worst flaws of
their constitutional handiwork before seeking legislative approval.
If they refused, Trudeau hoped that his arguments would force
them to respond to political pressure. Ideally, an irate public would
convince at least one premier, fearful of defeat at the polls, not to
ratify the accord. Initially, it appeared that neither strategy would
succeed. Senator Lowell Murray, the minister of state for federal-
provincial relations, took on the challenge of rebutting Trudeau's
critique. In the press and before the Special Joint Committee of
the Senate and the House of Commons on August 4, Murray
described Meech as a "seamless web and an integrated whole" that
could not be amended. His approach convinced committee members to support the accord. Several concerned citizens as well as various women's, social, ethnocultural, aboriginal, and civil liberties

organizations expressed their opposition to elements of the accord, but their interventions had no impact. At this early juncture, Canadians appeared reasonably pleased with the accord, expressing only modest concern over the "distinct society" clause.

Trudeau loyalists in parliament arranged for him to be invited to testify before the Special Joint Committee as well as the Senate Committee. Trudeau made the best of both occasions and expanded on the general criticisms he had outlined in his public letter. He also countered Murray's attack on his role in the process of constitutional renewal since 1968. Coming at the end of month-long hearings that had barely ruffled the government's feathers, Trudeau's intervention on August 27 strengthened the sagging determination of the accord's critics. It also focused public attention on the radical nature and consequences of the Meech provisions. Few commentators appreciated the significance of the moment: the beginning of the end for the ill-fated accord. Inexorably, Canadians were drawn into a debate over what they came to perceive as an anti-democratic constitutional renewal process, one dictated by the 1982 amending formula controlled by the first ministers. Once this perception formed, it became easier for critics to draw attention to the accord's substantive flaws. Eventually, this criticism emboldened the public to pressure the three wavering premiers who had not been part of the original deal.

What was it that Trudeau found so objectionable in the Meech Lake accord? It was revolutionary, Trudeau informed the Special Joint Committee, because its provisions would quickly transform Canada from a genuinely balanced federation, one in which the Canadian nation-state was greater than the sum of its provinces and territories, into a decentralized confederation dominated by provincial potentates intent on serving their own agendas. The accord would destroy any possibility of a truly national spirit by undermining the heart of the federation, the central government's executive, legislative, and judicial powers. Once the provinces controlled appointments to the Senate and the Supreme Court, the premiers would exercise a de facto "kind of remote control," almost a veto, over Ottawa's sovereignty. The mandatory annual federal-provincial conferences, one on the constitution and a second on the economy, would cripple the federal cabinet by subjecting it to constant pressure from ten premiers. The provincialization of immigration, the curtailment of the federal spending powers in areas of provincial jurisdiction, the extension of the unanimity amending formula to a whole range of federal institutions and prerogatives such as the creation of new provinces, and the designation of Quebec as a distinct society (combined with a clause empowering the Quebec government to preserve and promote that distinctiveness) contributed to an irreversible enhancement of provincialism. In short, the accord said "goodbye to the dream of one Canada" and created a "sort of confederation or directory of eleven first ministers getting together to try and determine what direction the entire country . . . should take."

For committee members, the two most controversial issues were the distinct society clause and the devolution of powers to the provinces. Initially, Trudeau had chosen not to dwell on the distinct society clause except to point out that, if it was an interpretative clause, then the drafters intended that it mean something. Murray's contention that the clause was meaningless—that it had no constitutional impact and would not give Quebec any additional powers to preserve or develop this distinct society—was insulting and misleading. The real problem was to determine exactly what the distinct society clause meant; otherwise, Canadians could be in for some nasty surprises. Trudeau noted that the federal and provincial governments had protected their section 91 and 92 powers of the Constitution Act with a non-derogation clause, but refused to extend that protection to citizens' rights protected by the Charter. This omission required rectification. The distinct society clause, Trudeau said, was a hidden form of special status, something that was insulting, humiliating, and patronizing to every Quebecker. More important, since the clause, according to Bourassa, would override the Charter and transfer sovereignty in certain grey areas from Ottawa to Quebec, it was a fast track to sovereignty-association, the political option that a majority of Quebeckers had rejected in 1980.

Trudeau also dealt with the charge that his government had offered the provinces, at some point during his time in power, virtually everything in Meech. He conceded that he had been willing to negotiate matters pertaining to Senate and Supreme Court appointments, Ottawa's spending powers, and immigration, but always on condition that Ottawa gained something in return. What, Trudeau asked, had Mulroney asked for in return for the accord's gifts to the provinces? Nothing. Determined to set the record straight, Trudeau, waving his letter of March 31, 1976, to the premiers, demonstrated that he had never offered an amending formula based on unanimity. Trudeau's preferred amending formula remained the one based on four regions, a formula agreed to by all provinces, including Quebec, in the Victoria Charter of 1971.

Trudeau's appearance before the Senate on March 30, 1988, was a *tour de force*. Fully briefed, he expressed his profound disappointment that the Special Joint Committee had refused to carry out its legislative responsibility by recommending amendments to the accord despite the express recognition of its flaws, especially the impact of the distinct society clause on the Charter. He hoped that the senators would take their legislative responsibility more seriously, and he challenged them to "become a focal point for the most important constitutional debate, or certainly one of the most important, in this period of our history" by proposing amendments. With any luck, Canadians would be shocked into taking a closer look at the accord and insist that their provincial legislators analyse and amend it. If changes could not be made, the premiers had no other recourse but rejection.

Referring to a letter by Murray in the *Globe and Mail* of May 30, 1987, Trudeau agreed that the Constitution Act, 1982, had three main flaws: the absence of the Quebec government's signature, the notwithstanding clause, and the opting-out provisions in the amendment formula. These flaws had resulted from the dynamic tensions of federalism. Various prime ministers, beginning with King at the federal-provincial conference of 1927, had attempted unsuccessfully to patriate the British North America Act. After 1945, Ottawa succeeded in building "a national will, a sense of national identity," thanks to progressive domestic and foreign policies. By the 1960s, this development began to be undermined by the rise of Quebec nationalism, separatism, and provincial rights. Beginning with the 1964 Fulton-Favreau amending formula negotiations and proceeding on through the Victoria Charter of 1971, several provinces, copying Quebec, demanded new legislative powers in exchange for patriation and an amending formula. The election of a secessionist Parti Québécois government in 1976 accentuated the pressures for special status for Quebec and more powers for the provinces.

Trudeau reminded the senators that his government, after the 1980 Quebec referendum, tried to get provincial agreement to a limited package of amendments including patriation, a charter, and a version of the Victoria amending formula. When, at the September 1980 federal-provincial conference, Trudeau was presented with a greatly expanded list of provincial demands, he concluded that the premiers' appetite for power was insatiable. If the constitutional logjam was to be broken, he knew that his government had two options: accept the unanimity rule and abandon his referendum promise to renew the federation, or proceed unilaterally to Westminster with a citizens' constitutional package comprising patriation, a charter, and an amending formula.

Trudeau took the opportunity to deny that his referendum promise of constitutional renewal entailed a recognition of Quebec as a distinct society. "Honourable Senators," declared an irate Trudeau, "how could it reasonably be inferred that I was attempting to win the referendum by setting Canada on a course that I consistently had denounced as deleterious as even losing the referendum itself would be? I really take objection . . . that, somehow, we have made promises to give the Province of Quebec, in a reformed Constitution, what the Separatists and some ultra nationalists were asking. There was no point in winning the referendum if we were going to give those who had lost it everything they were trying to get by winning it." His government, he explained, might have been able to avoid the three flaws in the Constitution Act, 1982, had it not been for a highly questionable decision of the

Supreme Court, on a reference forced upon the government by the Senate, which declared that the unilateral approach was legal but "was not conventional by virtue of a convention which was so obscure that they [the Supreme Court Justices] could not define it." Trudeau had reconvened the premiers one last time on November 5, 1981. To obtain the support of a majority for the Canada Bill, he had accepted the notwithstanding clause, which allowed for an override of most sections of the Charter and the dissident premiers' Vancouver amending formula. This formula, based on the equality of the provinces, included a veto over federal institutions and an opting-out clause for certain programs with full compensation. All the provinces, including Quebec, received additional powers over natural resources as well as the entrenchment of equalization grants. In short, Trudeau had compromised. He expected no less of Mulroney and Bourassa.

Was the Meech Lake accord a natural outgrowth of Trudeau's previous constitutional offers since 1968 or the Constitution Act, 1982, as the Mulroney government repeatedly claimed? Trudeau reponded with an emphatic no. His government's proposals had been structured to strengthen Canadians' national will, their *"vouloir vivre collectif."* In contrast, Quebec's demands ran counter to the spirit and the letter of the 1982 Constitution since they "destroyed the existence of a national will and submitted it to the unanimous consent of the provinces." In short, the flaws of the 1982 Constitution considered so abhorrent by Mulroney were made worse by the accord. The Bourassa government had concocted the accord to enable it to drive a stake into the heart of the Charter and to undermine Ottawa's sovereignty in several areas. Successor Quebec governments would use their new powers to enhance Québécois political identity and the drive for secession.

Nowhere was this gambit more apparent, according to Trudeau, than in the distinct society clause. While Mulroney preached that the clause was meaningless, Bourassa proclaimed loudly that it was an all-powerful tool to obtain, through the courts, more powers in grey areas of jurisdiction. Quebec, Trudeau agreed, was a distinct society. Indeed, Ottawa had contributed immensely to fostering

that reality. Furthermore, he reminded Mulroney that his government had proposed to entrench a reference to Quebec's distinctiveness in a constitutional preamble, never in the body of the
Constitution as an interpretative clause. These offers had always
been rejected by Bourassa and René Lévesque as insufficient because Trudeau insisted on a reference to "the Canadian people."
Consequently, Trudeau said, "when you deliberately do not put it
into a preamble but put it into an interpretative clause, that can
mean only one thing—you are giving to the government of that
distinct society powers that it did not have before." The distinct
society clause could only be construed as a mechanism for the
Quebec government to obtain by stealth what it could not obtain
directly—additional powers not available to the other provinces.

Trudeau was not surprised that Bourassa had pursued additional
powers for Quebec. Constant juggling between the central and the
provincial governments was simply the political dynamic of any
federation. What was dangerous was that Mulroney proved such a
weak defender of Canada's sovereignty. Demonstrating his incompetence as a negotiator, he threw away "all the trump cards he had"
by abolishing the National Energy Policy, handing Newfoundland
shared administration of the offshore fisheries, and granting Quebec the right to sit at international summits. A weakened Mulroney
then sat down with the premiers to haggle over Quebec's demands.
Little wonder Bourassa boasted he had obtained more in the field of
immigration, appointments to the Supreme Court, and the distinct
society clause than he ever dreamed. In return, Mulroney asked for
and obtained absolutely nothing, not even the remedy of the flaws
of 1982. His determination to obtain reconciliation at any price
threatened to entrench the compact and *deux nations* theories at the
heart of the Constitution.

"In 1987 the Quebec government was in [the Constitution],"
concluded Trudeau, "but the Quebec people stand divided between themselves and from the rest of Canada as a distinct society.
In 1980 there had been a victory of people over power; 1987 was a
triumph of power over people." The problem with Mulroney's
bungling was that Canadians stood to be the losers whether or not

the Meech Lake accord was ratified. If it failed, Bourassa, backed by *nationalistes* and secessionists, would take Quebec out of the federation as he often stated they could. If the accord was ratified, it would create legal and political chaos, destabilize an already weakened federal government, and provide the opening for secession. Given this no-win situation, Trudeau argued, it was imperative that the senators call for a reference of the accord, especially its distinct society clause, to the Supreme Court, and that they propose significant amendments before sending the government's resolution back to the House.

Did Trudeau's intervention have any impact on the public's perception of the accord? In June 1987, 45 percent of Canadians considered the accord a good deal, while just over 25 percent rejected it and nearly as many had no opinion. After Trudeau's intervention, public support declined to 35 percent by October 1987. Support rebounded to 40 percent by March 1988, thanks to a concerted campaign by the prime minister and the premiers. Nevertheless, by this time, a well-organized, broadly based opposition had emerged that would gain considerable momentum by the spring of 1989. This opposition included women's groups, aboriginal organizations, linguistic minority and ethnocultural associations, civil liberties organizations, poverty and social groups, public sector labour unions, and an informal network of academics. Opponents were angered by the unwillingness of their political leaders to respond to what they considered were well-founded criticisms of the Meech accord. Indeed, they had no patience for political leaders who had lost their respect. The Charter, by granting citizens certain judicial powers over their provincial and federal governments, had given Canadians a sense of ownership in their Constitution. Only a few specialists and virtually no politicians understood this development.

Meech critics needed to convince just one premier not to ratify the accord and it would be history. They experienced momentary hope when New Brunswick's Liberal leader, Frank McKenna, became premier on October 13, 1987, but it soon became obvious that McKenna was no Trudeau Liberal. His objections to the accord were purely provincial. The first real breach in the accord's armour came when voters threw Manitoba's NDP premier Howard Pawley out of power in April 1988. Conservative leader Gary Filmon now headed a minority government, with Liberal Sharon Carstairs holding the balance of power. Pressured by Mulroney, Filmon introduced Meech into his legislature on December 16, 1989, a day after the Supreme Court's decision outlawing the French unilingual commercial signage requirements of Quebec's Bill 101. Despite a warning from Filmon, Bourassa used the Charter's notwithstanding clause to introduce Bill 178, which reimposed unilingual signs. Manitobans, who had just re-embraced official bilingualism for their legislature and courts after the Supreme Court's restoration of section 23 of the Manitoba Act, 1870, were incensed. Bill 178 proved the rightness of Trudeau's warning about the real intent of the distinct society clause. Indeed, as Bourassa candidly explained, his government intended to use this clause to fire-proof all of Quebec's current and future language legislation from legal attacks stemming from the Charter. Realizing the risks to Meech, Bourassa declared that he had to protect the integrity of the French language in Quebec. Given Carstairs' strong opposition to Bill 178, Filmon had to withdraw the Meech resolution from the legislature because it was now clear that Quebec intended to use the distinct society clause to achieve special status.

The architects of Meech were thrown on the defensive, never to recover. By March 1989 support had dropped to 30 percent, and it continued to erode. In the eight turbulent months leading to the eventual demise of the accord in June 1990, opposition climbed to near 50 percent, while an all-out blitzkrieg by the accord's supporters never managed to push public support above 35 percent.

Meech's fate was sealed when a new premier of Newfoundland, Clyde Wells, arrived on the scene. A constitutional scholar and lawyer who argued the Trudeau government's position successfully in critical constitutional cases, Wells led his Liberal Party to office in April 1989. He succeeded, in part, by promising to rescind the accord, and his preference for the Trudeau constitutional school of thought was reinforced when he hired Deborah Coyne as his constitutional adviser in October 1989. A friend of Trudeau's, Coyne had caught Wells' eye with her scathing critique of the accord published in the June 1989 issue of *Policy Options*. The Newfoundland premier quickly became the political rallying point for all Meech opponents, confronting and eventually turning back a tidal wave of pressure from Canada's élites.

Ironically, it was Filmon who was responsible in the end for the demise of the accord. What Mulroney had not counted on was that Filmon, because he required the unanimous consent of the members, would not have time to push Meech through the Manitoba legislature. Filmon and Carstairs, sensing tremendous opposition from Manitobans, simply allowed the clock to run out. This unanimous consent was denied by Elijah Harper, a Cree member of the NDP caucus who took the opportunity to express the aboriginal community's wholesale rejection of the accord. The Meech Lake accord died in Manitoba on June 23, 1990. Furious at Senator Murray's last-minute effort to lay the blame on Newfoundland and its premier, Wells promptly adjourned the House of Assembly without a vote.

■

Mulroney and Bourassa decided to exploit the feigned outrage of the nationalists and secessionists, the majority of whom had rejected Meech, to make a second attempt to impose the accord on the Canadian public. Encouraged by Mulroney, Bourassa adopted a "knife to the throat of English Canada" constitutional strategy. First, he called on the Quebec Liberal Party's Constitutional Committee to prepare a report outlining his government's constitutional options. The Jean Allaire Report, *Un Québec libre de ses choix* (January 1991), sanctioned the political/juridical dismantling of Canada to enable the creation of a Quebec/Canada confederal system. It called for a massive devolution of powers to Quebec along with the abolition of all appeals, including those under the Charter, to the Supreme Court. Most important, the report proposed a fall 1992 referendum to approve either this radical constitutional restructuring or the secession of Quebec along with an economic association with Canada. This political bombshell was reaffirmed in the March 1991 report produced by the Special Committee of the National Assembly on Quebec's political and constitutional future. Its report, signed by Bourassa and Parti Québécois leader Jacques Parizeau, called for an October 1992 referendum on either the secession of Quebec or a binding constitutional offer from Ottawa and the provinces. Bourassa put the strategy into operation by having the National Assembly pass Bill 150, which required a referendum. Under this scenario, Mulroney had to deliver a constitutional package acceptable to Quebec or face a referendum on secession by late October 1992.

Mulroney forged ahead with his part of the plan. In September 1991 he initiated the Canada Round, with a set of twenty-eight constitutional proposals entitled *Shaping Canada's Future Together.* Attempting to reconcile competing Canadian, aboriginal, and Québécois nationalisms, the document contained a pot-pourri of amendments from the Meech Lake accord and the federal government's Charest Report, the concept of aboriginal self-government, the devolution of substantial powers to the provinces, a triple-E Senate, and the entrenchment of executive federalism through a permanent Council of the Federation. Between March and July this complex package was fine-tuned during a closed-door process involving aboriginal representatives and federal and provincial ministers. Then, in August, Bourassa was drawn into a series of secret first ministers' meetings that produced the Charlottetown Report, listing more than sixty amendments and twenty-five yet-to-be-negotiated political accords. This Charlottetown accord was subjected to a referendum, the ultimate democratic test, on October 26, 1992.

Between June 1990 and late September 1992, Trudeau had made no public statement on the constitutional renewal process or its substantive elements. Some Liberals had consulted him, but he remained critical of both the post-Meech process and its substance. Trudeau encouraged Chrétien to insist on a national referendum, but he refrained from participating in the campaign until late September. The small but well-connected No organization, Canada for All Canadians, co-founded by Deborah Coyne, Robert Howse, Robert Jackson, and Michael Behiels, encouraged Trudeau to join the fray in early September. The No forces outside Quebec had only a fraction of the financial and human resources available to the Yes forces led by the Mulroney government, the NDP and Liberal parties, and corporate Canada. Canada for All Canadians believed that Trudeau's participation could redress this imbalance. Its founders were informed that he would intervene on his own terms and at the time of his choosing. Trudeau's judgment proved impeccable, and the impact of his timing and critique devastated the Charlottetown accord.

His intervention, an article entitled "Quebec's Blackmail" published in the late September issues of *Maclean's* and *l'Actualité*, was a bombshell. Trudeau castigated Quebec's corrupt "blackmailing" political culture as well as the dishonest myths perpetrated by Quebec's "humiliated" chattering classes. He charged that the master blackmailer was Bourassa: the premier had commissioned the Allaire Report, which demanded that "the rest of Canada must hand over nearly all its constitutional powers, except of course the power to give [Quebec] lots of money. And to put a bit more kick in the blackmail, no opportunity is missed to point out that Quebec's [alleged] right of self-determination is written in this premier's program." Trudeau heaped scorn on the nationalists and ridiculed the distinct society concept that the Parti Québécois had fashioned in 1982 as a tool to obtain the sovereignty-association rejected in 1980. But this was merely his opening volley.

On October 1, 1992, at the now-famous Maison Egg Roll, a Chinese restaurant in working-class St-Henri, Trudeau regaled supporters and critics of the recently revived *Cité libre* magazine with a damning critique of the report. Characterizing Charlottetown as "a mess that deserves a big NO," Trudeau dissected the deal's contradictions, myths, assumptions, and erroneous principles. He warned Canadians that they should take their democratic responsibilities very seriously by basing their choice in the referendum on reason rather than passion. Their individual choices would determine whether they would "live in a society in which personal rights, individual rights, take precedence over collective rights . . . in which all citizens are equal before the law and before the State itself." Indeed, if the theory and practice of collective rights prevailed over individual rights, Canadians would find themselves facing "a dictatorship, which arranges citizens in a hierarchy according to their beliefs." Charlottetown's omnibus interpretative Canada Clause turned the 1982 Charter on its head by creating a hierarchy of collective rights.

At the top of the pole, thanks to the distinct society clause, was a Franco-Quebec community that had at its disposal a legislature and a government to preserve and protect it. Next came the aboriginal peoples of Canada with their vaguely defined third order of discretionary, non-democratic ethnic governments, empowered to promote aboriginal languages, cultures, and traditions. Under the third category, Canadians and their governments were only "committed" (in the French version Bourassa insisted that the weaker term *attachment* be used) to the vitality and development of the official language minority communities. Such language ensured that provincial rights would always trump minority rights in disputes before the Supreme Court. The court-enforceable equality rights of the Charter, in Trudeau's view, were weakened considerably by the Canada Clause, which merely required a vague, redundant commitment by Canadians to racial and ethnic equality, "a respect for individual and collective *human* rights and freedoms;" and the equality of female and male persons.

While the clause stipulated that "Canada is a democracy committed to a parliamentary and federal system of government and to the rule of law," Trudeau reminded Canadians that aboriginal governments could replace parliamentary democracy with non-elected traditional forms of government. Furthermore, while the clause confirmed the principle of the equality of the provinces, it was clear that Quebec was more equal than the others, since it constituted the "*only* distinct province in the Constitution." Not mentioned, but clearly at the very bottom of this hierarchy, were ordinary Canadians, "the little people" as Trudeau sarcastically reminded his audience. Invariably the courts would be clogged trying to sort out interminable conflicts between these competing collective rights and commitments. The Canada Clause, the counter-revolution of the political classes, strengthened the power of the state at the expense of the Charter and the sovereignty of the people.

Trudeau reminded his audience of the lies and the procedural absurdities that offended democratic sensibilities and common sense. First, Canadians were being asked to approve a counter-revolutionary package of constitutional amendments without being shown either the legal texts or the twenty-five yet-to-be negotiated political accords. Second, the proponents argued dishonestly that ratification would bring an end to Quebec's constitutional demands. Finally, "high-level politicians and even high-level bankers want us to believe that voting YES is 'a yes to Canada' while NO is a 'no to Canada.'"

Not a single intervenor in the audience or during the media press conference laid a glove on Trudeau. He parried all questions with sarcasm and wit, refusing to back down. He reminded the media that the No votes of Canadians were not the same as the No votes of the separatists. Parizeau's No was intended to advance secession. The No vote of ordinary Canadians was simply a vote against a bad constitutional package rather than a vote, as the Yes propagandists maintained, against Canada. Separatists "say NO because they want a weaker Canada. I say NO because I want a stronger Canada."

When the ballots were counted on the evening of October 26, the Charlottetown deal was soundly defeated by a margin of nearly 10 percent, 54 to 45. The No side won by over 60 percent in the West, while the Yes side carried the Maritimes and the Northwest Territories. Ontario, where all the pundits expected the Yes side to win by a wide margin, produced a draw, 49.8 percent for the Yes side and 49.6 percent for the No side.

Did Trudeau's intervention in the referendum campaign have a dramatic impact on the outcome? Was he responsible, as some have claimed, for the No victory? Without doubt, the large and well-funded Yes coalition would have preferred that he remain silent. Mulroney was very conscious of the mauling Trudeau had inflicted on the defunct Meech accord, and, most assuredly, he was not anxious to see him attack the Charlottetown deal. With Trudeau's intervention, the hundreds of small, unconnected No organizations gained legitimacy, as well as an enhanced sense of purpose. The No forces believed that their cause was just and that they were expressing the sovereign will of the people. After Trudeau's interventions, activity at the Ottawa-based Canada for All Canadians took on a feverish pitch as requests for speakers and literature poured in. Increased access to the media was dramatic—in fact, too overwhelming to handle. Most important, Canada for All Canadians' television and radio advertisements, featuring non-political talking heads explaining the deal's flaws, proved influential with ordinary Canadians.

Nevertheless, there are two schools of thought on Trudeau's impact on the campaign. One argues that his intervention was not the dramatic turning point in Yes campaign fortunes. While its members point to the many tensions within the Yes coalition and its inept, fear-mongering advertising campaign, they conclude that the primary explanation for the rejection resides in the complexity and confusing nature of the deal. In fact, Canadians were aware of the deal's many problems and contradictions before Trudeau's intervention, which simply confirmed their opposition. For the second school, Trudeau's timely intervention in the referendum debate had a cataclysmic impact, one that crossed party, class, gender, ethnic, religious, and regional lines. Indeed, support for the Charlottetown deal outside Quebec declined by an incredible twenty points to 40 percent immediately after Trudeau's speech. Many Trudeau loyalists, they maintain, had mistakenly believed, because of his silence, that he favoured the agreement. The moment they realized this was not the case they felt free to express their opposition openly.

The real explanation for the resounding defeat of the deal resides somewhere in between. Trudeau's participation in the debate prompted many Canadians to educate themselves about their Constitution. Most important, Canadians came to understand more fully than at any time in their history that the Constitution belonged to them and that it was they who ultimately held the only effective sovereignty over changes to it. The 1992 referendum gave Canadians their opportunity. Trudeau had merely reminded them how far they had come since 1982 and that they must exercise their democratic rights without fear of reprisal from the political and economic élites. Indeed, by acting on their democratic instincts, Canadians moved closer to defining themselves as a sovereign people.

■

And yet, this new-found sense was challenged severely by the Quebec secessionists in the 1995 referendum. In 1993 Jean Chrétien's Liberal Party trounced the moribund Conservative government of Kim Campbell as the voters vented their rage at the retiring Mulroney. Québécois voters elected fifty-four Bloc Québécois members under the leadership of Lucien Bouchard. For health reasons, Bourassa resigned as premier and his successor, Daniel Johnson, was quickly defeated by Jacques Parizeau, who promised Quebeckers their first referendum on outright secession. Bouchard, realizing that a forthright question would bring yet another humiliating defeat, pressured Parizeau into accepting a convoluted, ambiguous referendum question that stressed an economic partnership between an independent Quebec and what remained of Canada. Bouchard was confident that his *partenariat* formula would win the support of the 20 percent of the Québécois voters who are strong nationalists. Indeed, he helped persuade them that only a direct threat of secession would force Ottawa and the provinces to accept Quebec's demands outlined in the Meech Lake accord.

An overconfident Chrétien decided not to lead the No forces in the referendum, convinced that his strategy of devolving powers to the provinces through administrative arrangements would appeal to Quebeckers. While the prime minister remained aloof from the battle, the leader of the No forces, Daniel Johnson, unwisely decided not to challenge the constitutionality of Parizeau's disingenuous Bill 150, which set the parameters for a Unilateral Declaration of Independence. Nor was Johnson effective in demonstrating either the blatant dishonesty of the referendum question or the undemocratic nature of Quebec's referendum law. Johnson erroneously believed that he could win the votes of Québécois nationalists by getting Chrétien to offer Quebeckers a variant of the Meech Lake accord. During the last week of the campaign, when it became clear to an astonished Chrétien that the No forces were about to lose the referendum, he panicked and promised Quebeckers a distinct society clause and a constitutional veto. In a further desperate move, the Liberal government helped organize a mass rally in Montreal of some 100,000 Canadians from all parts of Canada. Some argue that these developments prevented a catastrophe by enabling the dispirited No forces to eke out the narrowest of victories. While the jury is still out, it is clear that the referendum result inflicted great damage on the cause of Canadian unity. Many Canadians recoiled at the fact that a majority of francophone Quebeckers had rejected Canada, and they insisted that Ottawa take the lead in setting terms and conditions for any subsequent referendum or possible secession.

On February 3, 1996, Trudeau broke his silence with a blunt attack in the press on Lucien Bouchard, accusing him of betraying the population of Quebec during the referendum. In his usual meticulous fashion, he dissected the distortions at the heart of Bouchard's powerful, demagogic rhetoric: "By calling upon fallacies and untruths to advance the cause of hateful demagoguery, Lucien Bouchard misled the electors during last October's referendum. By his actions, he tarnished Quebec's good reputation as a democratic society and he does not deserve the trust of the people of his province." The close referendum result and the near defeat in the June 1996 election forced the Chrétien government, guided by Stéphane Dion, to adopt Trudeau's strategy of attacking the propaganda, ideological dogma, lies, and distortions of Bouchard and his supporters. Chrétien was also convinced by many of Trudeau's supporters, as well as by Guy Bertrand, lawyer and former separatist turned federalist, to challenge the constitutionality of Quebec's Bill 150 in a reference to the Supreme Court. As a result, Canadians will be much better prepared come the next referendum on secession. Trudeau's constitutional legacy, then, has proved to be both enlightening and enduring.

What Makes a Country?
Trudeau's Failure
as a Leader

■

GUY PRATTE

Guy Pratte, an Ottawa lawyer, has acted as counsel for the Liberal Party on matters of constitutional reform, including the Charlottetown accord. He believes that a strong commitment to federalism can be consistent with sensitivity to the legitimate concerns of Quebeckers.

WHAT MAKES A COUNTRY? The British thought they knew the answer to that question. As the American historian Francis Parkman wrote of Britain's conquest of Canada in 1763:

> England imposed by the sword on reluctant Canada the boon of rational and ordered liberty. Through centuries of striving she had advanced from stage to stage of progress, deliberate and calm, never breaking with her past, but making each fresh gain the base of a new success, enlarging popular liberties while bating nothing of that height and force of individual development which is the brain and heart of civilization; and now, through a hard-earned victory, she taught the conquered colony to share the blessings she had won. A happier calamity never befell a people than the conquest of Canada by the British arms."
> (*The Old Regime in Canada*, 1888)

The inherent superiority of English customs and institutions was not immediately apparent to French Canadians, and British authorities soon concluded that some tolerance of indigenous French institutions was necessary to earn the allegiance of the conquered. So, the Quebec Act of 1774 was passed by the British Parliament allowing the *habitants* to keep their religious institutions and their civil laws. And in 1791, Lower and Upper Canada were created to afford some greater measure of autonomy to the French-speaking majority. But this policy of accommodation was not working particularly well and, following the recommendation of Lord Durham, the Canadas were reunited in 1841.

Reunification itself turned out to be short-lived as a constitutional solution to the Canadian problem. By the mid 1860s, "confederation" emerged as the magical formula that might rally a majority of disparate views and interests within the bosom of a single state—albeit still constitutionally dependent on Britain. The genius of federalism, which had imposed itself on the founders of the American union a century earlier, had by now conquered the minds, if not the hearts, of Canada's political leaders. It seemed that federalism held the promise of a long, durable political association between French and English Canadians.

But squaring the constitutional circle turned out to be much more difficult than the Fathers of Confederation apparently realized. By the 1960s a significant minority in Quebec was beginning to think that Quebec should get out of Canada completely. Thereafter, Quebec premiers behaved as if they could gain and keep power only by representing themselves as "nationalists." It began with Maurice Duplessis, but once Jean Lesage had proclaimed his provocative "Maître chez nous" slogan, nationalism, regardless of party affiliation, became the essential condition for political survival in Quebec politics. The question "What makes a country?" was implicitly being posed by the repeated demands of the political leadership in Quebec, and federalists, including those sympathetic to Quebec, were at a loss for an answer.

At this point Pierre Elliott Trudeau arrived on the scene as the third man of the trio summoned by Prime Minister Lester Pearson, along with Jean Marchand and Gérard Pelletier, to help fashion a solution to the perennial constitutional dilemma facing Canada ever since its conquest by Britain two hundred years earlier. Trudeau certainly thought he knew what was needed to make a country and, for a long while, Canadians must have thought so too, for he led the country as prime minister for nearly sixteen years. During this long tenure, he devoted his considerable energies and ferocious intellectual powers to convincing or forcing Canadians to accept that official bilingualism and a constitutionally protected charter of individual rights afforded the only sure means of effective, durable country building. Indeed, it would only be a slight exaggeration to say that Trudeau and his Liberal government—to paraphrase Parkman—imposed on a reluctant Canada the "boon of rational and ordered liberty" when they forced a majority of the provinces to accept a Charter of Rights and Freedoms as the price for patriating the Canadian Constitution.

As a strategy for keeping this country together, it was a failure. Fifteen years after the Charter of Rights and Freedoms was enshrined in the law, Canada is more divided than ever, as demonstrated by the results of the recent federal election. Moreover, virtually every Canadian is resigned to the inevitability of another Quebec referendum sometime soon. Trudeau's national unity strategy, as Kenneth McRoberts convincingly argues in his book *Misconceiving Canada*, "has failed abysmally to change the way Quebec francophones see Canada. Indeed the attachment of Quebec francophones to Quebec as their primary identity is stronger than ever, and they are more determined than ever that Quebec be recognized as a distinct society."

Faithful Trudeau followers will blame Brian Mulroney and Robert Bourassa for reopening the constitutional debate with the Meech Lake accord of 1987. But if the Charter really was the miracle cure to constitutional woes, why did the malady resurface with increased virulence just a few years after the prescription had been administered? As McRoberts observes:

> It is ironic that the national unity strategy, although conceived primarily in relation to Quebec, has had its main impact, not in Quebec, but in the rest of the country and has transformed the way many English Canadians think of Canada. As such elements of the Trudeau strategy as a charter of rights, multiculturalism, or the equality of the provinces have become central to English Canadians' view of Canada, so they have destroyed any willingness to recognize Quebec as a distinct society. Indeed, within the Trudeau strategy these principles were intended to negate Quebec's claim to recognition.

Trudeau's failure was to confuse his personal convictions with the ultimate needs of the country and to refuse to adjust his official views, notwithstanding the mounting evidence that his political beliefs were not producing the desired unifying effects. In this regard, it will be enlightening to compare Trudeau to another leader who fought for rights and equality, Abraham Lincoln.

Trudeau's Solution

From the outset, Trudeau was viscerally opposed to any modification of the prevailing constitutional arrangements that would sanction nationalistic feelings in Quebec, which he abhorred. For him, nationalism and emotionalism were inextricably linked, and as such they were opposed to federalism and reason:

> I would like to see emotionalism channelled into a less sterile direction than nationalism . . . Within the sufficiently advanced federal countries, the autodestructiveness of nationalism is bound to become more and more apparent, and reason may yet reveal itself even to ambitious politicians as the more assured road to success . . .
>
> Thus there is some hope that in advanced societies, the glue of nationalism will become as obsolete as the divine right of kings; the title of the state to govern and the extent of its authority will be conditional upon rational justification; a people's consensus based on reason will supply the cohesive force that societies require.
>
> The rise of reason in politics is an advance of law; for is not law an attempt to regulate the conduct of men in society rationally rather than emotionally? (*Against the Current*, 1996)

Reason, federalism, and law were related notions essential to the establishment of viable and durable government. But how could French Canadians be made to feel a part of Canada if their nationalist tendencies created centrifugal forces difficult to contain in the existing federal state? How could Canada itself become a nation whose own nationalism was not destructive for being based on emotionalism? Trudeau's answer to this dilemma was to posit that only the establishment of legally entrenched individual rights could create a collectivity that was not doomed to internecine and perpetual conflict.

Instead of race or religion, the nation would define itself in terms of every citizen possessing certain inalienable rights shared by everyone else. In this scenario, individual rights were not only required as shields against the possible oppression of the majority but were the means by which to transcend a petty and destructive nationalism based on emotion. Rights and freedoms—of speech, religion, and thought—would make everyone equal and free, united by this common denominator.

In February 1964 Trudeau wrote in *Maclean's*:

A constitutional entrenched bill of rights seems to be the best tool for breaking the ever-recurring deadlock between Quebec and the rest of Canada. If certain language and educational rights were written into the constitution, along with other basic liberties, in such a way that *no* government—federal or provincial—could legislate against them, French Canadians would cease to feel confined to their Quebec ghetto, and the Spirit of Separatism would be laid forever.

The express purpose of official bilingualism and of the Charter of Rights and Freedoms that came into force on 1982 was, therefore, to serve as a unifying force that would make Quebec nationalism obsolete.

It is hard to find any evidence that the Charter, or official bilingualism for that matter, has had any effect whatsoever in creating the bonds of rational nationalism which Trudeau so fondly hoped for. Still, he remained absolutely committed to his Charter. He vehemently opposed any dilution of its legal force, particularly in the name of granting any special status to Quebec, as was his perception of the attempts made by Mulroney and Bourassa in the Meech

Lake accord of 1987. At that time, Trudeau wrote in a blistering article published in the *Toronto Star* and other newspapers: "The real question is whether the French Canadians living in Quebec need a provincial government with more powers than the other provinces. I believe that it is insulting to us to claim that we do."

From a legal point of view, the arguments against the "distinct society" clause are weak, as is obvious from Trudeau's intervention before the Senate. The vagueness of the clause could hardly be held against its drafters. Indeed, we would never have had a British North America Act in 1867, with its exceedingly vague and elastic "Peace, Order and Good Government" clause as a major source of federal power, if the Fathers of Confederation had insisted on utter limpidity of constitutional drafting. Similarly, the Charter of Rights itself, with such notions as "equality" and "fundamental justice," would not have passed the standards of precision that Trudeau and his constitutional groupies insisted on when the Meech Lake debate was raging.

Nor can the distinct society clause be objected to on the basis that it is an interpretive clause likely to benefit one particular group, for the Charter already contains several interpretative clauses explicitly designed to yield interpretations favouring distinct groups like aboriginals, women, and cultural minorities. In any event, it is up to the Supreme Court of Canada to apply the distinct society clause and it is hard to see why that Court, federally appointed with a majority of 6–3 of the judges from provinces other than Quebec, could sanction a legal interpretation detrimental to the well-being of the nation as a whole.

The most potent argument against the distinct society clause is not a legal but a sociological one—that it will foster a society within Canada that will tend to define itself in terms of itself, with no reference to Canada. There is some force to that argument, except that, even without this clause, Quebec is inexorably inching towards, if not outright separation, a major redefinition of the country likely to result in a much more asymmetric Canada than that which could possibly emerge from the enactment of the distinct society clause.

This sociological argument also ignores the goodwill that recognition of Quebec as a distinct society would engender among Quebec nationalists who believe in Canada as a rational political construct, but who resent the impression, partly based on experience but increasingly fuelled by historical mythology, that English Canadians consider French Canadians as inferior, as unwitting and ungrateful benefactors of the superior wisdom of British colonialists. This group would easily represent 10 to 15 percent of the 49.6 percent that voted Yes in the last referendum. It is certainly large enough that, once committed to the federalist cause, it would make it virtually impossible for separatists to win a referendum. Polls show that, between 1995 and 1997, 74 to 80 percent of Quebeckers agreed that it was important for the future of Canada that Quebec be recognized as a distinct society in the Constitution. Indeed, it could be argued that many Quebec francophone federalists would strengthen their commitment to this country on the recognition of Quebec as a distinct society. It would also be a mistake to believe that only Quebec nationalists harbour feelings of vague and latent resentment towards English Canada.

The generosity of spirit that would be demonstrated by making this concession—the proof that English Canadians wanted to keep Canada as including Quebec to such an extent that they were willing to acknowledge the special place that Quebec occupies—would generate a new bond with Canada that no legal or rational argument could duplicate. But this concession would also require a compromise to Trudeau's theory of nation building, a pragmatic recognition of the limits of the acceptability of his political theory which he was utterly unwilling to make.

Trudeau and Lincoln

Trudeau's determination that only a Charter of Rights would keep the country together was based on logic: If every citizen has the same fundamental rights as every other, then all citizens who enjoy those rights will be bound together in a single nation regardless of their other, less important differences, such as culture and language. This theory was not without precedent: The United States of America was founded on a similar creed. Indeed, when the political axiom that "all men are created equal" was challenged by the southern states, the North, led by President Lincoln, engaged in a massively destructive war, ostensibly to affirm its fundamental primacy. In light of that example, it might seem that Trudeau and his followers' uncompromising attitude towards Quebec nationalists was justified, even at the risk of separation.

Such an interpretation of Lincoln's political motives would, however, be simplistic and misleading. First and foremost, Lincoln was fighting to keep the nation whole. Although he, personally, profoundly believed in the tenet of equality of fundamental rights between people, regardless of religion or race, he stated clearly that he would compromise those principles if it was politically necessary to do so:

> If there be those who would not save the Union, unless they could at the same time *save* slavery, I do not agree with them. If there be those who would not save the Union unless they could at the same time *destroy* slavery, I do not agree with them. My paramount object in this struggle *is* to save the Union, and not either to save or destroy slavery. If I could save the Union without freeing *any* slave I would do it, and if I could save it by freeing *all* the slaves I would do it; and if I could save it by freeing some and leaving others alone I would do that. What I do about slavery, and the coloured race, I do because I believe that it helps to save the Union; and what I forbear, I forbear because I do *not* believe it would help save the Union. I shall do *less* whenever I shall believe what I am doing hurts the cause, and I shall do *more* whenever I shall believe doing more helps the cause. I shall try to correct errors when shown to be errors; and I shall adopt new views so fast as they shall appear to be true views. I have here stated my purpose according to my view of *official* duty; and I intend no modi-

fication of my oft-expressed *personal* wish that all men every where could be free.

(Letter to H. Greeley, August 22, 1862)

For Lincoln, there was no dishonour in pragmatism. The supreme objective was to keep the nation together and, to ensure that this goal would be reached, he was willing to compromise substantially on the principle of absolute equality among citizens. He would allow the southern states to keep slavery in the belief that, ultimately, perhaps only after hundreds of years, this peculiar institution would die on its own. If that is what it would take to keep the nation together, he was willing to wait.

Lincoln was routinely vilified by northern strict abolitionists for his position of tolerance of slavery in the states that already had it. But he was convinced that his belief in equality could rally the nation only if this compromise were allowed. He was willing to make this concession because it seemed to him that imposing absolute equality would only further divide the country. But the South, unwilling to compromise with the newly elected president, wished slavery to be extended to the new western territories. Inevitably, war ensued.

Trudeau, like Lincoln, was a staunch believer in individual rights. But for Trudeau there was no compromising on rights. He was ready to sacrifice the nation on the altar of individual rights. Then a grabbag of Trudeau followers, political opportunists, and anti-Quebeckers—from Clyde Wells to Preston Manning—seized on this notion of individual equality and appropriated it for the benefit of the provinces, asserting that the equality of individuals necessarily meant that all provinces had to be equal—to have precisely the same powers. This group is now willing to push the nation to the brink of destruction by insisting on the perfect equality of the provinces. The problem is that neither the equality of individuals nor the equality of provinces has served to convince a sufficient majority of Quebeckers that the current constitutional arrangements are satisfactory.

We should know by now that perfect equality, be it of individuals or of provinces, is not an idea that can overcome a widespread feeling in Quebec that it is somehow different, entitled to some form of different treatment. We may not understand this feeling or even accept it, any more than Lincoln personally understood or accepted the morality of slavery. But should we reject it to keep our principles untainted, at the cost of losing our country?

What the Country Needs

On a rational plane, the case for Canada is unanswerable. That is why sovereignists, except for wide-eyed, frustrated emperors like Jacques Parizeau, sell their nationalist jump into the unknown with a solid, foolproof parachute made in Canada, complete with a Canadian passport, Canadian money, and full partnership in the Canadian market place. Indeed, there is no semblance of proof that economically, politically, or culturally, Quebeckers would be better off in an independent Quebec. Nor is there any evidence that, from the governance point of view, Quebec politicians would better administer their affairs if left to their own devices. The educational system, for example, which is of exclusive provincial jurisdiction, is in a mess in Quebec at least as much as in the other provinces.

Special status, let alone independence, is not required. But sometimes people "want" what they don't "need." Indeed, people often want what they know will be economically disadvantageous. From that point of view, the most important decisions in life are irrational. Getting married is not—usually—a profitable venture, particularly if children follow. But how many actually calculate the cost of family? *Le coeur a ses raisons que la raison ne connaît pas!*

Reason is not sufficient to bind us all together as a nation. Nor is economic prosperity, although this was not apparent to those who designed the federalist strategy in the 1995 referendum on the premise that economic self-interest would dictate that a strong majority of Quebeckers would choose Canada. Our relationships as citizens will require—just like all worthwhile and important relationships—significant compromises. Parents who want to keep their family together will not insist that each one of their children attend university and become a doctor or a lawyer, in the face of one "black sheep" who wants to write poetry or play in a rock band. Sometimes, imposing uniformity will only lead to disunion.

Perhaps what makes a country is the same ingredient that makes relationships between individuals last—compromise, giving something to the other person even when we don't understand why that is so. Perhaps it requires giving something that we consider important. Trudeau's failure as a leader is that he could not make any compromise to his theory of equal individual rights for the purposes of satisfying Quebec. It is true, of course, that nothing would have satisfied the true separatists and those who want all power for themselves. But those people are irrelevant. What is relevant is to see what compromise would be sufficient to rally a substantial majority of Quebeckers so as to doom the hard-core separatists to eventual extinction. Entrenching the distinct society clause in our Constitution, with the consent of a strong majority of provinces, is such a compromise.

But Trudeau could not abide this compromise; he could not admit of this weakness. He could not bring himself to give to others—even to his fellow French Canadians—what he did not need himself and what he felt they should not need either. He did not realize that his leadership could have been strengthened by an act of compassion; he revelled instead in his lifelong intransigence, so relished by his disciples. Perhaps there is much pride in standing firm—a justifiable courage in risking the nation for a principle. But, surely, great political leadership consists in advancing a principle as far as the nation will admit, and no farther. That is what Trudeau failed to comprehend: one can't be a philosopher and nation builder at the same time.

We shall not fight a civil war to keep Quebec in Canada. But we shall lose Quebec without a fight if we insist on our principles as if *any* principle were worth risking the destruction of such a worthy national ideal as Canada. For we are not asked to sanction

Hitlerism or condone slavery in Quebec, nor are we asked to condone any form of human repression. We are merely asked to show our respect by acknowledging a difference, when this recognition is important to those who seek it. Where is the leader who will convince Canadians that there is nothing demeaning in accepting this difference for the sake of this country?

Pierre Elliott Trudeau:

Quebec's Best Friend

■

MAX NEMNI

Max Nemni, *a professor of political science at Laval Univer-sity in Quebec City, is particularly interested in the relation-ship between nationalism and liberalism. His recent essays, in both English and French, analyse the effects of ethno-cultural nationalism on the viability of Canada. With his wife, Monique, he is editor-in-chief and publisher of* Cité libre, *the magazine founded by Pierre Trudeau and other Quebec intellectuals in June 1950.*

Trudeau and the Second Coming
of Quebec Nationalism

THE MIGHTY WAVE of Quebec nationalism which has thoroughly shaken Canada's political institutions first through the failed Meech Lake accord from 1987 to 1990, then through the failed Charlottetown accord from 1990 to 1992, and once again through the Quebec referendum of October 1995 on secession has brought with it many harsh criticisms of Trudeau's ideas and policies. On the face of it, this criticism is quite surprising, since the Trudeau political era came to a close in 1984 and the crowning achievement of his political life, the patriation of the Constitution accompanied by a Charter of Rights and Freedoms, was achieved in 1982. Because his policies were meant to tackle the very complex and still unsettled "unity" question, however, it is fair to judge him for a situation that may have derived from his policies.

Many intellectuals—francophones and anglophones, academics and journalists, politicians and bureaucrats—levy a harsh judgment on Trudeau's legacy. In *Trudeau and the End of the Canadian Dream* (1995), for example, Guy Laforest, a prominent representative of the new generation of "soft nationalists," interprets the 1982 constitutional reform as a mean-spirited attempt by Trudeau "to break the spine of the Québécois community in the interest of an idealized vision of the Canadian nation." In his most recent book, published in 1997, Kenneth McRoberts presents the same idea from an English-Canadian perspective. He claims that Trudeau's strategies, widely adopted in English Canada, have "destroyed the basis on which the stability of the Canadian polity had rested." McRoberts believes that only by abandoning the Trudeau vision can Canadians hope to unite their country. Hence the title of his book, *Misconceiving Canada: The Struggle for National Unity*.

In 1994, in a book titled *Reclaiming the Middle Ground*, a similar judgment of Trudeau's legacy was brought by two of his former collaborators who were then top civil servants, Gordon Robertson and Roger Tassé, and by Donald G. Lenihan, a research associate at the University of Ottawa. The "middle ground" to be reclaimed, in the eyes of the authors, is the one occupied by the so-called soft nationalists. A brutal version of this harsh critique appeared in *Maclean's* special report of April 22, 1997, on the ranking of Canada's prime ministers. There, Desmond Morton, a well-known friend of the soft-nationalists and the director of the McGill Institute for the Study of Canada, declared, "Trudeau was the disappointment of the century."

The main target of most of Trudeau's critics is the constitutional reform of 1982. To them, this reform was marked by a spirit of confrontation rather than accommodation with Quebec. Interestingly enough, this critique was mainly expressed at the time of the failed Meech and Charlottetown episodes. For example, the very first sentence of *Reclaiming the Middle Ground* states that "the clearest lesson of the debate over the 1992 Charlottetown Accord is that Canadians are divided in their vision of the country." A few lines later, those who still remember that this event happened under the Mulroney régime are surprised to learn that the objective of the authors is to "examine how the political philosophy of liberalism— especially as incorporated into 'pan-Canadianism' under former Prime Minister Trudeau—contrasts and conflicts with the more federalist aspirations of moderate Quebec nationalists." At the very outset of the first chapter one reads that "the intensity of the reaction in Quebec following the collapse of the Meech Lake Accord in 1990 stunned many in English-speaking Canada. The surge in support for sovereignty that followed sent shudders through the political class in the rest of Canada." Although it is common to attribute the recent rise of nationalism to Trudeau's policies, concrete proofs are rarely given. To these authors, the fact that nationalism is still present proves that Trudeau's policies have failed: "The proof is in the pudding."

Laforest adopts a different slant. He directly accuses a group of persons, labelled Trudeau's fellow travellers, of having worked hard "to influence a number of politicians in English Canada . . . against the ratification of [the Meech Lake accord]." Laforest brings two charges against the constitutional reform of 1982. First, he bemoans the fact that "the Quebec government was excluded from the constitutional negotiations of 1981–82." Second, and more important, he claims that the powers of the National Assembly were drastically reduced without the consent of the people or the government of Quebec. Invoking Locke, for whom the "legislative power is supreme and sacred," he claims that because the Quebec legislature did not consent, Trudeau committed a grievous mistake that delegitimizes the entire Canadian political system. He writes: "If my reading is correct, the Canadian political system has a fatal weakness at its core."

A second theme in the latest wave of criticisms rests on the notion that Trudeau's concepts of liberalism and nationalism were too abstract. A common picture of Trudeau is that of a man with noble but essentially obsolete ideals typical of the Enlightenment. Stubbornly clinging to an abstract vision of liberalism, individualism, and pan-Canadian nationalism, he abandoned reality and neglected federal principles. This abstract idealism, critics say, had dire consequences. First, Trudeau's purported attempt to apply individual rights across Canada caused him to disregard the legitimate needs of various communities. To Laforest, for example, the 1982 constitutional reforms were "unjust and reprehensible measures," nothing more than "a continuation of Lord Durham's policies by other means." Robertson, Tassé, and Lenihan double the stakes. To them, Trudeau's uncompromising desire to impose a single approach to the interpretation of rights across Canada was "a kind of imperialism [which] far from uniting the community, only serve[d] to alienate important subgroups within it." So fixed was he on abstract ideals that he was blind to the value of communities. They attribute his neglect of the values of community to the fact that he did not keep abreast of "communitarianism," which they depict as an exciting new current in liberal theory. Trudeau's outdated philosophy was translated, they claim, into already outdated policies premised on the view that "shared culture, language or history [were] of marginal concern, if not irrelevant, to what the Canadian Charter, in section (1), calls the 'reasonable limits' that can be placed on rights."

These mistaken philosophical perspectives, say the critics, had dire political consequences to the extent that they denied the validity of the claims of moderate nationalists: that, as the only province with a French-speaking majority, the Quebec government had a special mission in Confederation. Quite unjustifiably, Trudeau placed all nationalists in the same boat. He failed to see that moderate nationalists, unlike the extreme nationalists who sought separation, were merely seeking means to promote the development of their cultural community. As a result of this absence of nuance in Trudeau's ideas and of his doctrinaire espousal of classical liberalism, he failed to understand the needs of "cultural communities." The most damaging of all his failings was his inability to empathize with the struggle of francophone Quebecers to strengthen their culture "through membership in a healthy, developing cultural community."

Laforest puts this point very bluntly. He claims that by failing to recognize Quebec as a "nation" in its own right, "the reform of 1982, in its very principle, is a veritable war machine unleashed on the spirit of political and national duality." McRoberts expands on this theme and claims that "the Constitution Act, 1982 . . . violated the basic view of Canada, including the notion of a 'double compact,' held by generations of francophones."

The case against Trudeau is crushing. He tragically misunderstood the true nature of Quebec nationalism, was blind to the legitimate aspirations of cultural communities, and failed to empathize with the moderate nationalists and others who believed in a more flexible type of federalism. And because the Charter is skewed towards abstract individual rights, the antagonisms that Trudeau's policies created are now deeply embedded in the very structure of Canada's basic institutions. "Many Quebecers, Aboriginal peoples and Westerners," says McRoberts, "have dug in their heels and steadfastly refused to accept that what they regard as essentially community affairs must be subordinated to the new pan-Canadian vision of their common interests." In essence, then, Trudeau's policies have weakened rather than strengthened Canada. Thus, he is directly responsible for our present predicament. The proof, they claim, lies in the second coming of Quebec nationalism, which resulted in the slimmest of victories for the forces of Canadian unity after the October 1995 referendum.

Trudeau's Concepts of Liberalism and Nationalism

To assess Trudeau's vision in light of such weighty criticism, let us start with his understanding of Quebec nationalism. This concept is at the root of the current intellectual wave, critical both of his philosophy and his policies. Nobody would ever deny that Trudeau was a critic of nationalism. Similarly, few would deny that he is a major architect in constructing a new Canada. Should we conclude that his anti-nationalism was selectively directed against Quebec as a mean-spirited way of building a pan-Canadian nationalism? Did he, in fact, misunderstand the nature of Quebec nationalism? Worst of all, was he "anti-Quebec" rather than "anti-nationalist" in the abstract? We can answer these questions by examining both his writings and his record. But first, we must briefly recall Quebec's political climate in the early 1960s.

On June 22, 1960, a triumphant Jean Lesage—the father figure of this new era—announced the end of Quebec's nightmare by shouting, "Ladies and gentlemen, we have crushed the infernal machine, with its hideous face." The infernal machine was, of course, the corrupt Duplessis régime. Yet, in the election of November 1962, armed with a catchy new slogan—*Maîtres chez nous*—Lesage and his *équipe du tonnerre*, in which René Lévesque was a star performer, completely forgot the infernal machine. This time a potent political idea was intertwined with the powerful symbolism of a nation determined to rid itself of the oppressors. In effect, the new élite was arguing that a Quebec state was the only instrument available to the Quebec nation in its historic march towards full emancipation. The élite loudly proclaimed that the frontiers of nation and state should coincide.

The 1962 election marked the beginning of our present political era of relations between Quebec and the rest of Canada—an era characterized by the belief among all Quebec parties that the provincial government is essentially the political instrument of francophone Quebecers. To "federalist" parties, this belief has meant seeking as distinct or special a status for Quebec as possible, using all kinds of "knife at the throat" strategies to achieve their goal. For separatists, it has meant devising various formulae, such as "sovereignty-association" or "sovereignty-partenariat," to bring a reticent Quebec electorate to accept a secessionist agenda. The preliminary report of the Royal Commission on Bilingualism and Biculturalism, published in 1965, declared that Canada was going through the deepest crisis in its history. And, in July 1967, Charles de Gaulle crowned his visit to Canada with the cry that has echoed long after his departure: "Vive le Québec libre!" When a few weeks later, opinion polls showed that a majority of Quebecers approved de Gaulle's action, a motion was passed in the National Assembly expressing gratitude to the French president. Lesage, who was then in opposition, declared that "he was very happy with the way the population received the general." In this atmosphere, between 1961 and 1968, Trudeau expressed some of his most important thoughts on Quebec nationalism and Canadian federalism. Between 1968 and 1984, he attempted to deal concretely with these issues.

A good starting point for Trudeau's ideas is his famous article, "New Treason of the Intellectuals," first published in *Cité libre*. It is rarely mentioned, but worth noting, that this essay was not written during the Duplessis regime but in April 1962, well into the Quiet Revolution. What was this treason?

Nationalism, Trudeau claimed at the time, was an absurd and contradictory idea because "every national minority will find, at the very moment of liberation, a new minority within its bosom which in turn must be allowed the right to demand its freedom." It was a "retrograde" and "reactionary" idea because it led to "a definition of the common good as a function of an ethnic group, rather than of all the people." Good government cannot afford to be nationalistic because it must respect its citizens equally, without prejudice to their ethnic or racial origins, their cultural or religious values. Whenever a government deviates from its fundamental responsibility to promote the general interest, civil strife inevitably ensues. "This is why a nationalistic movement is by nature intolerant, discriminatory, and, when all is said and done, totalitarian." Finally, nationalism is a "barrier to progress" because the trend throughout the world—a very hopeful trend, according to Trudeau —was towards the tearing down of frontiers and barriers between peoples, rather than the erection of new ones. For Trudeau, the most pernicious barriers were the ones meant to protect a specific "cultural community" from contacts with the outside world. So far as Trudeau was concerned, no better recipe could be devised for stifling culture. Hence his resounding cry in his article "Nationalist Alienation" in 1961: "Open up the borders, our people are suffocating to death!"

"The New Treason of the Intellectuals," unquestionably Trudeau's sharpest and most eloquent critique of nationalism's failings, opens with the much quoted but still ambiguous statement seeming to condone certain varieties of nationalism: "It is not the concept of *nation* that is retrograde, it is the idea that the nation must necessarily be sovereign." To unravel the ambiguity of this sentence and to understand Trudeau's critique properly, one should keep in mind the context described above, where, after a brief respite of two years, Quebec's political and intellectual élites resorted once again to the ideal of nationalism as a means of rallying French Quebecers. This time, however, a new and important twist was added: Nationalism began to assume a territorial and political hue. For the first time in Canadian history, Quebec's government was openly and

systematically seeking to restructure a provincial state so it would fit
the contours of a nation. This was precisely what Trudeau regarded
as extremely dangerous. It is the theme he developed throughout
the essay and on which he concluded with the words of Lord
Acton: "Nationalism does not aim either at liberty or prosperity,
both of which it sacrifices to the imperative necessity of making the
nation the mould and measure of the state."

The opening and closing statements of the essay capture the
kernel of Trudeau's critique of the newly emerging nationalism in
Quebec, as well as his vision of the kind of Canada that would
respond to the aspirations, not only of French Quebecers, but of all
Canadians. Underlying these statements lies the fundamental
distinction Trudeau drew between "nation" and "nationalism."
Unfortunately, while obvious when placed in context, this distinction was sometimes obscured by the inconsistent use of the word
"nation," taken occasionally to mean either "nation-state" "or nationalism." It was only in 1964, in his other celebrated piece entitled "Federalism, Nationalism and Reason," that Trudeau clarified
his terminology. He noted the inherent ambiguity of the word
"nation" and attempted to resolve it by distinguishing between its
"juristic" and "sociological" meanings. Aware of the enduring lex-
ical ambiguities, he warned that "lawyers and political scientists
cannot remake the language to suit their convenience; they will
just have to hope that the context makes it tolerably clear which of
the two [definitions] we mean." The context demonstrated that, as
far as he was concerned, the nation "in the sociological sense" was
an existing reality. Throughout history, Trudeau argued, human
beings have constituted themselves into communities characterized
by various cultural traits, common traditions, and shared memories. It was just as absurd to set oneself against the "nation" as against
social life. The nation, he asserted, was "the guardian of certain
very positive qualities: a cultural heritage, a community awareness,
historical continuity, a set of mores; all of which, at this juncture in
history, go to make a man what he is." In today's vocabulary, one
would say that the nation was for him a specific, historically con-
tingent type of cultural community. Tomorrow, the nation could

well be replaced by another form of organization of individuals within a collectivity. In any case, the nation was a historical reality and he had nothing against this fact.

As his policy of multiculturalism would later illustrate, Trudeau was clearly in favour of measures that would enhance and enrich the cultural heritage of any group of people. His problem lay with the political use to which the idea of a nation was put—with the ideology of nationalism. More specifically, within Quebec, he was strongly critical of what he referred to as "this self-deluding passion of a large segment of our thinking population for throwing themselves headlong—intellectually and spiritually—into purely escapist pursuits." Chief among these sterile pursuits was the idea that "only Quebec as a state would appear to belong unquestionably to French Canadians; and the fullest power for that state is therefore highly desirable. Democracy having declared all men equal within the nation, so all nations should enjoy equality one to another, meaning in particular that ours should be sovereign and independent." This was *la nouvelle trahison des clercs*, the new treason of the intellectuals, which he was intent on denouncing.

Interestingly enough, in 1962 Trudeau was already critical of the logic of communitarianism, the school of thought that defends the idea that communities, especially national communities, should in some respects be treated as individuals. From this perspective it becomes possible to say that Quebec is or is not "humiliated" or that it seeks "recognition." The Trudeau critics mentioned above admire the writings of Charles Taylor from McGill University and Will Kymlicka from the University of Ottawa, for they see there a just mixture of communitarianism and liberalism most suitable to the Canadian situation. They express regret that this school of thought has passed Trudeau by.

In fact, Trudeau was at least one step ahead of his critics in terms of theory, and he never engaged in abstract philosophy. His critique was specifically aimed at those nationalist intellectuals who squandered vast amounts of energy in a dead-end pursuit. Thus, while Trudeau's evaluation of nationalism had a rich theoretical content, it was also a powerfully reasoned reaction against the concrete manifestations of nationalism that choked "his people"—the French Canadians. This "nation," as well as the English-Canadian one, was a historical reality that simply had to be accepted: "The die is cast in Canada: there are two main ethnic and linguistic groups; each is too strong and too deeply rooted in the past, too firmly bound to a mother-culture, to be able to engulf the other. But if the two will collaborate at the hub of a truly pluralistic state, Canada could become the envied seat of a form of federalism that belongs to tomorrow's world." In terms of abstract idealism, this is as far as Trudeau ever went. In terms of pragmatic realism, his entire political life was premised on the conviction that the ideal of a pluralistic Canada was achievable.

However, just as there existed in Canada two linguistic groups with a great potential for mutual enrichment, there were also two nationalisms with a similar potential for mutual destruction. In Trudeau's words, "if, in the face of Anglo-Canadian nationalism, French-Canadians retreat into their own nationalistic shell . . . Canada will become a sterile soil for the minds of her people, a barren waste prey to every wandering host and conquering horde." It was clear to Trudeau that the two linguistic communities, which had shaped Canada and each other, could not just be wished away or absorbed one by the other. He developed this theme more extensively in his "Federalism, Nationalism and Reason," where he showed a keen awareness of the political usefulness of appeals to ethnic sentiments. But it was the English-Canadian community that took the brunt of his criticism. The repeated attempts by the anglophone community to put francophones in a subordinate position, not to say to dominate them, had simply produced a countervailing and equally ugly French-Canadian nationalism. But reason, Trudeau claimed, had to prevail if we wished to avoid disaster. Jealous and inward-looking nationalisms could destroy what had been achieved and what could yet be achieved. It was time to forget past grievances. The challenge was the promotion of "national values," the danger was nationalism, and the solution was pluralism and federalism: "We must separate once and for all the concepts of state and of nation, and make Canada a truly pluralistic and polyethnic society." This reasoning was the basis of Trudeau's critique of nationalism, his trust in federalism, and his search for a genuinely pluralistic society.

In concrete terms, Trudeau believed that good government required good institutions; good institutions, in turn, required counterweights. Canada's problems would not be solved by longing for great leaders, but through the improvement of existing institutions. Trudeau felt that Canada was already endowed with the institutional arrangements perfectly suited to the tasks at hand. He greatly appreciated, in particular, the distribution of powers between the two levels of governments. The jurisdiction of the federal government concerned itself with all matters devoid of ethnic or cultural dimension, whereas the provinces had jurisdiction over education, property, civil rights, and the administration of justice. In order to "make Canada truly pluralistic," what remained to be done was, first and foremost, to ensure that French Canadians occupied their rightful place within Canada's institutions. The reform of existing institutions was also necessary to fertilize the flowering of cultural and "national values." To succeed, these reforms required the creation of a sense of Canadian patriotism that could only be achieved by transferring sovereignty to the people.

The Constitutional Reform of 1982: Orthodox Liberalism or Pragmatic Federalism?

Trudeau's response to these challenges is well known. His political philosophy was founded on a liberal conception of justice, emphasizing the moral and political primacy of the individual as well as the pursuit of tolerance and equality of opportunity. All his political initiatives were informed by these principles, foremost among them were those policies that had a direct impact on the unity question: official bilingualism, multiculturalism, and the Charter of Rights and Freedoms. As we have seen, these policies are now increasingly perceived as part of an abstract pursuit of lofty ideals rather than as pragmatic answers to real problems.

By entrenching official bilingualism, Trudeau hoped to put the two historic language communities on an equal footing, politically and juridically. The policy was never meant, as many of his critics contend, to make every Canadian bilingual. Certainly the objective was ambitious, but it was doable, and history has proved that, to a great extent, Trudeau's policies have indeed been realized: Government services are now available across Canada in both languages; the ranks of the civil service in Ottawa are fully accessible to all; French immersion has opened bilingual education to countless anglophones; and a political career in Ottawa, especially in the higher echelons, can hardly be envisaged without a sound knowledge of both languages. These very concrete achievements negate the accusations of "abstract idealism" that are so frequently aimed at Trudeau's policies. Of course, by recognizing both official languages as absolutely equal in juridical and political terms, and by entrenching language rights within the Constitution, a big step was taken towards the creation of a Canadian political nationality.

Multiculturalism was another pragmatic response to the reality of Canada. When Trudeau came to power, in the late 1960s, at least one-third of the Canadian population was already neither English nor French in origin. The constitutional reform of 1982 reacted to this situation by recognizing that the Charter must be interpreted "in a manner consistent with the preservation and enhancement of the multicultural heritage of Canadians." This right has undoubtedly helped to foster the strong sense of Canadian patriotism that is so prevalent within Canada's increasingly multi-ethnic population.

The main target selected by Trudeau's latest wave of critics is, however, the constitutional reform of 1982, and especially the Charter of Rights. But the critique is accompanied by a new twist. In the first few years after patriation, the reform was criticized essentially on the grounds that it abandoned the British tradition of parliamentary supremacy and unduly increased the powers of the judiciary. The critiques now take a different slant. The reform, and in particular the entrenchment of the Charter through its emphasis on freedom, equality, and individual rights, is seen as a move away from federal accommodation of national diversity, and hence as a flawed instrument in view of the aspirations of Quebec's soft nationalists. Let us attempt to deal with this accusation by briefly reviewing the effects of the Charter on Quebec's citizens.

First, the Charter guarantees certain basic rights to all Canadians. Although civil liberties are not as fragile in Canada as they are in many other countries, abuses do occur. Moreover, polls have systematically shown that Canadians, including Quebecers, identify very strongly with, and appreciate the protection of, the Charter. Second, the Charter has provided powerful support for the French language by putting it on an equal footing with English in the eyes of the law, and by protecting the educational rights of official minority languages. These constitutional guarantees clearly strengthen the French presence and its vibrancy across Canada, while the continuing presence of francophone minorities beyond Quebec is an essential condition for the preservation of official bilingualism. It is evident that measures which favour the promotion of French are in the interest of all French Canadians, within Quebec and outside. The Charter is thus an indisputable asset to francophone Quebecers.

But there are two aspects of the Charter that Quebec nationalists bitterly criticize. They claim, first, that it has substantially reduced the power of the Quebec government and, second, that it has created a pan-Canadian nationalism which excludes Quebecers. Certainly, the Charter has changed the role of the judiciary. Some believe this judicial prominence has in turn weakened the powers of the legislature and the power of the people over their governments. But this perspective minimizes an important aspect of the judiciary within a federal system: the arbitration of disputes between the two levels of government. In federal systems, the courts necessarily become part of the political process. The choice is between providing a legal framework for this role or leaving it loosely structured. Canada's history is replete with examples of the latter approach. One easily recalls, for instance, the series of appeals to the Supreme Court by a number of provinces, including Quebec, intended to prevent the federal government from patriating the Constitution unilaterally. The Supreme Court held that while unilateralism by the federal government was legal, political conventions required that the consent of some unspecified number of provinces be obtained. This extra-legal decision clearly had serious political consequences. Foremost among them was the fact that the federal government sought and obtained the consent of all provincial governments except Quebec. The separatist Parti Québécois government, which had no interest in improving Canada's political institutions, used this situation to its political advantage: it proclaimed loudly that Quebec had been "excluded." The extra-legal ruling lent a measure of credibility to this point of view which entered the political imagination of Quebecers in various guises, such as the "night of the long knives" or the "*coup de force*" of 1982. The same powerful themes were used by the Mulroney government to great advantage between 1987 and 1990, when the Meech Lake agreement was presented as the atonement of "English Canada" for the "humiliation and isolation" of Quebec in 1982.

This is where, in a federal system, a Constitution and a Charter of Rights can create a framework that minimizes encroachments in the political domain. When the rights of citizens and the powers of governments are spelled out, the courts have less leeway in resorting to "political conventions." Trudeau envisaged the effect of a Charter of Rights on the judiciary and on intergovernmental relations in this way. His position was clearly expressed in April 1963 in a brief but highly laudatory review of Edward McWhinney's *Comparative Federalism*, which, he claimed, "should be a requirement for anyone running as a candidate in Canadian elections." Trudeau seems to have learned a number of important lessons from this book which he later applied to the Canadian context. Foremost among them were the benefits to be derived from a Charter in a federal system and the special role of the courts in dealing with minorities. In his words:

> I am increasingly coming to believe that Canadian federalism will reach full maturity only if we entrench in our Constitution a declaration of human rights and freedoms. Among other

things, the existence of such a declaration would make it possible to restrict the actions of the Supreme Court to the area of public law. In this way, provinces could exercise their autonomy with all the more freedom, since this freedom would come within certain civilizing and democratic standards guaranteed by the declaration of rights and applied by the Supreme Court.

Trudeau saw in the Charter a powerful instrument to vest sovereignty in the people, thereby strengthening Canadian institutions rather than governments. He was convinced that the power transferred to the people would come principally from the federal government: "An examination of the categories of all fundamental rights, however described, for which we propose protection, reveals that the bulk of them now fall under federal jurisdiction. This means that in this process of surrender of power [to the people] that we are proposing, Parliament will be giving up far more than will the provinces."

With constitutional reform now well behind us, we know that the only effective reallocation of powers between the two levels of government was accomplished in favour of the provinces, all of which gained greater control over natural resources. It has also become abundantly clear that the reform's greatest impact, which deeply disturbs Quebec nationalists, lies in the reallocation of sovereignty.

By embedding fundamental rights in the Constitution, the reform in effect placed citizens above their government, both in symbolic and practical terms. For the first time in Canada's history, the locus of sovereignty moved away from governments towards the people. The era of "executive federalism" was over. But, by the same token, the "compact theory of confederation," in both its "two founding peoples" and its "founding provinces" varieties, became inoperative. As we shall now see, this changing focus profoundly disturbs Quebec nationalists.

The nationalists repeatedly complain that the Quebec government was excluded from the constitutional negotiations of 1981–82. This phrasing is at best a figure of speech. In fact, the Quebec government was not only a party to these negotiations but the leader of the famous "Gang of Eight" that nearly succeeded in scuttling the entire process. The Quebec government officially refused to endorse the final accord, and it managed to obtain the support of the provincial Liberal Party. It is also true that Quebec's refusal to endorse the Constitution constitutes a serious political obstacle to Canadian unity systematically exploited by the nationalist élite.

However, as we have seen, patriation was effected in full respect of the law, and with full respect for the "political conventions" referred to by the Supreme Court. In no instance did the Court even vaguely allude to the necessity of Quebec's specific consent. And this is where the difficulty lies. To Laforest and others of the new generation of soft-nationalists, Quebec is not just another province—it is a "nation" living side by side with another "nation." Its people constitute a "political community" distinct from the rest of Canada. The only Canada they may be willing to accept is a "bi-national" Canada. In all likelihood, they would not even welcome former prime minister Joe Clark's "community of communities." To them, what matters first and foremost is the recognition of a "dualistic" Canada. But, as we noted above, by transferring power to the people, Trudeau has entirely dispensed with this possibility. Hence Laforest's lament for the loss of a "Canadian Dream."

But let us stop dreaming and deal with the nationalists' solitary concrete critique. Loudly and repeatedly, they assert that patriation of the Constitution reduced the powers of the National Assembly without its consent and without the consent of the Quebec people. This argument rests on one central premise: Quebec's National Assembly is a supreme legislative body similar in all respects to that of a unitary state. This, of course, would only be true if Quebec were indeed an independent country or if Canada were a confederation of autonomous states. But let us delve a little deeper into these critiques, since they contain a degree of empirical substance.

The claim that the Quebec government has lost substantial and important powers is made over and over again. Very rarely, however, are the precise extent and nature of these powers clearly defined. The closest we come to such precision is when Laforest writes that "the legislative powers of the National Assembly of Quebec were reduced, notably with respect to issues of language." The accusation has been repeated time and again by Quebec's intellectuals and politicians. It was one of Lucien Bouchard's most effective weapons during the October 1995 referendum campaign. On October 7, 1995, for example, referring to Prime Minister Jean Chrétien as Trudeau's underling, Bouchard shouted: "We shouldn't forget the man of 1982 . . . He is the one who has imposed on us a Constitution which has forced us to retreat in such crucial areas as our powers on language, on culture and on education."

But what powers actually were lost? This information is extremely difficult to come by. Politicians, journalists, and even academics rarely, if ever, specify the missing powers that, they claim, have crippled Quebec. Here and there, Laforest is less imprecise and points an accusing finger at Article 23 of the Charter. He claims that the provisions of this article, on the language of education, are so nefarious as to empty the Canadian legal and political system of all legitimacy. They warrant secession and, Laforest hints, possibly civil disobedience and revolution. Let us take a thorough look at this article.

Article 23 of the Charter: Confrontation or Accommodation?

Because Article 23 is the focal point of this section, it is necessary to quote in full subsections (1) and (2), which specify the extent and nature of the rights involved and their intended beneficiaries. These rights apply only "where numbers warrant," according to subsection (3). This subsection, having no other purpose, will not be quoted here. Here, then, are the sections of the Charter which, according to Laforest, have rendered all Canada's institutions illegitimate:

Minority Language Educational Rights

(1) Citizens of Canada

(a) whose first language learned and still understood is that of the English or French linguistic minority population of the province in which they reside, or

(b) who have received their primary school instruction in Canada in English or French and reside in a province where the language in which they received that instruction is the language of the English or French linguistic minority population of the province,

have the right to have their children receive primary and secondary school instruction in that language in that province.

(2) Citizens of Canada of whom any child has received or is receiving primary or secondary school instruction in English or French in Canada, have the right to have all their children receive primary and secondary school instruction in the same language.

The clear purpose of this section of the Charter is to protect the educational rights of "official language minorities" across Canada "wherever numbers warrant." This protection leads some of Trudeau's critics to claim that the Charter imposes a homogeneous concept of individual and minority rights and maintains a "national" vision of Canada contrary to the spirit of federalism and to the particular character of Quebec. But this claim is not true. The actual effect of these articles is to protect French minorities *outside* Quebec, and the French majority *inside* Quebec. We will see that this protection involves an adaptation of liberal principles to the Canadian context to suit the specific needs of francophones, inside and outside Quebec.

Let us first examine how these rights apply beyond Quebec where French is the minority language. There are two categories of francophone Canadians: Those whose first language learned and still understood is French [section (a)] and those who, although not native francophone, took their primary schooling in French anywhere in Canada [section (b)]. As official minorities, these francophones can avail themselves of the rights spelled out in the Charter to have their children educated in French, where such numbers warrant. In contrast, anglophones outside Quebec obtain no specific educational rights with regard to the language of instruction. They cannot have recourse to the Charter if they are refused admittance to a French school. Indeed, in some recorded cases, francophone school boards turned away anglophone students in order, they claimed, to preserve their language and culture. Since anglophones have not historically fought for the right to an education in French, and since for the last thirty years or so they have enjoyed the benefits of "French immersion" in the English-language schools, the restriction has not created much turmoil. Nevertheless, denial of freedom of choice to anglophones outside Quebec cannot be defended on the basis of liberal principles.

Within Quebec itself, anglophones constitute the minority and are therefore protected by the Charter. There are two types of anglophone Canadians: Those whose first language learned and still understood is English [section (a)] and those who, although not native English speakers, had their primary schooling in English anywhere in Canada [section (b)]. While Article 23 grants the same rights to both groups of francophones in the rest of Canada, the rights of anglophones as defined in Article 23 (1) (a) are restricted in Quebec by Article 59, which states that Article 23 (1) (a) will apply only after it has been "authorized by the legislative assembly or government of Quebec." Whereas the definition of a francophone is not subject to the approval of any provincial legislature, the Quebec government is given the power to decide whether this subsection will effectively apply or not. Since the National Assembly of Quebec has not approved it yet, this means that immigrants in Quebec whose mother tongue is English cannot avail themselves of the rights spelled out in Article 23 unless they previously resided in another province and received their primary education in English.

Why does the Charter make Article 23 (1) (a) conditional on the approval by the legislative assembly of Quebec? And why not Article (1) (b) as well?

The answer to the second question is obvious. To create two categories of anglophones, those educated in Quebec and those in the rest of Canada, and to grant special rights to only one category, runs counter to the basic liberal principle of equality under the law. If Canada is one country, then its citizens must be able to keep their constitutional rights as they move freely throughout the country. Canadian citizens must be in a position to retain their rights when they become part of the English minority in Quebec.

The answer to the first question, which involves a relatively small departure from liberal principles, can only be attributed to Trudeau's empathy with the needs of francophones within Quebec. Immigrants whose native language is English who settle in Quebec fall under Article 23 (1) (a). However, they cannot avail themselves of their prescribed rights because Article 59 leaves them in abeyance. This means that even when anglophone immigrants become Canadian citizens, they never acquire the same constitutional rights as those anglophones educated in English in Canada. It is evident that the creation of two categories of anglophone Canadian citizens residing in Quebec, one having fewer rights than the other, constitutes an infringement of individual rights. Moreover, one could argue that it is an unnecessary infringement, since so few people would have gained access to English schools by means of this clause. But that is another question. In the present context, it is one more example of the Charter's adaptation of liberal principles to suit Quebec's concept of minority educational rights.

But this is still not the whole story. Let us look again at the Charter to evaluate the rights of individuals who are not members of official minorities. In effect, within Quebec, only one group of people, anglophones as defined in section (1) (b), benefits from complete freedom of choice with respect to the language of education. All other Quebecers, including native-born francophones, have no constitutional right to English schools. Through Bill 101, the government of Quebec has imposed the French school system on these people and, with the minor exceptions noted above, the Charter in effect has provided constitutional support for these measures.

But in order to understand the loud complaints of the nationalists to the effect that the Charter has reduced the powers of the National Assembly, we have to come back to the category of anglophones as defined in Article 23 (1) (b). This is the only empirical basis of Laforest's rejection of the reform of 1982 as a "veritable war machine unleashed on the spirit of political and national duality." Beyond the rhetoric, the bone of contention lies in the fact that, according to the Charter, anglophones are Canadian citizens educated in English in *Canada*; Bill 101 defines the equivalent category as those who were educated in English in *Quebec*. Thus, "this formidable war machine," this *coup de force* against Quebec, is nothing more than the fact that the few anglophone Canadians from other provinces who settle in Quebec have educational rights in their language. This right is hardly a valid reason to claim that "Trudeau has betrayed the trust of Quebecers," especially when we keep in mind that the Charter has bent liberal principles to accommodate Quebec. On the contrary, one finds here another example of the adaptation of liberal principles to the Canadian context in order to promote French in Quebec.

By protecting the rights of the anglophone minority alone, the Charter, by default, fails to protect the freedom of choice of the language of education for all other Quebecers. Here, however, an important difference is noted between the Charter and Bill 101. Whereas the Charter specifies the rights of minorities, it does not *forbid* access of the majority to the schools of the minority. To respect the constitutional division of powers, this decision is left to the provinces. In contrast, Quebec's Bill 101 formally forbids instruction in English. Article 78.1 states: "No one can allow or tolerate that a child be given instruction in English unless he is admissible to it." The Charter is silent on this infringement of individual rights. This omission can only be explained in terms of respect for federal principles and for Canada's history. In effect, the Charter recognizes that French, being a minority language in

Canada and North America, requires special measures of support. The Charter shares with Bill 101 its most fundamental objective: the protection and promotion of French in Quebec.

The provisions of the Charter with respect to the language of education depart from a strict adherence to the basic liberal principle of freedom of choice. As Trudeau explained in an interview with the directors of *Cité libre* in 1997, he accepted this departure from basic values because he refused to interfere with provincial prerogatives in education. He also endorsed some aspects of Bill 101 for pragmatic reasons. He simply recognized the lesson of history: The two language communities had an equal right to flourish, and French, being vulnerable, needed special protection. Everyone who desired could learn a language and be personally enriched in the process. However, with regard to culture, what was imperative was tolerance and the acceptance of diversity. Cultures should not be treated as holistic entities or as endangered species that needed political protection to survive. What needed protection was the right of individuals to cultivate themselves in as many ways and directions as they pleased. To this end, the indispensable prerequisite was a political system that favoured tolerance and cultural pluralism.

Let us now summarize the effect of the Charter. Outside Quebec, francophone minorities are fully protected and benefit from full freedom in the choice of their language of instruction. The anglophones outside Quebec receive no special protection, which in effect means that their access to French is left to the discretion of the French educational system. Outside Quebec, therefore, the francophone minorities are the only beneficiaries of the Charter.

Inside Quebec, only a limited group of anglophones—Canadian citizens who were educated in English in Canada—have rights protected by the Charter. Bill 101 restricted this choice to Canadian citizens educated in Quebec. For all other Quebecers—the huge majority—Bill 101 imposes attendance in the French school system, and the Charter does not invalidate this restriction of freedom of choice. The Charter has merely placed moral pressures on Quebec's legislators to open the English schools to all native English speakers.

Fundamentally, therefore, and this point is left unsaid by Trudeau's critiques, the Charter has provided a constitutional foundation for most educational requirements of Quebec's language legislation.

Clearly, the Charter is not inspired by an abstract liberal philosophy and a rigid concept of individual rights mechanically applied to all regions of Canada. On the contrary, fully respectful of federal principles and of the specificity of Canada's bilingual character, the Charter has adapted fundamental liberal values—foremost among them freedom of choice in education—to the Canadian context. In the final analysis, it is the French language that is protected and promoted within Quebec and outside Quebec. By embedding in the Canadian Constitution the means of protecting the specificity of Quebec society, the Charter has, in effect, granted a "distinct status" to the French language.

Conclusion

Trudeau's policies have not "solved" the problem of Quebec nationalism once and for all. But is there such solution? Nationalism is an extremely powerful ideology, and it has been part and parcel of Canada's history for many generations. Before Trudeau came to power, the Royal Commission on Bilingualism and Biculturalism had already declared that Canada was facing the most serious crisis of its history. Yet we now forget that from 1981 to 1987, right after the constitutional reform, Quebec nationalism almost disappeared.

Trudeau was not against the "nation," in the sense of a community of people sharing certain attributes and certain values. He was against appeals to ethnic or cultural traits for political purposes. He knew that nationalism engendered other nationalisms, and that territorial divisions engendered other divisions. The powerful rise of the "partitionist movement" in Quebec, after the October 1995 referendum, is the latest example of Trudeau's acumen. Nationalism, to him, was a barrier to cultural pluralism and tolerance.

He believed that the simultaneous promotion of French and of cultural pluralism were extremely valuable objectives that need not be antithetical. The embedding of French and English as the two official languages, the protection of the education rights of the English-speaking and French-speaking minorities, and the encouragement of multiculturalism were all concrete means of achieving this goal. These policies strengthened French and thus strengthened "Quebec."

How can Quebec nationalists claim that the Quebec National Assembly lost huge powers through the constitutional reform of 1982? In fact, it lost no powers at all. It gained powers, since its language legislation, crucial to Quebec francophones, was strengthened through constitutional measures. The grievance of the nationalists lies elsewhere. They bemoan the loss of the myth of the "two founding peoples." They bemoan the non-recognition of Quebec as a "nation" in its own right. This loss is true. The constitutional reform of 1982 had no room for recognition of any form of "national principle." It was premised, rather, on the most fundamental of democratic principles—that governments were answerable to the people and not to the "nation."

Yet so-called soft nationalists still seek a dualistic Canada, by which they mean a bi-national Canada. This is an unreasonable demand for all the reasons Trudeau so clearly identified many decades ago. It is unreasonable because the Canada of today, the Canada moulded by the constitutional reform of 1982, has given Canadian citizens effective means of control over their government. The Meech Lake and Charlottetown sagas are here to remind us that the unanimous agreement of all governments is no longer sufficient to change Canada's institutions. The people have acquired a keen sense of their political rights and the means to exercise them. Finally, a dualistic Canada is not a reasonable demand because the Canada of today, Trudeau's Canada, has plenty of room for tolerance, for cultural diversity, and for the promotion of French. Trudeau's continuing popularity in Quebec and Quebecers' continuing attachment to the Charter and to Canada are signs that these values are appreciated by the people. It is to be hoped that intellectuals and politicians, be they federalists or nationalists, "soft" or "hard," will stop catering to the "nation" so they can lend an ear to the people.

5

THE LION
IN WINTER

Pierre Trudeau:

The Elusive I

■

B. W. POWE

B.W. Powe teaches at York University and is the author of five books, including Outage, *a novel,* The Solitary Outlaw, *and* A Canada of Light, *a reflection on the country's hopes and possibilities. He is a popular speaker and a frequent contributor to the* Globe and Mail.

A T WHAT POINT do you become . . . enigmatic?"
Trudeau smiled—that tight Asiatic (Attic?) grin, at once mildly mocking and supremely amused at the complexities of life.

"Why do you ask?" He spoke slowly. It was, after all, a strange, probably self-indulgent question. "Why are you thinking about that?" Again the slow speech. I have observed, lately, how his speech has slowed. But then, he is an elderly man now, close to his eighties.

I explained: "I've been referred to as 'almost' enigmatic in a newspaper. Sometimes I puzzle over it. When do you go from being 'almost' to 'completely'?" Those words had cried out for quotation marks.

Silence. Laser-blue stared across the desk. The eyes not blinking. The smile lingering. He was no doubt continuing to think, why am I being asked such a question? His Jesuit leanings would have taught him that there are always meanings within meanings. Finally, the shrug; and a reply:

"Just stick around."

"Stick around?"

"Longevity. The longer you're at it, the more of a mystery you'll be."

"Survival. That's the key?"

"Just staying alive in this business is mystery enough. For most people, anyway. Or so it seems."

The smile returned and didn't fade. Nor did the blue stare falter. Another silence. His answer, naturally enough, had been more elusive than illuminating.

Time: May 1997, the Canadian spring late (as usual) in Montreal, one month before the federal election. Place: Trudeau's office on the twenty-fifth floor of 1250 René-Lévesque Boulevard. Historians with a developed taste for ironic patterns and puckish synchronicities should take note of that street name. (A future scenario: A retired Lucien Bouchard, his separatist cause forever defeated, retreats to write his memoirs on the recently named Pierre Elliott Trudeau Boulevard in Quebec City . . . no, it's unimaginable.) Day: Wednesday, with the wind carrying traces of ice, a blue light like a subtle aurora in the sky. Me: taking a break from a round of interviews and readings. PET: thirteen years out of power, deep in his implacable retirement. And yet for many people his resolute remove had become mythic—the persona of this former prime minister ever more impenetrable.

I had come for lunch, but I'd also come with questions. It is hard to visit a myth without having questions. And though I remember him that day as being kindly, receptive, almost serene, and certainly articulate, I had the sense of him being turned more inward than on other occasions when we'd talked. There was an intensity of inwardness about him. Day-dreamy or contemplative? I wondered. Or maybe an individual all too aware of ends, life's narrowings? At any rate, if I'm remembering precisely, he wore a light blue suit with a tie; oddly formal, more so than some of the times when we'd met before.

His mood was unhurried, and he was willing to let our conversation wander. We talked of mutual acquaintances, books, trips we'd taken, and poetry—zeroing in on Yeats and Rilke, two poets he said he was reading closely. Their last poems, he told me. Unexpectedly he quoted a long section from Yeats' "The Second Coming." He stopped after the famous first stanza, almost daring me (so I thought) to complete the lines. They were lines from Yeats' mid-career that (luckily) I knew, so I obliged. Before I arrived at that passionate arching query to time, he broke in and finished the poem: "And what rough beast, its hour come round at last, / Slouches towards Bethlehem to be born?"

He laughed quietly to himself—and I thought, abruptly, of how many citizens had sometimes thought of him as being monstrous long before the hazy, soft-focus light of myth had descended like a halo. But the "rough beast" of those lines meant many things—prophetic, ironic, allegoric, symbolic, literal. They also alluded to coming chaos. Maybe there was some other monster, another presence looming, in his mind? He gazed off, withdrawing, becoming thoughtful, then privately amused, that amusement gradually turning back into a reflective look.

I always entered his office with the mild sense that I was breaking into an utterly private domain. The room was welcoming enough. Large, angular, a wide bright view of the new hockey arena to the south, a clear aerial view to the east of the park between Peel and Cathédrale where the Rally for Canada took place during the 1995 referendum on separation. I wanted to ask him about watching that rally alone from this perch, but first I made a mental note of the haunting stillness that pervaded his space.

Books were stored precariously on top of other books, the stockpile threatening to teeter over like some personal Tower of Babel. Manuscripts and special advance reading copies. T.C. McLuhan, Andrei Sakharov, John Ralston Saul, Rilke; theology, philosophy, politics, history, memoirs. Little fiction anywhere. ("Old men read few novels," said George Steiner. Why? Because reality and the imagination have fused for an individual who has lived with vehemence and keenness? Maybe at a certain point your own stories become vivid enough?)

His office seemed as removed as he himself had—mostly—been for the past years. No computer, no fax, no cellular, no typewriter, no TV, no gadgets of any kind. Pens and notepads only. The desk remarkably clear. Pictures of his boys—paintings, photographs, of the four together. Awards, medals. Not much to indicate his political life.

"This is where you stood during the rally in '95?"

He rose from his cushioned chair, walked to the window.

"From here. Yes. I looked down that day at the people and the flags. I could see it all."

"You weren't asked to speak?"

(Note to myself: I was being too inquisitorial. Do most encounters with him turn into interviews? People wanting to ask, to know. Looking for a way inside. That ache for answers. Well, I did have many questions.)

"No, I wasn't asked."

"You weren't asked to just show up?"

He looked off, then down into the park. The turning inward again. A look that seemed vaguely as though he was waiting, or searching, for something. Looking down from that spot in his office you can see the statue of Sir John A. Macdonald. When I'd passed that statue earlier, I paused to stare at the patch of graffiti, a white-paint smudge, streaked across the cenotaph's base. FLQ, the letters had said.

"No," he said. "The organizers felt they didn't need me." Strong emphasis on the word "organizers." Pronounced implications of anger. "It was their show. They thought they knew what they were doing. What they really wanted to accomplish."

"And with the referendum."

"It was poorly handled. No backup plan. Looked like desperation in the end. Which I suppose it was. Giving everything away like that."

"It's quite an image. You standing up here, looking down at the flags, the celebration, the speakers, the crowds."

He turned away from the window, and made a gesture with his right hand, like a farewell.

"I didn't stay for long. I went out to lunch. And I walked in the *other* direction." Emphasis precise, intention clear.

"It was cold," he went on quietly, almost incidentally, it seemed. "I had a long lunch."

Quiet. While he'd been talking I'd kept trying, precisely, to catch the mood of this room. Then it dawned on me: The mood was uncannily quiet. I was tempted to say quietist. Some absorption in contemplation, some surrendering to interior life. Despite his flashes of wit and anger, there was a calmness to him, a conscious unfastening from the affairs outside. His office located at the end of a long corridor. No one else nearby, except for his discreet assistant, Michelle. An office at the edge of a tower. Quiet in the way that certainly signalled, Be careful about disturbing the peace. Quiet in the way that also said, I'm thinking about things here. The carpeted corridors, the assistants in separated booths. A silence in these chambers. A place not quite part of anything directly. You had to walk up stairs; find your path down corridors; then find yourself in a place which was, while friendly enough, almost invisible, untraceable.

Turning to leave for lunch. (He: "Will I need my coat?" I: "You will. It's cold out there." He: "Still? It *is* May." I: "I know. But it's Canada." He: "Did I need reminding?") We went out into the tower lobby, then into the streaming street, the sudden shout and wind of crowds and traffic.

And our conversation changed to talk of our children. Mine, twins, a boy and a girl, still very young; his boys now young adults, so he was remembering his experiences. I almost had the impression that, chameleonlike, our exchanges were taking on the quality of our environment. Here we were among people—couples, groups, trios, soloists, all heading somewhere for lunch—and we had modulated into talk of connection. We talked of reading to our children at night before sleep, and of learning how to be fathers. Talked of watching our children grow, of missing them when you travel. We both remarked on how the scent of your young children, and their touch, lingered with you and sharpened your longing to return home. Talked of the questions children often ask, of the pleasure and difficulty of getting to know what it is they dream of, and what it is they want.

"When they were around ten, eleven, thirteen," he said, "every Saturday night I would get away from my commitments and read to them. It was our Saturday night together. I read them Rousseau, history books, poetry, Victor Hugo. Later, Stendhal, and Tolstoy. We'd talk about what we read. Read out loud to each other. Every Saturday night for years . . . It was," he paused, "one of the happiest periods of my life."

He made it seem like this happiness was in the very distant past.

"It doesn't sound like you've raised any of your children to be politicians."

"It would be better," he said, "if they were teachers."

"No money in that," I said, aiming for irony.

"No, maybe there's a great need for people who can truly teach. Maybe now more than ever. With all the machines around. So many pressures . . . I still like to help my kids with their studies. Read what they're reading."

We stopped to cross René-Lévesque. Waited for the lights to change. And waited. And waited. Waited longer than I expected we would. A decade before I'd watched Trudeau sprint off into traffic—"Well, I guess we're off," he'd called over his shoulder—running against the light, impatiently jogging and halting cars, vans, trucks, and cabs, with drivers mouthing his name in a pantomime of surprise when they recognized who was dodging through, dashing to the other side, leaving me stranded while the cars picked up speed again. That day he ambled out when the lights finally changed, and I slowed my pace to stay beside him.

We were heading for a Chinese restaurant called the Chrysanthemum.

People emerged from towers, hurtling off to lunches of meetings, people leaning into the wind clutching spring coats to their necks, people out sidestepping others on the narrow sidewalks, people suddenly struck with the recognition that here was a well-known face passing them by, a face with scars and curves and gashes and prominent bones, so familiar to most people that, startled, they paused to say something but did nothing other than nod or smile or raise a hand or blink, no doubt gathering thoughts of what to say over a meal, back in a tower, on the way home, in the evening, to colleague or date or spouse or parent or child or friend, some registering in their faces an uncertainty about him—was it a ghost? an eerie lookalike?—maybe shocked at his aged appearance, people roaming off to liaisons and appointments, passing by a part of their history, each with a memory of the special intensities of that history—Trudeaumania in 1968, the War Measures Act, the election defeat of 1979, the election victory of 1980, the referendum battle with Lévesque, the patriation of the Constitution, the skirmishes with Bouchard after the second referendum—people passing and showing amazement, sometimes a touch of scepticism and even annoyance in their astonishment, because time and magic and unpredictability and the human presence had intersected.

"Do you ever miss it?"

"Miss what?"

I pointed to the people regarding him.

"Do you miss politics? Being prime minister?"

"No."

"Not at all."

"Not in any way."

I inclined my head towards him to pick up the words that strayed away.

"What about the exercise of power?" I persisted. "Dealing with issues, with people. Finding solutions, or compromises. Finding ways to bring about justice."

He spoke softly again, maybe answering more for himself than me. "Being in politics was a role I was content to play for a time. Now I'm content to play another role. To be away from it all. You have no idea. I miss nothing."

I was tempted to ask what role he thought he was playing now; but I didn't pursue it. Let this pass, I thought. Another time, another question.

We walked up steps to the doors of the Chrysanthemum and entered. We found a table, sat, ordered two plates (shrimp, chicken, with a bowl of hot-and-sour soup for me), and resumed our conversation—shifting to questions of government's role, to representation from regions, to Thomas Jefferson, to the neoconservative movement in the United States. I noted to what degree Trudeau identified any stormy strain of nationalism with rabid tribalism or racism, how much he feared the encoding of tribal rights—ethnic rights—into the Constitution. While he applauded the debate of these issues through political symposia, he thought the encoding of such rights would be "a formula for tyranny."

"Any elevation of collective rights—language rights, provincial rights, tribal rights, government rights—over the individual strikes me as a recipe for disaster. We have to watch."

"It should be a tension between the individual and the collective?"

"Always. A balancing of rights and obligations. Too much liberty for the individual leads to anarchy—chaos. Too much power for the collective, for institutions, leads to oppression—to statism."

His form of Canadianism—was it a kind of quixotic, rooted cosmopolitanism?

"Contrary to what Samuel Johnson said, patriotism is usually the *first* refuge of the scoundrel. Yet one must have a strong feel for where you are, be capable of seeing your own place, of wanting to make a place for yourself."

This was his form of Canadian Liberalism: social conscience and universality mixed with native caution and a persevering, powerful ability to imagine one's locale.

Shifting subjects, back to books. Trudeau told me he'd been reading Thomas Mann's *The Magic Mountain* (which happens to be one of my favourite novels), and that he'd returned to the Bible.

"The Bible?"

"I'm reading through it. Genesis to Revelation. And I'm reading it all . . . slowly. Studying different translations to see how certain words have been changed. I find it all fascinating, this question of translation. The differences in interpretation. The mistakes that were sometimes made over the translation of one word."

I noticed his preference for classics. His readings seemed entirely centred in the past—works that had formed him when he was young. He mentioned few contemporaries. Was this another sign of withdrawal into contemplation? I still had the sense, nothing I could pinpoint, that his words carried levels, evoking inner concerns, worlds within worlds.

People in the restaurant sometimes surged towards him. Looks of hope, eagerness, irony, regret; a sneer here, a gaze of blunt fear there. Words passed, greetings.

I have often been asked where the security officers go when I have lunch with Trudeau. People gravitating, circling close. How do the RCMP guard him? How do they shadow him without intruding? My answer: I've never seen any security around. American ex-presidents travel with a phalanx of praetorians. Ex-PMs shuttle unattended in the relatively—temporarily?—civil streets of this country. (One exception to this unwritten rule is Mulroney, who, I've been told, never goes anywhere without the RCMP—no doubt to protect himself from an adoring population.)

We went on, talking quietly about large ideas that were surely passions while we finished our meal. He made a brief, affectionate reference to his toddler daughter, who lives in Toronto with her mother. Again he became lost in thought, maybe some faraway memory.

And back to books, and to ideas about society. He described his recent interest in the legend of Faust (Faust!), listing a few of the great works written on the scholar who sold his soul to know more, to have absolute power. He talked of the "redistribution of wealth," that apparently taboo phrase, currently banished by our hardened political mood of remorseless self-interest. Fair distribution and a flexible constitution of the rights of all citizens—these were the touchstones of his dream of a just society. A crucial declaration, I thought. This dream still moved him.

Then he paid our bill (he always has), and we stepped back into the street and walked off to his office.

Last exchange in the law-office lobby.

I said, "Chrétien will no doubt win this election. By a reduced majority, I think."

"Chrétien. He's a survivor. But I'm not really following all that closely."

A pause. I turned, getting ready to go.

"I am retired," he said flatly. He'd added this—for my benefit, or to remind himself? Paraphrase: Stop asking me for punditry. I smiled at the ambiguities. The statement could have had several interpretations, depending on how you stressed each word.

Glimpses. Trudeau offering his hand to say goodbye. Wishing me well with my "charges," he said, referring to my children. Saying come back, thank you for the talk. He turned and walked up the staircase, no bounding up steps or *Till Eulenspiegel* antics. (But there were no cameras around, either.) The only ones there to watch were receptionists and fellow lawyers—and they were clearly accustomed to his arrivals and departures. My last thoughts: He was an individual more and more eager to vanish, to disappear off the stage.

The taxi driver said: "Politics. People like to talk. With the election. Chrétien, Charest. Well, they come and go. I remember Trudeau best."

"Why?" I asked. The name card taped to the back seat said, Angelo. An older man; in his sixties, I guessed. A heavy accent; broad gestures. Angelo steered his cab through the maul and mew of traffic, whisking me to Dorval and an early flight home.

"Trudeau? Never had him in my cab. But there's no one like him now. And you know what? He was true to himself. Sure, he made mistakes. Plenty. But so do we all, right? He was different. When I first came to Canada, I thought about him all the time. But I never met him."

I told him I had, and that I'd just had a long lunch with him. Angelo shot me a look over his shoulder, then nearly jerked his cab off the road. I told him it was the truth. He wanted details.

"What's he like now?"

I described a gentler Trudeau than the one I'd met in other years. Lucid, aware, attentive, courteous, and yet—here came that word again—withdrawn. I described how this hadn't been the bristly argumentative Trudeau I'd once faced off with; nor had it entirely been the quick-fire legalist and philosopher with whom I'd discussed Mackenzie King and Laurier, de Maistre and Dostoyevsky— though this time we had certainly ranged over politics and literature. I'd found a melancholy man, gazing into spaces few could enter or fathom. There had been something elegaic in his speech and manner. In his inwardness I'd detected a growing apartness.

I'd wanted to say to Angelo that, for better or for worse, we were still in the grip of Trudeau's concept of country. No idea or concept, story or myth, had fully succeeded his dream. And I'd wanted to say that, despite my public utterances to the contrary, I was unsure about the destiny of Canada. Had we already stepped away from the difficulty of being here?

I'd found a complex man in Trudeau, of course, but absorbed now by loner reveries. He had seen a great deal. Maybe enough was enough. When the world one dreams begins to fade before reality's limiting, when the imagination wears out because the need to transform reality has left the dreamer exhausted, maybe then the individual turns to introspection, and contemplations of loves and losses.

"Never his kind again," Angelo said.

Some might say—this is good. The dream of changing the world can be too much to bear for people. The mood in politics has become more livid and overwhelmed than explorative, impassioned, transfiguring, or transcendent. Maybe Trudeau, and his kind, must pass. Maybe the concerns of country and identity, of selfhood and place, must pass, too. In the mingling of amped circuits and souls will come heated shapes to intrigue us, though I continue to believe that we need those who dream well first, then encounter some of the delusive configurations of the real.

Angelo hauled his cab up to a halt in front of the Air Canada doors at the terminal.

"Will you see him again?"

"I don't know." Who could say?

"If you do, tell him I remember him."

I smiled, said I would. Made a mental note—remember this man, record what he said.

"You think he'll come back?"

"I doubt it."

"He'd win. Easily."

"Maybe. But his time is finished. Could we bring him back like Sir John A. for one last campaign? The old warrior. Well, there are different players now. Trudeau knew when to get out. Someone else has to come up with an idea for this country."

Angelo leaned over the seat, gazing back, while I climbed out to the curb. "I tell you I worry," he said. "Things are not so good here. Sure, sure, I make a living. Sure, I have a good life, business is pretty good for me. Sure, but my children, their children. I worry. What will be here for them someday?"

I stopped, half in the cab, half out, and said, truthfully, that I didn't know, but I hoped for the best. I had children, and often wondered about what they would inherit. Then I paid him, tipped him, thanked him, said goodbye, clambered out fully, entered the airport, joined the lineup for Toronto—a serpentine sprawl that looked like a queue for an urgent exodus elsewhere—and thought about the mystery of ourselves and the unexpected links we make with people, like Trudeau, who live such public lives, realizing how difficult it is to truly grasp anyone, thinking that trying to grasp someone's mystery could be a wrong turn in thought because the self always slips away and tenderness must come from knowing you can't hold on to anyone or anything, that we all pass one another, never quite knowing what it is we can or will make of ourselves or for ourselves, whether it is an identity and a place, a family and a home, a business or a venture into the wilderness, a grand unifying theory or a single clear perception, a poem or a country.